JOURNEY
TO THE
LIGHT

By George Noory and William J. Birnes from
Tom Doherty Associates

*Worker in the Light: Unlock Your Five Senses and
Liberate Your Potential*

*Journey to the Light: Find Your Spiritual Self and
Enter into a World of Infinite Opportunity—True Stories from
Those Who Made the Journey*

Journey
TO THE
Light

Find Your Spiritual Self and Enter
into a World of Infinite Opportunity

TRUE STORIES FROM THOSE

WHO MADE THE JOURNEY

GEORGE NOORY
AND
WILLIAM J. BIRNES

A TOM DOHERTY ASSOCIATES BOOK

NEW YORK

The names, places, and other identifying characteristics in the anecdotes submitted to us for publication have been changed to protect the privacy of the people being described in the stories.

JOURNEY TO THE LIGHT

A Forge Book
Published by Tom Doherty Associates, LLC.
175 Fifth Avenue
New York, NY 10010

www.tor-forge.com

Forge® is a registered trademark of Tom Doherty Associates, LLC.

ISBN 978-0-7653-2103-9

First Edition: November 2009

Printed in the United States of America

0   9   8   7   6   5   4   3   2   1

To my three wonderful children, Wendy, Kristina, and Jonathan, and to my special friend, Monica, who lights up everyone's life.

—George Noory

To Casey Birnes Grindle, Reese Birnes Grindle, and Marcus Charles Walker Birnes, this is their journey. And to Nancy Hayfield Birnes, Class of '79, the real creator of *UFO Hunters* and the editor in chief and driving force behind *UFO* magazine. If there ever is disclosure, it will be because Nancy found the secret. She is the true-life Nancy Drew.

—Bill Birnes

CONTENTS

ACKNOWLEDGMENTS

To my parents, Georgette and Gabriel, and my sisters, Gail and Glinda, who have put up with this human creature for all these years. And to my producers, Lisa Lyon and Tom Danheiser, who work effortlessly to keep me going!

—George Noory

To my children, Geoff and Carly and Holly and David, who keep me honest and grounded in reality. And to the producers, cast, and crew of *UFO Hunters*: Pat Uskert and Kevin Cook, execs Jon Alon Walz, Dave Pavoni, Aaron Kass, Steve Nigg, line producer Daniel Zarenkiewcz, Kyle Crosby, and to our network execs at the History Channel, Dolores Gavin and Mike Stiller, thanks for giving me this wonderful opportunity to talk about my favorite subject, UFOs. And thanks as well to my talent agent, Mark Turner at Abrams Artists, who urges me to step back when I, as usual, have gone too far.

And to my wife, Nancy, who defines reality, not just on television, and keeps everything going.

—Bill Birnes

To our publisher Tom Doherty at Forge Books, Tom Doherty Associates, and our editors Bob Gleason and Eric Raab, the real brains behind both *Worker in the Light* and *Journey to the Light*. And to assistants Katharine Critchlow and Ashley Cardiff, who keep the process flowing. To the fine literary agents at Vigliano Associates under David's guidance.

—George and Bill

FOREWORD

by Kira Ra and Sri Ram Kaa

Our dear friends George Noory and Bill Birnes asked us to contribute a foreword to their new book about the stories of those who are working their respective ways toward spiritual attainment. We are happy to offer our thoughts from a recent column we wrote also for *UFO* magazine.

Are we really ready to embrace a new year? More than ever before, we ponder the question of how quickly this past year has come to closure, and collectively, we find ourselves often wondering what has happened to the time. Many are acknowledging that the world is rapidly entering into a new paradigm, and that the current state of affairs needs to change.

Computers are faster, technology is seemingly limitless, and in the surge of world change we find ourselves asking, what is it we really know? What fundamental truths are still evident within our consciousness that offer us the gift of navigating the mounting chaos without fear, and for that matter, do these truths really exist?

We are indeed living in the age of great communication. It is abundantly available on all levels and from all sources. When we open ourselves to receive information, and especially as we ponder yet another year before us, ripe with possibility and filled with challenges, how do we sustain our peace and balance? In the midst of chaos is there an attainable and fundamental bliss?

There is an inner wisdom available to us all, and this universal source offers us the "Four Knowns." These are four fundamental and universal truths that have for the ages sustained spiritual seekers and religious devotees. Understanding and reconnecting with these four simple yet profound truths bring forth for us all a centered recognition and allow us to move forward with clarity and abundance.

In this moment, take a breath and imagine what your life would be like if you no longer embraced any self-doubt. Perhaps this could be a resolution for this very year, one that could quite possibly simply reconnect with the Four Knowns, this stunning clarity that is yours and available in this very moment for you to claim.

Each new year offers great and abundant facts, revelations, and paradigm shifts toward phenomena, multidimensional existence, and, of course, our beloved UFOs.

What if for just a moment you no longer needed any form of external evidence except your own ability to trust that which you know inherently? What if your paradigm was expanded enough to allow all dormant memories, DNA, and wisdom to be the door of universal truth swung open for you? What if you could simply release your need to investigate while embracing your birthright to know? This is the gift that you begin to unwrap as you revisit the Four Knowns.

While connecting with the content of the Four Knowns is simple, they do come with a caveat, however, a fail-safe program. To be fully understood and embraced, these powerful truths will burst forth for anyone who is conscious of their heart-centered existence. And to anchor a truly heart-centered life is to recognize that each precious being is having the experience that fully supports his or her own soul evolution, even when we may not understand or appreciate it. We have found that by simply adopting the habit of consciously bringing your hand to your heart often, you will empower this shift in perspective simply and quickly because the movement itself acts as a kind of reminder and signal.

So, what are the Four Knowns, and how can you best reconnect with them? We have listed all four below and suggest that as you review them, bring your hand to your heart, read each one independently, and then close your eyes. Let yourself feel the energy of each ancient universal truth before continuing on to the next one.

> I *am* not my body.
> The mind is my servant.
> I *am* the Divine at all times and in all actions.
> All is in divine order.

When we can anchor ourselves in a universal truth, we will find a new stability and peace in a changing outer world. Now that you have gifted yourself with a moment of presence with each of the Four Knowns, we suggest that you offer to yourself the simple gift of bringing your hand to your heart and repeating just one Known for a full week. Treat it like a mantra in the same way that George and Bill suggested in their first book, *Worker in the Light.* Try doing this many times during the day, every day for seven days. Can you break through all doubt of this truth as you do this? Are you able to be present with just one truth in its fullness for a full week? To completely flush out any hidden resistance to your greatest beingness? Are you worth just four weeks of simple practice, one Known per week, to fully illuminate yourself and prepare to step into a period of your life with extraordinary clarity and a heightened sense of purpose? Are you ready to embrace a life without any doubt?

To break through doubt is not easy. Most of us have culti-vated a dependency on outside authority. It is simple if we let it be, however. The simplicity comes from recognizing that we need only discipline ourselves to consistently reinhabit our daily pat-terns so that we become accustomed to living in our deepest truth.

This begins with complete self-honesty, which unravels doubt. The old adage "The truth shall set you free" fully aligns to support your journey when you apply it to all aspects of yourself. This gift, in conjunction with the freedom that unfolds from the recog-nition that you are the Four Knowns, is a dynamic combination that opens limitless possibilities and life choices.

As we stand ready to move forward into another year on our beloved planet, now is the time to fully remember that we are all teachers for one another, and we are in every sense the ones we have been waiting for. When we keep our eyes on the Divine at all times, everything in our life and our beloved world becomes sim-ple. Navigating the coming years may be best described as a tu-multuous time of buoyant joy when we are holding the recognition of the Four Knowns through all circumstances.

May your heart unfold ever more this coming year, and may your life be filled with abundance and joy as you keep your eyes on the Divine. May each of us be ever present with Divine humility for the great gifts that we are being offered at this very moment, on this wondrous planet, right here, right now.

If you've ever attended one of the conferences hosted by Kira Ra and Sri Ram Kaa, you will not need to read their short bios. Both Sri and Kira have brought solace to many people who have sought out their extensive experience as spiritual healers and sages. They graciously agreed to write this foreword because they have spoken and worked with many individuals who have had the very same experiences as our contributors.

Wisdom Teacher Sri Ram Kaa is a gifted psychotherapist,

skilled medical intuitive, and Master Avesa quantum healer. Angelic Oracle Kira Raa has been clairvoyant since childhood, and was declared clinically dead of cancer in 1989. She is now widely accepted as the most profound archangelic oracle of our time, and is also a Master Avesa quantum healer. Bestselling authors, columnists, and radio personalities, they are internationally recognized for lovingly "walking the walk" of authenticity. Together they have founded the TOSA Center for Enlightened Living, the 2012 One Heart Foundation, and the Avesa Quantum Healing Institute (www.selfascension.com).

PREFACE

HOW INTUITION SAVED A LIFE
WHEN MOMENTS COUNTED

BY GEORGE NOORY

Sometimes, despite whatever logic tells you, and certainly despite whatever advice you hear, you have to follow your intuition, your searchlight into the universe. All of us have intuition. None of us is spiritually blind. We may not listen to it, but we have it. If the only thing you learn from the stories that follow is that folks should listen to their intuition, then you've learned a lot. A man I'll call D told me how intuition, literally, saved his life:

D was only a youngster thirty years ago, a self-described hippie with long hair and an aggressive independence that drove him to venture out on his own whenever he could. D lived in Des Plaines, Illinois, a Chicago suburb, and he spent a lot of time at the local bus depot checking out where he wanted to go next and, upon his return from one of his trips, waiting for his father to pick him up.

On one particular day, D remembers very well, he had just

called his father to pick him up and was waiting outside the bus depot when a stranger pulled up in a pickup truck. The stranger caught his eye, locked on, and asked him if he needed a ride anywhere. Sure, D could have told his father to stay at home because he had just caught a ride with a kind person who offered to drop him off at home, but there was something about this stranger that bothered him.

First, he did not address D in the kind of casual, conversational way that passersby would. There was an intensity about this person that was disturbing, and something else about this man made D think twice about hopping alongside him in the pickup. Maybe it was a look in this stranger's eye that said he was thinking about an agenda, planning something way in advance. D couldn't tell you whether it was the way he cocked his eye, or looked right past him to a faraway point in the distance, or the lack of a smile on his lips. It was none of these things. It was, D says today, simply something in his intuition that picked up on a visual signal and said, "Beware."

From his travels and encounters with people on the road, D had learned to trust his intuition. He learned to get beyond self-doubt, the seemingly rational voice that tells you intuition is just a bunch of New Age garbage, something they burned witches for five hundred years ago, something that old ladies may swear by but strong men dismiss. D didn't buy into that way of thinking because he believed that his intuition was even more valuable than logic.

So, as D looked this man over, the stranger in the pickup became more insistent, almost leaning over to take him by the arm and pull him into the passenger seat. Other people began to take notice as well. Why was this stranger so intent on getting D into that truck? Why was he so interested in D?

The more the stranger pressed, the more D demurred until, finally, D saw his father pull up and he bolted for the car. The stranger just stood by the door of his pickup truck like a jilted lover.

Over the years, D put that incident behind him, burying it under sediments of memory until he barely thought of it again years later when he read a headline in the national news that the police in Des Plaines had just arrested John Wayne Gacy. At that time he was one of the country's most prolific serial killers, targeting young boys at local bus stations outside Chicago. D realized that had it not been for his intuition, he would have been one of Gacy's victims, buried in the soft dirt under the foundation of Gacy's house.

Today, D will tell you with a straight face that it was his intuition that saved him, his intuition that picked up on some danger signals and kept him from going with a very convenient stranger, and thereby saving his life.

This is just the beginning of what I hope will be a series of stories, instructive, illustrative, and exemplary, that will show you what people do when they become workers in the light.

JOURNEY
TO THE
LIGHT

INTRODUCTION

WORKER IN THE LIGHT: ITS RATIONALE AND THE METHOD

Working in the light is so much more than a concept or an idea. It's a great idea, to be sure, an idea for self-realization and human empowerment. But to stop there is to stop short of the real purpose of working in the light. By following a process, a path to the light, people can tap into a power greater than themselves. I have found the path to this self-empowerment myself in my own daily life. But, since the publication of our book *Worker in the Light*, I have found that members of my *Coast to Coast AM* listening audience have found that path as well, and have infused their lives with the power that comes from making a connection with the universe at large.

How can this help you? First, it will empower you in ways that you might have thought impossible. As our contributors to *Journey to the Light* tell us, just by realizing there is an alternate reality in which people don't die, souls live forever, angels as well as the departed communicate with the living, we can control our dreaming, light beings can help us in our daily lives if we just welcome them in, and we can resonate with the entire universe. *Worker in the Light* and *Journey to the Light* are filled with the humbling experiences of those who, through enlightenment, gain a knowledge so exciting that they are true spiritual warriors, a powerful group of people who not only travel with spirits, but travel in time and tune in to the thoughts and feelings of others.

In *Worker in the Light*, we laid out the process for self-empowerment, opening up the mind to the spirit and opening up the spirit to the power of the universe. We said that it began with three things:

What is your mantra? You have to find a mantra, a statement, prayer, spiritual offering, or even a word that has resonance to you, that is yours and not to be shared with others. You start repeating that mantra to yourself, over and over again. You repeat it not just once, but ten to fifteen times a day. You repeat it when you are happy to express your joy. You express it to give yourself serenity during difficult moments. And you express it to express love. Just saying it and thinking about love will make all the difference in your life.

Learn how to breathe. Most people actually don't know how to do it. They suck in air, gulp in air, take a quick snatch of air, and move on. Again, what I've found is that if you learn how to expand your lungs with air instead of contracting your muscles and actually thinking about it as you do it, you will get more oxygen. Oxygen is fuel. If you restricted the fuel flow in your car, you would get a bucking and hesitation in the engine, especially when you try to climb hills. Now think about what would happen if you try to get through each moment of your day on a restricted airflow. Your brain slows down, you are more anxious, and you operate with a very limited capacity of fuel. You may still operate, but you are uncomfortable and always just this side of struggling for your next breath. Now try filling up your lungs to capacity. Do it every time. Own your breathing. You will start feeling better almost instantly.

Visualize your breathing. There's more to this than just breathing. Breathing correctly is a good start. You can't do too much without a nice lungful of air to keep you going. If, however, you think about what breathing does, you'll see what I mean about visualizing your breathing. With every breath you inhale clean—relatively cleaner—air than the air that's already in your system. The oxygen from your lungs is picked up in the alveoli, the tiny air sacs in the lungs that mix the oxygen molecules with your red cells and carry the oxygen to all parts of your body. At the cellular level, there is an exchange of air. The used-up air goes back into the venous blood, oxygen poor at this point, and from there back to the lungs, from where it is expelled back into the atmosphere. You inhale pure air and you exhale used-up waste air. Now, if you can imagine this, you can see why poor breathing, holding your breath for an inordinately long time while doing something else, is actually a way of poisoning yourself or starving your system. If you take in lungs full of healthy air and expel the used-up air, you are feeding yourself, feeding your brain.

Now you have to translate all of this to a visualization. You close your eyes and imagine that you are inhaling clean air and the air that you exhale is filled with toxins. Picture this as you breathe with your eyes closed and when you're in a safe and secure place. You spend time forming an image of the clean air coming in and the foul air going out. As you do this you can't help but relax as you nourish every single cell in your body. Look at the exchange of air as it takes place. If you tell yourself that you can see it as it happens, you will. You will be an observer as well as a participant of the process that is nourishing you many times a minute every day of your life, keeping you alive and functioning.

There are breathing therapists who actually teach their clients how to breathe because most people, believe it or not, don't do it correctly. Respiration may be natural, but in our lifestyles, the way we drive ourselves and the positions we contort ourselves into, we often interfere with the natural flow of air. That's why learning how to breathe correctly is one of the first steps to working in the light.

Visualizations. If you combine repeating your mantra with your breathing exercise, you will start to feel a kind of gentle tugging away from reality and into a state where you are at one with the universe. Ultimately, your goal is to free your consciousness from the details of your life and the demands upon your time and energy. It's like taking a spiritual vacation.

Here's the process. Find a place where you can be free from the phone, your boss, or those who place demands on your time. Maybe it's in the privacy of your bed at night or in a quiet room in your house. Maybe it's just going outside for some contemplation. But wherever you choose to do this exercise, it should be in a place where there won't be any interruptions for about twenty minutes. Once you've found the place, start by breathing consciously: taking nice, deep, cleaning breaths and filling your lungs. Hold that breath for a couple of seconds while you imagine that air is exchanging in every single cell of your body. Picture it as if you're looking through a camera into the cell itself. Molecules of air are penetrating the cell walls and infusing all the good stuff in the nucleus with healthy air.

At the same time you breathe and say your mantra to yourself, you have to find a way to keep day-to-day thoughts from intruding. How to do this? Usually, it's very hard to make your mind a blank. Our minds are made to think, to conjure up images, to transfer emotions and thoughts back and forth between the hemispheres. So we need to have an exercise that not only tries to make the mind blank, but that pushes out the negative, day-to-day stuff that clogs our minds with worries and cares. Here's an easy exercise you can practice as you breathe and say your mantra.

Let's say that you are lying there in your bed at night and reciting your mantra to the universe while you breathe in and out and see the exchange of air taking place in your body. And let's say that as you do this, your overly demanding boss pops up in your mind, or the traffic cop who gave you that ticket, or someone who keeps bugging you on your cell phone. You wonder, if that happens, what can you do? Erase them? No, you don't have to. What my guests on *Coast to Coast AM* have explained to me is that you can't just take an eraser to these thoughts and rub them away. Won't work. What you should try to do is to send them gently on their way. Float them out of your mind positively and willfully by imagining that they are leaves on a stream that float downstream with the current. By carefully sending every day-to-day intrusion downstream as a creative act, you will develop the skill of clearing your mind from negative thoughts so that this process becomes habit. You will be able to enter this state within a few minutes of doing your breathing and saying your mantra.

Ultimately, you will find that, contrary to the state of powerlessness that this exercise presupposes, you will have the extraordinary ability to free yourself from the constraints that everyday living places you under. Most of us live under the pressure of jobs we have to do and people we have to deal with. Even though we try to find solace, most of us simply can't get out from under the pressure of what we have to do each day. That's why this exercise in breathing, chanting, and letting your cares simply float away like leaves on a stream can put you in a whole new place where you surrender to the fact that you need some spiritual privacy. The paradox is that when you achieve this spiritual privacy, you actually link up with the entire universe. And here's where it really gets heady.

When you link up with the big universe, it's like you've entered a world where everything is possible because everything is potential. Werner Heisenberg postulated all the way back in the early twentieth century that when you look at a quantum of matter—a wave or a particle—what you see is exactly what you expect to see. If you think the quantum is a wave, then that's what you'll see. If you expect to see a particle, then it's a particle. In essence, if you expect it, it will be. That's a very compelling possibility in and of itself. But wait, there's more.

Theoretical physicists also believe that quanta of matter are linked to one another throughout the universe. These are not just pairs of quanta, but trillions of quanta that are linked so that if you expect to see a wave, then trillions of quanta linked to the quanta you're looking at suddenly turn out to be waves. Now, if you consider that possibility, you can quickly arrive at the conclusion that what you expect to perceive is exactly what you perceive in the big world, the world you live in. Does this sound familiar? It should, because it's the scientific basis behind the now-famous Law of Attraction as well as the less well-known, but hugely powerful, Army Remote Viewing Program of the 1980s that author Paul H. Smith talks about in his book *Reading the Enemy's Mind* and in his interviews with us in *UFO* magazine and on *Coast to Coast AM.*

Simply stated, the Law of Attraction posits that if you inhabit a reality, expect to see that reality, then that reality will become your reality. Believe that you're life's biggest loser and it will be a self-fulfilling prophecy. Believe in yourself as a success, and you will be a success. This is not a new concept. Back in the early twentieth century the writer Napoleon Hill wrote the famous book *Think and Grow Rich,* and years later Norman Vincent Peale wrote *The Power of Positive Thinking.* Both books stressed what we're suggesting now, that the way you perceive things is the way they turn out to be. Far from being an alternate reality, we suggest that this is the actual reality because, in the end, we create our own realities based on what we believe to be there. Accordingly, when we suggest that connecting with the larger universe connects you to a fundamental reality from which you can derive enormous power, we are basing this proposition not only on over three thousand years of philosophical teachings, but on hard science and official U.S. military operations.

What happens when you connect with this larger universe? We have found, and our contributors to *Journey to the Light* corroborate this, that you can actually travel in time, into the future. You can read the minds of other people and perceive what is going on around you. You can lucid-dream, exercise control over your dreams so you can travel to different places, and even stretch your mind's superpowers. You can even defy gravity and fly. That's the basis for the stories that our contributors sent us for *Journey to the Light*.

The folks who have contributed stories tell us of how, perhaps in moments of crisis or in emergencies, they surrendered their belief in the reality around them to the larger reality in which all things are possible. In so doing, they were able to see angels manifest themselves, talk to spirits of their loved ones, receive messages from those who might have departed from this life but are still in a neighboring dimension, see visions of loved ones, dream dreams of the future, and tap into the flow of all time so as to perceive the future. Our contributors have, many times without even consciously realizing it, reached out into the larger reality of the universe to experience the light. And once there, their lives forever changed so that they became workers in the light.

Also once there, our workers in the light, also feel the one unifying force in the universe that cannot be defeated. That is the force of love, and it is the natural emotion that arises out of working in the light. Love defeats anger, hopelessness, pride, selfishness, and all the other deadly sins. *Amor vincit omnia.* Love conquers all. This is what we learn from working in the light.

GHOSTS AND SPIRITS

If I weren't a radio talk-show host speaking every night with callers who have had paranormal experiences in their lives, I would be downright astonished at the number of people who said they have seen, and communicated with, the spirits or ghostly manifestations of their departed relatives. Mainly these communications come from parents or grandparents, but I have also heard stories about communications from departed children.

GHOSTS AND COMMUNICATING WITH THE DEPARTED

On *Coast to Coast AM* we discuss the question all the time: what are ghosts? Do all of the departed become ghosts or just those spirits who don't know they're dead? In his forthcoming book, *Haunting of America*, my friend and repeat guest Joel Martin tells an amazing story he heard about a person recovering from surgery in a hospital. One night he was awakened from a deep sleep by the jingling of bottles. He thought that it was one of the nurses bringing him some medication on a tray, but when he looked up, he could see no one in his room. The jingling was coming from outside his door. So he got out of bed and crept to the door where he saw a very pale, strange-looking man in a white laboratory coat rolling a medicine cart down the corridor.

Odd, he thought. Why would a person be making that much noise with a medicine cart at night? Normally it's the nurses who deliver the nighttime meds to patients. So he followed the strange figure as he walked right by the nurse's station, where the nurse on duty didn't even look up. This was even weirder. Didn't she see him?

So he asked her, "Hey, who's that guy?"

The nurse looked up and said, "What are you doing out of bed and walking the halls?"

"Wait a minute," the patient said, "forget about me. What about that guy? Who is he?"

"Oh, him," the nurse on duty said. "That's just a guy who used to work down in pharmaceuticals. He's delivering the prescriptions to the nurse's stations."

"Used to?" the patient asked, now getting very nervous about this.

"Yeah, used to," she said very nonchalantly. "He died a few months ago."

"You mean that's a ghost? And you're not scared to death?"

"We know the guy. He's been the night pharmacist at this hospital for decades," the nurse said. "Everyone here knows him. He's just doing his job, then he disappears. He doesn't know he's dead and we don't want to tell him."

Sounds very blasé, I know, but people who are used to ghosts, and know the ghosts they're used to, remain very unfazed.

Take, for example, a story from History Channel's *UFO Hunters* as they made their way across England. They were shooting a scene one night in a 450-year-old pub-and-restaurant near Leeds. As they were interviewing retired police officers there about UFOs they'd seen, one of the pub managers, who had just sent her two teenaged daughters home for the night, walked up to the producer and told him about the UFO sighting she'd had right down the road from the pub. "Let's get her on camera," the producer said.

During the ensuing interview, the UFO hunters asked her about her sighting, when she had it, and what the UFO looked like. Finally they asked, remarking how calm she seemed about her sighting, whether or not she was scared at having seen this pulsating orb of light right in front of her on a dark country road.

"Oh," she said almost casually. "After seeing the ghost we have down in the basement at night, nothing like that frightens me that much anymore."

"What?" the team asked. "Who?"

It was an old ghost, she said, who'd been killed in the pub sometime in the 1600s during the wars between the Cavaliers and the Roundheads after King Charles I was overthrown and was still angry about it.

"Angry. You mean he kills people angry?" they asked her.

"No," she said. "He fumes and he fusses and sometimes even throws things at people in the basement, but he's never killed anybody that I know of. I just tell him to go away, and he does. Everybody knows about him here."

Ghost stories can be exciting and thrilling. I hear them on *Coast to Coast AM* all the time, and the people who tell about visitations from their relatives seem to have experienced a sense of peace at having heard from the other side. Ghost stories are so common, in fact, more common than UFO sightings in my opinion, that I've often wondered whether there are ways to open yourself to ghostly visitations so that you can almost call them to you on command so as to communicate with them.

There are plenty of stories of mediums who claim they can communicate with the departed, stories that range all the way back to ancient times. Those who say they can communicate with the departed have been both celebrated and reviled in popular culture and even host their own radio and television shows. Even in American political history there are stories of mediums and channelers who visited presidents in the White House to reach the spirits of the departed.

In one of the most famous stories, Nettie Coburn wrote a book about her experiences in the Lincoln White House. She had originally been asked to conduct séances to contact the spirit of Willie Lincoln, who died during Lincoln's first term of a fever said to have been caused by bacteria in the White House water supply. But young Nettie Coburn found herself more involved in presidential policy-making than just trying to reach out to Willie to provide solace to the president and Mary Todd Lincoln. During one of her invitations to the White House—called there to provide advice on a very serious matter—Nettie was asked to contact a spirit to help the president reach a very serious decision that could affect the outcome of the war. Lincoln had written the Emancipation Proclamation, but, he said, he was still not certain whether to sign it. Nettie's ghostly contact was the great American orator, Daniel Webster, who, speaking through Nettie, urged the president in an impassioned plea to sign the Emancipation Proclamation and so give a high moral purpose for the Union to pursue the war that had ravaged the nation. Whether this story is accurate or not—after all, it was recounted by Nettie herself years later in her book, *Was Abraham Lincoln a Spiritualist or Curious Revelations from the Life of a Trance Medium*—we do not know, for we only have Nettie's version of the story. Lincoln himself, however, does not attribute his decision to issue the Proclamation to Nettie Coburn's channeling of Daniel Webster. Rather, as he wrote to Albert G. Hodges, he was "anti-slavery because if slavery is not wrong, then nothing is wrong." For President Lincoln this was an absolutely moral decision.

Nettie's story, however, has captivated historians of the paranormal because it shows just how almost conventional it was for presidents, Franklin Pierce and Woodrow Wilson included, to seek advice from people who said they could talk to the "other side."

Can you talk to the other side? Many of our contributors recount stories of their loved ones communicating with them just after death or even years later. Some—and you can do this, too— have told and written to me that all they had to do was to ask for a sign from a loved one in order to receive a message. In one particularly warm story, a woman recounts her years with her live-in boyfriend, a man who was abusive to her, but whom she loved nevertheless. After his death, our contributor, still hoping for a sign from him, began dating other men. Then, one day, lonely and disconsolate over the loss of her lover, she asked for a sign that he was still with her. That was when the refrigerator died. *Oh, great,* she thought. *That's all I need. To spend hundreds of dollars on a new fridge when I barely have enough money to buy food.*

So she opened the refrigerator to see what she could make out, and what do you think she found inside? There, on the top shelf, were three cans of beer. Three cans that her deceased boyfriend always kept on the top shelf, right in front. That was her sign, she said, that her boyfriend was there by her side, staying with her through the rest of her life.

Ghosts, it seems, don't have to materialize or even talk to people. They can just perform acts that let others know they're still present.

We suggested a number of exercises in *Worker* that can help people communicate with the departed in waking life as well as in dreams. In dreams, we said, because the logical mind has stepped back from its mediating function over our sensory input, you are open to all sorts of images that might not make sense or might challenge your grip on reality in a waking state. But in a dream state, all possibilities are open. Therefore, if you want to try to communicate, try it as a form of a lucid dream, as many of our contributors have done. As you do your deep breathing and repetition of your mantra, hold the person's image you want to communicate with firmly in your mind. Actually begin the conversation, even conjuring up mentally what you think you might say and hear. Doing this enough times over a repeated sequence of evenings, I have been told, will actually bring the person into your consciousness while you are asleep. And in that state, you may discover things about that person, things the person might have wanted to say to you in life, that you could not otherwise discover. Our contributors have reported this, and I have no reason to dispute any of their stories.

As for communicating with a loved one in a waking state, I can think of no story more charming than the one the late George Burns often repeated. George Burns was one of our country's greatest entertainers. A comedian, dancer, singer, and radio, television, and movie star, his career stretched all the way back to the earliest days of vaudeville in the early 1900s when he and his partner Abie Kaplan soft-shoed their way in bars on Manhattan's Lower East Side. George soon teamed up with Gracie Allen and, from the vaudeville stage, through two-reelers and feature-length movies in the 1930s, on into radio and then television, Burns and Allen became the most celebrated husband-and-wife comedy team in America. But Gracie retired from television in 1958 and died in Los Angeles in 1964. Thereafter, for thirty years, George Burns visited her tomb almost every day to talk to her. He would tell her about his business plans, how he wanted to sell his successful McCadden Productions, and about his returning to motion pictures in the 1970s to star in *The Sunshine Boys.*

Did George Burns really talk to Gracie Allen all those years, or was she only a figment of his imagination? Was her spirit actually present in the mausoleum, or was George Burns merely expressing his own thoughts, listening to his own voice, and giving himself the answers he knew that Gracie Allen would give him? You see, Gracie Allen wasn't the "dumb Dora" character she and George had created for her onstage and on television. Far from it. She was a savvy partner who, along with George Burns, had guided the couple's career from the 1920s all the way to network television and the creation of McCadden, one of the early independent producers of situation comedies. But Gracie only spoke to George.

Therefore, I'd like to believe that, seemingly all alone next to his wife's burial place, George Burns was not really alone. It was there that he could summon the spirit of Gracie Allen, the one person he could talk to without being onstage, and open up his heart to her for thirty years. It was what kept him going long after his contemporaries had left the business and died. It completed his every day after stopping at the Hillcrest for a cocktail and some lunch. George Burns did what any one of us could if we only believed in the possibility that people really don't die.

Therefore, just as my listeners and our contributors have done, and tell you about in their anecdotes, you can do. You can start by using the exercise that we've talked about: breathing, reciting, opening up your mind to the universe, and then visualizing that person you want to communicate with. Do this enough times while not allowing any logical, judgmental thoughts to intrude upon your practice, and you will have summoned the spirit of your departed loved one with whom you will be able to communicate.

Soon you will see, just as our contributors have seen, that we really don't die, and that the barrier between the living and the dead is a lot thinner and more malleable than people think.

Sometimes the reason for a ghostly manifestation is that the spirit doesn't know it has died. However, the living, by opening themselves up to what they're seeing and not denying it, can communicate with a spirit and help it on its way, just as Melissa Arkin did.

MY TRUE-LIFE GHOST ENCOUNTER

This took place in 1992. I had just lost my job as an assistant manager and I had started working full-time with a security company that up to that point I had only worked part-time for on weekends. I had the graveyard shift at a new shopping center that had just recently opened.

Although the shopping center was new, in a far corner of the parking lot was a medical arts building that had existed there before the shopping center. It was a two-story building with a variety of clinics lining the second floor. The second floor was just a long hallway with offices on either side and two restrooms that were kept locked and only for the patients to use. To reach the second floor you could either take an outside elevator, which was extremely slow, or you could walk up the stairs, which were open on the outside of the building. To enter the second floor hallway there were double glass doors on the elevator end. At the back end of the hallway was a single glass door that led to an enclosed stairway down to an exit door no one ever used.

One of my responsibilities was to conduct a walk-through of the second floor every night, checking to make sure that everyone was out, including inside the locked restrooms (I had a key) and checking that all the office doors were locked before I locked both doors at either end. This occurred at 11:00 P.M. nightly. It was then my responsibility to reopen the doors to the second floor at 6:00 A.M. and conduct another walk-through.

Almost immediately I started noticing strange occurrences while on the second floor. The AC shut off automatically at 10:00 P.M. so by 11:00 P.M. when I went to do my walk-through it was extremely hot and stuffy inside that enclosed second-floor hallway. It was also extremely quiet. The hallway was carpeted. I was not afraid or even concerned to be checking the floor by myself and in truth was usually lost in thought of something else and just going through the routine on autopilot.

One night I thought I heard something as I was walking down the hallway. I stopped and strained to listen. There was just silence but then, there it was again. It sounded like someone crying and sobbing. It was extremely soft but grew louder as I walked ever so quietly down the hallway. It sounded like a young girl, perhaps a teenager, and it was coming from inside the locked women's restroom. As I stood in front of the door listening, the sound suddenly stopped and I felt a sudden cold chill run through me, even though the air was hot and stuffy. The hair on the back of my neck stood up and I got goose bumps. My thought was that a patient or perhaps an employee of one of the doctors' offices was inside, and I would just let them know that I was there to lock up the building and that they would have to leave now.

I knocked on the door and announced, "Security! Are you alright? I need to lock up the building now!" There was no response. I repeated the same announcement several times and knocked loudly on the door. I then announced that I was coming in and used my key to unlock the door and enter the women's restroom. I checked both stalls. There was no one inside. I checked inside the men's restroom next door. Nothing. I chalked it up to my imagination and didn't think anymore about it.

The next night the same thing happened, and I tried to think of ways to explain it. Perhaps I was hearing someone who was actually inside the clinic on the first floor and the sound was carrying up through a ventilation duct. No, that couldn't be it, because the clinic closed at 6:00 P.M. and the cleaning crew was done and gone by 8:00 P.M. The clinic was locked and the alarm set. If anyone was still inside it would trigger the motion sensors and the alarm. I was at a loss to explain it.

The third night I decided I would just do my run-through quickly and so as not to hear anything I would sing a song. As I approached the women's restroom, singing out loud, I heard a toilet flush inside. These toilets are not the type that flush automatically using infrared or whatever. These are the old-fashioned kind with a manual lever. Needless to say, there was no one inside. It was at this point that I started talking to whoever or whatever this was. I would say things like, "Oh, you think that's funny, don't you! You're a little joker, aren't you?"

The next night I heard laughing and giggling sounds instead of crying and sobbing. The laughing and giggling of a young teenage girl. As I walked down the hot, stuffy hallway I would continue to talk to "her," saying things like, "Where are you? I know you're here. Where are you hiding?" And then I would feel a sudden cold chill pass through me and I would say, "There you are, you little trickster!" Each night I got goose bumps again and again as we played our little games.

Some nights she would wait till I was at the far end of the hall, after I had locked the back stairway door and was walking back to leave. Then she would open the double glass doors at the entrance and let them swing closed right before my eyes. There was no wind. No logical way of explaining it. All the while I continued to talk to her as if she were really there, I just couldn't see her. "Very funny, you!" I would say to her.

Things continued on like this for months. Even though I kept it to myself and never told anyone, I began to hear comments from the guards who worked there on my nights off. They would say how they felt there was something strange about that second floor. One of them, another female guard, said she had had some very weird things happen while using that restroom, and it got to the point where she refused to go up there at all. She would get her boyfriend to go up there instead.

Another time when I was not on duty I happened to be talking with the supervisor from the security company while he was waiting for the guard to come back to the security office in the shopping center. The guard on duty was locking up the second floor of the building. Suddenly, the guard came running back across the parking lot, screaming. When he reached us he was babbling something about an earthquake. He said that while he had been in the second floor hall the walls had begun to shake and rattle and the floor was rolling in waves under his feet. He said the whole building seemed to be moving and making a loud roaring sound. When we assured him there had been no earthquake he refused to believe it. Needless to say, after that he, too, refused to go in that building at night.

Then one morning while I was unlocking the doors at 6:00 A.M., as I walked down the hall I noticed one of the plastic nameplates, which are beside each of the office doors, was on the floor. It had not been there when I had locked up seven hours earlier. I picked it up. It was the nameplate of one of the dentists in the office. It had sticky glue on the back and I carefully put it back in its place among the other nameplates and pounded it into place with my fist. It was a tight, secure fit. I thought that somehow it had fallen off by itself and didn't give it any more thought until the next morning when the same thing happened again. The same dentist's nameplate was on the floor again, and it hadn't been there when I had locked up seven hours earlier. I again pounded it back into place.

The next morning there it was, on the floor. Again I replaced it and thought to myself that the glue must not be holding it in place even though it seemed sticky enough. The next morning, as I unlocked the outer glass doors and began walking down the hall, I strained to see if the nameplate was missing from its place. It was missing, all right, but as I quickly scanned the floor, it was nowhere to be seen. I started thinking, *Is it possible someone is pulling a prank? Someone who has a key to the building and a grudge against this particular dentist?*

Up until then it hadn't been a big deal. But now, if the nameplate was gone, I would have to make a written report. I looked around to see if I could find it, but no luck. Then, as I reached the women's restroom, there it was, stuck to the door. I immediately thought, *OK, this is definitely the work of some prankster. Someone who has something against this dentist who has a key and is sneaking into the building at night and messing with his nameplate.* As I tried to pull the nameplate off the restroom door I was astounded that it would not come loose. It was as if it were welded to the door. Finally, after pulling on it with all my strength, it suddenly just released. I decided that this was the final straw and that I needed to let someone in that dentist's office know what had been happening.

I was off duty at 7:00 A.M. and the dentist's receptionist didn't come in until 7:30, so I took the nameplate with me and went to get some breakfast. I returned at just after 7:30 and entered the now unlocked dentist's office. I explained to the receptionist that I worked the overnight shift there and told her what had been occurring every morning that week with the dentist's nameplate, that I had found it stuck on the door of the women's restroom earlier that morning. Her reaction was, it seemed to me, a little extreme. Her eyes grew wide as if in shock. She looked at the nameplate and then looked at today's date on her appointment book. Her mouth fell open and her eyes grew even wider. She let loose a loud gasp and began to visibly shake. I asked her if she was alright, but she didn't answer. She took the nameplate from my hand and mumbled, "Thank you. Please excuse me, thanks again."

I left, bewildered by her reaction. As I walked downstairs one of the nurses from the medical clinic was outside having a last cigarette before going inside. She asked me if I worked security there overnight and I told her I did. She then asked me if I had ever had anything strange or unusual happen. I told her, "You know, it's funny you should ask that" and then proceeded to tell her all of the goings-on that had been occurring leading up to what I had found that morning and the receptionist's inexplicable reaction. As I finished the story she let loose an "Oh my God!" I looked at her and asked, "What's wrong? Why are you reacting like that?" She shakily lit another cigarette and proceeded to tell me the story.

She said there had been a teenaged girl who had been very depressed and was a patient of that dentist. One day, while sifting through old magazines in the waiting room, she had asked for the key to the restroom and had gone in there and cut her wrists. By the time they found her she had bled out most of her blood and the doctor had picked her up and carried her downstairs to the clinic, where they tried to save her but could not. That was one year ago to this very day!

I was able to ask the nurse what the girl's first name was. She told me it was Jenna. I did some research on the Internet and found out how to "send an earthbound spirit on its way." Later that same week I talked to Jenna and explained to her that she had died from loss of blood from the deep cuts on her wrists and that, as sad as that was, there was a better place waiting for her. I told her not to be afraid, that her loved ones and others who had gone before her would greet her and help her, but it was up to her to make the decision to move on. I told her to concentrate on wanting to go to a better place, "heaven," and if she wanted it enough, the way would appear to her. I told her to look for the light, a very bright light, and to go into that light. I repeated that several times and honestly felt I could sense her say good-bye and her spirit leave. After that I never sensed her presence again and there were no further incidents.

Can ghosts attack? People can be spirit-sensitive in particular places if the places themselves have a spiritual intensity. But a spiritual healer became a worker in the light and helped one of our readers recover from a ghost attack.

A "PLACE MEMORY" IN RURAL CONNECTICUT

This is something that happened to me about twenty-three years ago. I sent this account to a few other people, but no one could ever explain it to me. I was friendly with a few folks who were pagans. We took an overnight trip to a friend's parent's home in Northern Connecticut near Granby Notch. The home was built in the early 1700s. While we were standing around outside the home I felt something enter my chest. It was not a natural chest pain; the only way I can describe it is if a freezing-cold metal rod went into my chest. It stunned me initially, but the feeling was fleeting. I did not tell anyone about this occurrence.

A few seconds later a group member announced that we should take cover because we were under a "psychic attack." They said the attack was from Revolutionary War soldiers and Indians. I thought to myself, *I've gotten involved with a bunch of crazy folks!* Soon after the announcement we went back into the house. At the door was a member of the group who was a follower of shamanism. This person ran her hands up and down my body. At the *exact* location of where previously I had felt the icy cold rod enter my body, she made a motion with her hands and seemed to be pulling something out of me. She said, "Did you know you were shot with an arrow?"

I never understood who could have shot that arrow.

Here is a fascinating story a reader sent us about her experience in Ireland years ago, where she had a ghostly encounter at a spot that had been a ceremonial sacred place for thousands of years. Ghosts, our callers tell us, congregate around these sacred spaces because of their great power.

THE LOST LEGION AT BALLYNAHATTIN

When I was in Ireland many years ago, I visited Ballynahattin, often called "Ireland's Stonehenge." One night, as I walked home from a pub into a damp fog that swallowed me, I thought I heard noises, the clanking of metal. There was no one around, no one on the heath where I was walking. I shrugged off the noises. *Must be cars in the distance,* I told myself. But as I walked, the noises grew louder. I turned toward their direction and tried to see into the fog to make out the source of that clanking. Then I heard footsteps, footsteps that grew louder. I walked toward them, hoping to find a group of people with whom I could tag along back to my hotel room. Instead, what I saw was a group of soldiers dressed in armor and leather. They looked like pictures of Roman soldiers I had seen in history textbooks. They seemed oblivious to me, so I kept staring at them. Then one of them turned and looked me right in the eye. I ran as fast as I could back to the pub where the barkeep told me that this was a lost legion of Romans who appear out of the fog from time to time. They guard Ballynahattin. Next time I go back I'll bring a camera.

For those open to the belief that spirits of the departed walk among us, this is an inspiring story.

THE SPIRIT OF A YOUNG CHILD

My Aunt Muriel recently passed away at ninety-three-years old. She was a very spiritual person. One of the turning points in her life was when she was thirteen years old. She was living in Wellington, Utah.

One of her best friends, a young boy and playmate, had caught polio and was bedridden. After a battle with polio for a month the boy passed away. This bothered my aunt because she thought, "How can God take away such a young boy?" A couple of weeks after the boy's funeral my aunt went out to his grave site. While there, she was startled because she heard a voice behind her. She turned around and it was the young boy that had passed away. The ghost of the boy told my aunt, "Don't be sad, everything is OK when you die." Then he disappeared.

After this encounter with a ghost my aunt said she had a totally different view of death. She was a very spiritual person her entire life.

Last March she passed away but she kept her faith until the end. The day before she passed away all of her vital organs started shutting down. She had a lot of family around her. She asked if she could get her nails done, so my sister painted her nails. Auntie said there were a lot of friends she was looking forward to visiting in heaven and she wanted to look nice for them.

Sometimes we see ghosts and sometimes we feel them, as this reader has done.

RUNNING WITH SPIRITS

In 1978, I had a psychic blowout. I was running down the street with my right hand in the air as if someone was holding it. In front of me was a ghost standing still as stone and yet, when I was running, it never moved but stayed a few feet in front of me the whole time. I turned a corner to get away from it and when I ran into people sitting on the porch, it disappeared. The people made fun of me and laughed at my screaming. I was very hurt and cried even more.

A few months later, I was sitting in my living room and five beings appeared. They discussed my ESP and told me that I have to manage it. They gave me tips, and when I decided that it could not be exorcised out of me, they took me to school. There I learned to be true to myself always, no matter what condition I am in, physically, materially, and emotionally.

This had to be back in the early '80s. I went to my cousin's house to visit; we were very close then. While we were sitting around shooting the breeze his best friend's name came up and I told him I had a coffee with him a few days earlier. My cousin went white and asked me what day exactly. I told him and he almost fell off his chair. He asked what time, and I said I think it was around 10:00 A.M.

Back then I drove a school bus for a living and that particular day I wasn't off somewhere, so my boss asked if I could do her a favor and drive a charter bus on a field trip downtown. I agreed and picked up the kids at 8:00 A.M. When I dropped them off the teacher in charge told me what time to return. I parked the bus a few blocks away and walked to a neighborhood diner. When I came around the corner I saw my cousin's friend waiting at the city bus stop and approached him. We talked a while and then he said, "Can I buy you a coffee?" I said I was going there anyway and I would buy him one. When we got inside we just talked about nothing (you know what I mean). Then the conversation got around to his wife. He was worried about her security if anything ever happened to him. He asked if I would look in on her if such a thing would happen, and I said I would. I found that strange because I didn't even know him that well.

We finished our coffee and he left.

Keep in mind that in those days we had to keep a logbook, so times and places are documented.

I explained all this to my cousin, and he said it was impossible that I could have been talking to him because he died that same day and time a hundred miles away. Now I'm freaking out. He showed me a piece that was in the *Daily Ledger* and it mentioned how he died. I was floored. I went home and got out my logbook, and sure enough, same day and time.

Four of my cousin's friends were fishing when a storm came up and they had to leave quickly. They rowed back to shore and one of my cousin's friends realized he had forgotten his tackle box. His friends tried to talk him into not going back, but he went anyway. He didn't make it back. Same day, same time, I was talking to him a hundred miles away at a diner in town.

Even our close friends can bring their own spirit guides to help us and guide us along the way. Call them ghosts or spirits, it sometimes doesn't matter if you're open to the possibilities that a presence from beyond, from another plane, can help you make your way.

My Friend's Spirit Guide

I have been able to communicate with my friend's spirit guide for fifteen years. I have on occasion been in communication with various spirits in my life, mostly family, but never someone else's spirit guide. The experience is still ongoing. Bob (my friend Trevor's spirit guide) has been very helpful to both of us on many occasions and is considered a close friend to both of us.

I'm an average person who sometimes has had unusual experiences with the other side. I am not a medium, psychic, or intuitive. My friend Trevor also considers himself average, with some contact from deceased family members every once in a while. Nothing unusual had ever occurred at my trailer before. I had the trailer since 1985. I have been there on many occasions both alone and with guests.

In 1995, I invited Trevor up to my cabin in Mississippi to stay the weekend. The cabin is in a vacation park and it was early fall. Until that weekend, Trevor and I had been acquainted with each other for six years, through work location and job title, but both of us had been too busy even for casual conversation and coffee.

The first evening, after dinner in the cabin, while engaged in a conversation about spirits, Trevor's guide, Bob, made himself known to me. The cabin's interior is small and compact. I was standing next to the stove and Trevor was sitting on the sofa approximately twelve feet away from me in the living room area. We were alone in the cabin; not even a cat, dog, or bird was present. During the early part of the conversation, I was physically bumped on my right shoulder from behind. My body lunged forward and I caught my balance. I was very puzzled about what had just occurred. Trevor saw me lose my balance and asked me, "What happened?" I wasn't sure what happened, although I was aware that it was physical and I did not bump myself.

After a minute or two Trevor and I went back to our conversation. Again, I was bumped, this time on my left shoulder, and again my body lunged forward. It was weird, but I wasn't afraid, just puzzled. I knew something was there, and this something was attempting to make itself known to me, but for what reason I had no clue.

Trevor, who was still sitting on the couch, saw what happened to me a second time and asked, "Ethan, what's going on?" I wasn't able to physically see anything; neither was he. I remained near the stove, quiet and still. As I looked over to where Trevor was sitting, thoughts began to race through my mind. I felt that there was a male presence in the room standing behind Trevor. This male presence wanted me to know he was there (in the cabin) because Trevor was there.

I told Trevor about the impressions I was receiving. "This is a male spirit, he's here because you're here, and he wants to introduce himself to me through you. He says you know who he is. Now who is she?" Trevor said, "I don't know what you're talking about." I got another impression, this time a visual. "He's approximately six-foot-two, dark brown hair, blue eyes, dressed in farmer clothes, doesn't look like he's of this century. I'm getting the name Bob; does this sound familiar?"

"No, I still don't know what you're talking about."

"Trevor, this spirit has been with you a long time, you know he's with you, now who is he?"

Again he denied any knowledge of this entity.

OK, now I'm getting upset. There's a spirit in my cabin that I didn't invite here, and I'm not interested in entertaining any uninvited guests, known or unknown, seen or unseen. I definitely didn't want any spirits flying around the inside of my cabin without my permission.

"Trevor, I know enough about my intuition to believe what I'm feeling, and I definitely didn't bump myself. So, come clean and tell me who this is. If you don't tell me, I'll get angry and throw out the both of you. Remember, I asked you for the weekend, I didn't ask you to bring a spirit."

Finally, Trevor opened up and told me about Bob. He said he's been with him for as long as he can remember. I asked him why he didn't want to tell me this when I first asked. He said, "I thought you might think I was weird or crazy."

I said, "Trevor that's why I didn't want to say anything when I got bumped on the shoulders." I realized now that Bob used the bumping as a way to say, "Hi, guess who?"

Over the past fifteen years, Trevor and I have become best of friends. Bob has been there for both of us, separately and together, aiding us in times of trouble. Both of us can hear Bob although we can't see him with our physical eyes. Bob has said he must repeat things twice, once to me and once to Trevor, because we are on different vibration levels and cannot hear him together.

Bob has never bumped me since the episode in 1995, nor has he bumped anyone else to my knowledge. My own spirit guide is very quiet; I hear him occasionally. Bob said it doesn't matter whose guide helps you when you need it, only that you get the help you need. He's just doing his job, and sometimes a different spirit guide can help you more than your own in a particular facet of life.

Bob's message to all who read this is:

Begin to listen more closely to your thoughts, you know, the ones you hear and discard and later say, "I heard that. I should have listened to myself and this wouldn't have happened." If you listen closely enough and long enough you may just hear the voice of your spirit guide. The more you listen to your inner thoughts the easier life becomes. Everyone has a spirit guide, and several through life. Learn who your guide is.

My readers tell me that psychic experiences often run in families. Whether it's genetic or whether it's simply a matter of family tradition, I do not know, but this reader's experience is an example.

A FAMILY OF SPIRITUALISTS

My fraternal grandparents were spiritualists from the Midwest. I grew up attending a spiritualist church, complete with messages, séances, materializations, and something they called "Airport," which consisted of a cone-shaped object being passed around from which came other objects. I received a ruby cross one night. At the materializations, a black booth was used and entities would appear nearby in ectoplasm. I saw my grandmother, who passed in 1959, and my great-uncle Ned, who played the piano when he came through.

Readers can be workers in the light even when they're children. Sometimes the openness to the possibilities of the universe, without the negative overlay of adults, can be enough to open the door to a world of spirits and wonder.

When I was five, I had my first psychic experiences. I recall being in my parents' bedroom and my stepdad was getting ready to leave for work. He was an electrician. I remember telling him to stay home and play with me because if he went to work he would get hurt. He went to work and was pinned in between two trucks at a housing construction site, breaking his back.

Also, when I was five, I saw what my mother said was Uncle Ned because he always dressed in black. He was standing at our front door asking to see Mama. When I brought Mama to the door, no one was there.

It was difficult growing up this way because everyone else had a traditional belief and went to a traditional church. Being a child, the idea of seeing ghosts scared me to death . . . LOL . . . I blocked it and never spoke of it to the other kids. After both my grandparents passed, phenomena were prevalent in the house we had shared with them. I would be home alone at night, about fifteen years old. I remember sitting alone at the piano and suddenly smelling cigar smoke and knew it was Granddaddy.

My stepfather mentioned an incident in which Grandma opened the door to our living room and sat on his lap. These phenomena also manifested in Grandma's Bible. It routinely fell off bookshelves and once, my bedroom closet shelf, which I will get to later.

Sometime in my midteens, I received a letter from a spiritual medium. The letter started off with her writing to me, but then it was Granddaddy writing through her. He was talking about being with me and that when he touched my shoulder, I would kind of squirm. He mentioned going crabbing and other things that had a personal meaning for me. Granddaddy gave me everything Mama said I couldn't have.

When I was eighteen, a friend of the family moved in who read tarot cards. I bought my first deck, but the first reading I did showed financial devastation and a worker's strike. Stepdad's union immediately went on strike for over a year. I stopped reading my cards then. I could predict bad things and I was scared to know them. Then came college, and academia led me to challenge what I couldn't explain or identify by science. Religion was a body of folklore used to control the culture.

How do I know the spirit is good or not so good? I know from my own experience with the tarot deck and the ouija board that not all spirits are good. Remember the adage: Evil will come to him who thinks evil.

Treat the spirit world similar to our world. You wouldn't let a stranger into your house, so don't request just any spirit to come for a visit. I say a brief prayer of protection before I work with any other di-

mensional beings. After surrounding myself with Godly white light/healing light, I request that only those entities with my vibrational level or higher come to see me.

In the cabin case, I did not initially know good or bad and remained open for additional feelings and info from the spirit. Lucky for me, he happened to have a good spirit with him. Bob (spirit guide) was smart enough to do what he did quickly and then he identified himself, although Trevor denied it at first. Spirits know more about us than we know about ourselves. Good spirits are kind enough to know what each one of us is capable of accepting, and they allow us to decide when it's time to meet them on an individual level.

From bad spirits you can usually feel negative energy, also chills, shortness of breath, and hyperventilation, and after the encounter your energy level will be drained. I have also found that spiritual sensitivity can be cultural as well as personal.

As this reader tells us, don't assume that the departed have really departed. The spirits of loved ones may watch over us or they may just watch us. I like to believe that they are truly watching over us because love never dies.

WHEN GHOSTS RETURN TO THE BEDROOM

My wife passed away from a massive heart attack, leaving behind our then four-year-old son. My wife was Native American and very intuitive; in fact, she could see spirits. It is very common with American Indians, part of their culture. She used to wake me up at night to tell me to look at the people all around the bed. I could not see them but I had a friend at work that was very spiritual, very psychic, and always right. I asked him what to do, and he said to get some holy water and a Bible, opened to the Ninety-first Psalm, and put them near the bed. She finally started being able to sleep.

At the time of her death we were separated and she had some

hustler for a boyfriend. She died because the ambulance rescue team did not put the tracheotomy tube in the right passage. They got it in the esophagus, thus she died on the way to the hospital. Separated or not, we still were sneaking away for weekends, you know . . . *rendezvous l'amour!*

She is the one true love of my life even to this day. Well, after she died I fell apart. I was drinking rather heavily and went out a lot. I had let my young neighbor, Paloma, and her three small boys move in with me and my two sons. She was happy to cook (homemade Mexican food will *spoil* you!). She had a boyfriend named Scott that sort of came with her, and his father, though I never met him in person, gave me some very wise information that ended up helping my son financially.

When I had started to go out and about again, one night I brought home a woman for the first time since my wife had died. My roommates knew something was up because my bedroom door was shut. When I did make an appearance the next morning, I was in a doorway from the hall to the living room. Paloma and Scott were sitting on the couch and all four children were in various places in the living room.

Paloma, with an urgency in her eyes, told me that they were going to walk down to the park, taking all the kids, so I could enjoy a nice quiet breakfast. By the way she was looking at me I knew she meant she was giving me time to enjoy and get the woman out when the coast was clear. All of a sudden, the vase on top of the stereo rose straight up into the air about three feet, went sideways to the east, and when it got to the middle of the room, it simply dropped onto the living room floor. We were stunned, but I knew immediately what happened. My deceased wife was throwing a fit because I had brought a woman home to our bed. I know that's why it happened and no one can change my mind.

Some years or so later, I was dating another American Indian woman and we came back to that same apartment one morning after being out partying all night. We also were with a white gal that was a friend of hers. I had never met the woman before.

When we went into the apartment, my girlfriend went straight to the kitchen to get the beer and her friend and I went and sat down on the couch. Directly across the room was my stereo with the two tower speakers on each side. This time there were two vases with flowers, one on each speaker.

When we sat down on the couch, the vases started rising simultaneously, up a foot or two, then they both went north into the dining room where they landed almost side by side, and above them were their respective flowers!

The white gal was absolutely freaking out and I told her, "Don't worry about it, it happens all the time around here." I felt so sorry for her. She was pale as a ghost!

My feeling about this was that my deceased "wife" was *not* pleased with me and that she was jealous because I was dating another Indian.

These are two of my many stories; however, these stories are correlated!

Here is an out-of-body experience with a spirit vision similar to the shadow people my callers talk about.

THE FIGURE IN THE WINDOW

I saw and did not acknowledge. I felt myself first rise then descend at an awkward angle (and for the last time not in the physical sense, damn it) sort of how you would if you could descend from a hyperbolic cube, at a 45 degree angle, kitty-cornered to reality. I came upon a plush rain forest–type environment. A solitary figure rowed a boat through what was, judging by the oriental tapestry, a flooded rice paddy. As I descended, the figure, obscured by his rather large oriental coolie hat, raised (or should I say angled) his head to come into my field of vision. At once I was met by the most horrific set of eyes I had ever seen or imagined. Believe me, now I acknowledged and fast. Boom! Dream, vision, astro-projection or whatever, aborted, over and out.

According to Joseph Campbell, we learn that in all mythologies, the separation of one realm from another is usually marked by a river or perhaps other symbolic representation of water. Posted at these intervals are guardians whose mission it is to keep those on one side of the river ignorant of those on the other side, at least until the proper time. Jesus speaks of the gulf that divides the living and the dead. Charon the Ferryman transits the river of existences not only in Greco-Roman mythology, but in many guises and in many tales of lore of different cultures. These guardians or ferrymen will use at their will and command all the elements of fear, cunning, and collective memory to secure their post.

I was far too busy with matters of the material world to be dealing with dreams, visions, or whatever of this nature, so I opted to listening to (wimpy) lite-jazz music as a way of relaxing, a nasty habit I still have difficulty in relinquishing. Time passed. One night I found myself relaxing to some sugar-coated jazz saxophone music when, like the character in the Edgar Allan Poe poem, there came a tapping, a gentle rapping but at my window (instead of at my chamber door). Tap, tap, tap, I turned my head to the large bedroom window, which was adorned with venetian blinds. I had not fully closed the blinds and was startled to see a figure standing on my roof and apparently looking through my window. I slowly turned my head away from the figure and ever so gingerly moved my hand toward the phone. Naturally, I called the police; the response was quick and intense. They even sent a whirlybird, checking the rooftops, not just my buildings, but all the houses at least on that side of the block.

This was my first-ever call to the police department. Nervously, I gave my report, which was really not much because after the initial shock of seeing someone on my roof my attention immediately turned to maintaining bladder control, remembering the exact procedure needed to dial a telephone and, naturally, to thoughts of *Super Jesus, if you're out there, please save me.*

The police did not find anything unusual on that side of the block, except maybe for me. (Hey, don't you belong on the other side of the block? I shouldn't exaggerate—that opinion may have only been implied by a few raised eyebrows.)

I calmed my nerves and eventually made it to sleep. The next night there I was, lying in bed, when, tap, tap, tap. Once again my visitor had returned and was throwing stones at my window. I reenacted my phone maneuvers of the previous night, but this time I called my boyfriend. "Greg," I said. "He's back."

"Call the police."

"What if they come out and he's gone again?"

"What has that got to do with anything?"

Men definitely are from Mars. In any event, I called. The cops came, no whirlybird, no sympathy, no nothing.

"Mrs. B, do you have any friends who may be playing a practical joke on you?"

Wait a minute, there was something. It came to me when I was trying to give a description of the prowler. He was a perfect silhouette, although I guess a perfect female silhouette may have wished him a little taller. What I mean by perfect is his shadowy form was without edges, without overlaps, without caps, straps, or flaps, and so forth, or any other distinguishable shadow that would be cast from clothing.

I had seen, through the semiopen venetian blinds, only a form. Form without function, as it were; there was no shadow cast of anything belonging to the form except the form. I kept this observation to myself, however. There was something about the height and dexterity of the prowler that made me think that he was possibly a child or a preteen, perhaps on a seek-and-locate booty mission, acting in the service of more devious and criminally intentioned adults. But even as I was reporting this, the recollection of the prowler's movements weighed ominously in the back of my mind. The movements were strange, yes, very strange.

The next day I discovered something that made me dubious about the competency of the police department. When I had told them that the prowler was on the roof, they did not make a good assessment of the facts I had given them. They did not contest my view that the prowler had done what he done while standing erect on the roof. You see, the section of the roof on which I viewed the prowler do his Blue Man Group thing was constructed at such an incline that it would not have allowed for the ease of movement displayed by the prowler unless the prowler had some inside-trader information on the laws of gravity that most of us are not privy to. In my own investigation, the matter was not fully explored as I dared not to venture out on such an incline—with a three-story drop below—on all fours, yet alone try to stand upright and fancy-free as the prowler had.

I was now more intrigued than fearful. That night I anticipated that another meeting was in the works, but I still dreaded the outcome. Maybe I would arm myself. I knew where I could quickly obtain some weapons. After all, I was still technically a teen. However, there seems to be something inherent in my destiny that blocks my becoming affiliated with guns. Even today, after serving four years in the military, I have still never possessed a firearm or fired one off, not even once.

I thought more about the figure, his below-average height, his spastic yet graceful movements. Remembering the incident elicited a welcome yet unjustified calmness. He/it seemed to be manageable (OK, this time in the physical sense), so I thought I would be able to handle myself in a physical altercation if it came to that. I contemplated fully drawing up the blinds, thus allowing me a totally unobstructed view of the visitor if he/it decided to pay me another visit, but the metaphorical testosterone surge didn't hang around long enough for that to happen.

I did have enough residual courage left to leave the blinds fully open. This reminded me how, when as a kid watching a monster movie that happened to be exceptionally scary, I would clasp my thumb and small finger together on one hand and then repeat the formulation on the other hand. Slowly I would bring the joined fingers together so as to view the television set and the apparition within from the perspective of the tiny diamond porthole formed by my fingers, thus believing I had diminished the threat of the beast by encapsulating it within the boundaries of my very own hands. Hey, maybe there's a spiritual truth somewhere in that, but this ain't a yoga tale.

True to form (without any known function), the visitor appeared and once again threw his magic beans or whatever at my window, causing the tap, tap, tap. This time as I looked toward the window I was able to maintain my composure. I watched, without acknowledging the eerie dance of curiosity that was being performed as if for my pleasure. The figure's gyrations were reminiscent of a Marcel Marceau, executing the comical gestures of a ballet-trained mime. I felt no danger from the visitor, who performed a few more gravity-defying stances and struts and pranced out of view, never to be seen again.

The next several months went along as usual with no other incidents. But, I gather, things were happening unbeknownst to me behind the inter-dimensional scenes. My life was ever so slightly yet continuously beginning to unravel. I grew distant from my boyfriend over extremely silly issues and we broke up. Because of my active calendar, I thought it necessary and beneficial for me to quit college. I then had problems with the nature of my employer's mission and with my supervisor, which led me to resign. Although my political alliances were growing stronger, due to my grass-roots community agenda and my political activism, I was becoming unsettled in my own neighborhood and had differences with my landlord. So my picture-perfect life unraveled in less then seven months after my ethereal guest dropped by. (Because of that weird gravity thing, I wonder if he really would have dropped, if dropped!)

Eight months after the visit, I found myself bewildered and disillusioned. Wishing to lose myself, I left Norfolk. Boarding a Peter Pan bus, seven hundred dollars in my pocket, bound for destination unknown. But, this was a good thing, I *think*!

Can beloved pets see ghosts? I hear this all the time from my callers, and Joel Martin also tells a great story of how President Roosevelt's dog saw the president's spirit at the moment of his passing.

PET GHOSTS

Woofty the forever faithful dog is communicating with his deceased owner, Liz. Days after she passed is when the strange, wonderful, and remarkable nightly events unfolded. I awoke at 3:00 A.M. the first time and found him looking up from the foot of Liz's favorite chair, wagging his happy tail! I froze in disbelief. Jumped up. Left them alone and slipped back to bed. And it did not stop! Next time he was there with leash in mouth, same tail wag, same look up! Now don't get me wrong, I've loved *Coast* forever. But why me? These night things continue, with Woofty bringing new stuff to the chair, wagging and looking up. Now I've heard of man's best friend. But a ghost?

This story speaks for itself. I was almost there, but pulled back in the nick of time.

MEETING THE DEVIL IN PERSON

It was Halloween. My daughter Amanda came home from school and requested that I be at the YMCA because she wanted me to meet her best friend Molly's mom. So of course I was going to be there. I met her mom. We hit it off immediately, and before the night was over she was asking me whether I could come to her house because her daughter was having problems with what she described as "the man."

The next day I went to their house, met her daughter, and we sat in their breakfast nook while she told me a little about what was happening. I then asked her to call whoever it was to her.

The next event, I must admit, if I hadn't experienced it with my own eyes I wouldn't have believed it. Molly had brown eyes, but in a split second they were blue. Her face became distorted, and she asked for a glass of whiskey and a peanut butter–and-jelly sandwich. Then the spirit walked through me. The only way I can describe it is being on the highway on a very hot day and seeing in front of you the waves of heat from the road.

In the next couple of months we researched the history of the house and the history before the house. Someone, a man, had committed suicide on the property and the daughter Molly looked exactly like his wife. The only difference was that Molly had short blond hair and the man's wife had long blond hair. He was born, if I remember correctly, in 1789 because we found his grave.

The situation got really too big for me to handle, so I needed help getting rid of the spirit. He was really becoming mentally and physically trying on Molly. So I started asking around and re-searching for someone to help out with the situation. Ms. Clara was her name, the woman we found to help in our hour of need.

Ms. Clara was a very good-looking woman, very personable. She visited with Molly and me and said she could help. (As I am writing this I can feel her anger.) It's hard to write now. My thoughts are scattered but I will get this on paper no matter what.

Things got worse. We were led in all directions. Before I knew who she was I introduced her to other people who she started to control. We went to her house one time and she was very ugly. I was very surprised. I remember clearly entering and exiting. She started to talk and I went and sat on the floor by a fish tank and went into a trance. This is the only way I can explain this. Her voice became muffled. When I thought about her house, I could see a black veil surrounding it. This is when I found out I had powers she wanted. I couldn't let her in. She once explained to me how she could be in her bed and make love to someone in another place. She proved it. Another friend of mine called very upset because for a moment his son cried out that someone was on top of him and he couldn't breathe.

Then there was a second incident. Ms. Clara came to my house in spirit and made my daughter cry out in fear for a whole night. Then one night my daughter went to a friend's house and all the lights on the street went out. I went to bed with fear I never experienced before or since. I lay awake most of the night, shaking and saying, "God is with me. I am protected."

All of a sudden I saw above me three tiny figures with robes with hoods and yellow eyes watching me. The next day I talked to someone who told me they were the devil's disciples. Molly's mother and I became enemies over something small. My life crashed. Ms. Clara (the devil) was angry with me because I wouldn't fall into her trap. I don't call it a curse, but she has put a dark cloud over me.

Evil is all around us. How can you protect yourself and your family? Is there a sure way to guard against the penetration of evil? There is. As we wrote in our first book, if you think evil, evil will come to you. Even to those who send evil to you, think of them with love and that will blunt the evil and protect you with a white light.

An Evil Spirit

I am forty-eight years old, twice-divorced female and I had moved to Indiana, leaving behind my boyfriend. He was not a very good person, but I did actually care for him.

He visited me, staying several days, and after he left I started feeling a presence in my home. I had experiences that I never had before. I started waking up in the night, sitting straight up and screaming, feeling someone was in the room with me. Also, while in my living room watching TV I would feel that someone was behind me, so strong that I would quickly jerk around, thinking I could catch whoever it was. The strange thing is I never felt scared or threatened, I just thought maybe there was a ghost in the home.

While my boyfriend stayed at my home he constantly lay on my sofa, which was at the end of my recliner, both of which faced the TV. One night while watching TV I noticed out of the corner of my eye a black mist or fog similar to the shape of a cloud coming out from under that sofa. I was so shocked that the hairs on my arms stood straight out, and large goose bumps ran up and down my arms. I was suddenly very cold. I moved up to the edge of my recliner and watched as this cloud moved right in front of me. It was just above the floor and slowly hovered as a cloud would. Then it went out of my home under my front door. I sat in that position for what seemed like an hour, in shock, thinking and trying to figure out what to do. Should I call someone? Would they believe me?

After that happened I never had any more of the experiences, never felt someone was watching me or never woke in the night again.

The only person I could think to call was my father, but I did not until the next morning after I had gathered my senses. He suggested I discuss it with his priest, as I was not in a church and did not have anyone like that to consult. The priest told me he thought it was surely an evil spirit, or the devil himself that my ex had left, either knowingly or not.

Even now when I talk about it or relive it I have the same physical results all over again. I am hesitant about whom I tell; for some reason it just seems personal. But it has changed my life.

I'm more serious about learning more about God, and I feel so much more sensitive to everyone. This experience is making me a better person, and I know God has a special plan for me. I hope this can help make someone else think about what is possible and real.

I receive many letters from people who've seen ghosts from other centuries. I often wonder, since ghosts are timeless, if we can see ghosts from the future without realizing it.

SOMEWHERE IN TIME

A few years ago I had to get up at 5:00 A.M. to go to work, and I had a habit of sitting on the side of the bed for five minutes or so after the alarm went off to get fully awake.

This particular morning I was sitting on the side of the bed after I shut the alarm off. Suddenly, I heard a woman say, "Mel," a nickname I had not used in about five years. I knew I was in a locked room, so I froze. Then the same voice repeated, "Mel," only much louder this time.

I looked to my right and at the foot of the bed stood this woman about three feet from me, dressed in an 1800s-style dress with brown stripes on a white background. It was figure-fit from the waist up, the skirt was floor length, and it looked like it had a lot of petticotes underneath. It had no collar, just hemmed at the neck, and the sleeves were to the wrist, again just hemmed, with no cuffs. I also noticed she was not wearing a bra; it looked like she had a tight band around her chest. She had brown eyes and freckles with shoulder-length brown hair. She had an inner glow that did not appear to go beyond her person. Naturally, I was scared stiff; all that was working were my eyes. After staring at me for several minutes, poof, she was gone.

Until that very moment I never realized there were live spirits about. What a shock that was.

Ghosts can protect us, especially if the bond between the living and the departed never breaks and still connects people across the boundaries of life. Do parents still watch over their children even after death?

HOW MY FATHER'S SPIRIT WATCHED OVER ME

My grandfather lived with me for twenty-two years. He died suddenly at ninety-eight years old! Two weeks after he died I was sitting in the living room watching *Jeopardy!* as we all did every night, when we heard my grandfather laughing in his bedroom. We ran back and looked into an empty room.

I was very close to my granddad, as he practically raised me. I went into his room and sat in his recliner and started to cry. Out of nowhere the smell of his pipe tobacco filled the room. I knew it was his way of telling me he was there watching over me!

On the first anniversary of his death, I had the house we had lived in up for sale. The Realtor came over and took twenty-seven pictures of the outside and inside. Two days later she came over with the pictures and asked me to look at them. There were two pictures in the group of the hallway. All the bedrooms were off that hallway. The last room on the right had been my granddad's room. On the closet door right outside his room there was an image on the closet door of Granddad!

The Realtor told me she took *no pictures* of the hallway! The image was of a man from the waist up in a bathrobe and holding a cane—with a baseball hat on. That was Granddad!

There is no reasonable explanation for this, yet I know it was my granddad again, telling me he was there!

Granddad never liked the woman I was with while we were together, and he wanted me to break up with her, telling me she was violent. But during the nine years we were together, I never saw that side of my girlfriend, so I thought nothing of it. Well, five days later my girlfriend came home insane or high on something and wrecked my house and slapped me!

The fight was terrible. She raised a vase to hit me and all of a sudden she fell to the floor with a crazy look on her face! I ran out the front door smack into a police officer. They went inside and arrested her. She was sentenced to two years!

I went one time to visit her, and that's when she told me some-one or thing had pushed her down that day. Oh—and here's the good part. The police said someone had called 911, and when no one talked on the line they responded to the address.

I know it was my granddad!

After I got rid of the crazy chick I never heard my granddad again or had anything weird happen. But I know he is still watch-ing over me!

Here's another pet ghost story. I have received a lot of them since we completed our first book and we talked about it on the air.

GABRIEL

I lost one of my best friends last week. His name was Gabriel, and he was a wonderful Alaskan malamute. But this isn't just another dog tale. I was guided to Gabriel and blessed with him. He was a special one in my life because he came at a time when I needed him and he needed me.

About eleven years ago I dreamed of a dog who was out living alone and having puppies. They were in an old shed with water on the dirt floor. Some of the puppies had died. It was such a sad dream. Yet I knew the information was real because I have been having this type of dream most of my life.

I went to the local dog pound where a college friend was working and told him about the dream. I told him this dog was out there somewhere and to keep an eye out for it. He agreed to do so.

A few days later I went back to check. They had brought Gabriel in. He'd been picked up because farmers had been complaining of his raiding their own dogs' food. He was very wary of everyone, frightened, but an intern at the pound spent time sitting in his cage with him because she knew his background.

His former owner was a school janitor who had given him to a friend who lived in the sticks. This person did not feed Gabriel or care for him. He had to take care of himself. But Gabriel had a future! Our mather had already told me about him and he would never be alone or hungry again!

I spent four or five days going to the dog pound, talking to him, feeding him bits of food, until finally he seemed to respond to me. I felt a little uneasy. He was a big dog and strong, but I knew he was meant to come home with me.

I brought him home and had to keep him tied or in the house until he got used to me and the place, but he eventually adjusted and became my best guardian and friend. I was very depressed at the time and he was the best thing that could have happened to me. He needed me and I needed him. I know that's why we were guided as we were to find each other.

A few years later I finally found the original owner, and he told me that Gabriel was the offspring of his K-9. It was no wonder he had such a good temperament. Over the years I found he was extraordinary in many ways. He watched over and guarded my other dogs, who are all toy poodles. When the oldest, Jules, was allowed out he would not let any other dog get near her. And he patrolled at night, which was good for me since I lived out in the country and we have coyotes. He did his job well and without ever being asked or trained.

There have been so many experiences I could recount, but there is one that is totally unexplainable in the usual terms. He saved me from what would have been a terrible injury, and only God knows the whole story.

I was trying to remove a log by the paved road near the house, and, like a dummy, I was using a shovel to pry it up. Suddenly, the shovel slipped and flew backward like a bullet. If I had hit the pavement I would have injured my back or head, maybe seriously.

But there was Gabriel! He had laid down in the exact spot I was headed for as the shovel slipped. I landed right smack on top of him, dead center. How was he there? I have no clue . . . but he was. Maybe he was guided, too.

I've lost a dear friend, yet through it all I have seen the hand of God in my life and his. We were there for each other at the most needed time. I am thinking that in the end we have no material things to take with us and our bodies are gone, but we have what we have given and been given in soul and spirit.

We take that wherever we go . . . and I know Gabriel's spirit lives on and some day I will see my old friend again. We'll have sunlit meadows to run and play, we will both be young again, and there will be no more pain or suffering. He'll be there to meet me. There is no doubt about that!

And some callers will tell me that a pet's ghost can even save a life.

MY DOG'S SPIRIT SAVED MY LIFE

I have an incident that I use to remind myself that there's more to life than what meets the eye. I used to drive a bus out of Seattle a few years ago, and this one trip will always be my most remembered.

I caught a run that goes from Seattle to Woodmont Beach at night, and it made every little stop they had in between those cities. I was sort of tired driving in the middle of the night. I was preparing to make an exit, when all of a sudden I had a very strong memory/sense of my old golden retriever that died thirty years ago. I just loved that dog; he loved me too. He was my absolute best friend ever. Bart was his name.

When I got to the exit, this sense of my old dog was startling to me. I had not thought about him in a long, long while. What was startling was he was giving me hell! He was barking and barking and quite agitated as I crossed a railroad track. I continued into the next town, dropping off a few people and picking up a couple more, almost filling up my bus, and most of the passengers were dozing, trying to sleep. I reversed my course and headed back out toward the highway with the image of my dog barking away at me. I slowed down close to the intersection where the train track was, gave an extra look to the right, and then I saw it, a big, bright light shining down thirty yards away. No horn, just light—a freight train rolling through at 2:00 A.M.!

I am a safe driver; I stop at the tracks, but after the train passed and I pulled out on the highway, Bart jumped in my arms and licked my face! I believe the spirit of my old dog was looking out for me. I also think I more than likely would have spotted the train before I proceeded, but I think he did just what he needed to do to warn me, and be safe! When I die, I hope to see him again and I will bring him a milk bone, and we will play ball again. I still love that dog.

Why believe that only particular religions can have spirits? Many spirit and ghost stories come from Native American traditions.

DEATH IS THE END OF LIFE...

I was raised in the Catholic tradition where there was talk about the "communion of saints," and where All Souls Day was celebrated, but despite that there was a fear of and a distance from the whole subject of death, dying, or life after death, and positively no talk about any spirit other than the Holy Spirit. When I reached the age of forty, I started hanging around and learning from some Hopi elders. Two of them adopted me into their families, an adoption of the heart. One died in 2005 and the other died in bed on March 7, 2006, at 7:00 P.M. after my best friend prayed that if she needed to transition that she would transition at the perfect time.

Soon after her death, her husband had a "strange" experience, strange in the white world but apparently not so strange in the Native American world. She came back to her family and was seen walking on two legs even though she had lost a leg, and argued with her husband over who would take the children to school as he had no driver's license, then climbed into the van to drive the children to school. But he realized that she was dead and got spooked all of a sudden after she got into the car. He did have a relative drive the children to school. She also talked on the cell phone to two of my friends, saying the words that she always said to them after they delivered food and money to her family, "You are my family. You are my family." My friends called me as they were blown away by the experience. They tried to trace the call, but the cell phone provider could not trace the call.

On my birthday I was missing my friend badly. Of all things to miss about her, that day I was missing the stones that she used to carry around with her and gave to me for my birthday, the polished stones that she sometimes would carve as a jeweler. I thought, *She is gone and I will never get another stone from her for my birthday.*

As I was crying in my room, I felt her presence near me, warm and comforting. I dried my tears and left my apartment for work. Just as I was getting into my car, I happened to look down and found a stone next to my driver's-side car tire. It was not just any stone. It was a polished dog tooth, amythest, also known as the "breath of life" stone. Both deceased friends believed that every breath should be a prayer "for all of my relations," so that was very special. It was also very special that the stone is similar to the amythest that I put in front of the picture of her.

I am a psychoanalyst, working with at-risk teens, and have carried the stone with me and used it with my suicidal clients who believed that there was nothing to look forward to after death. I told them this story and let them hold the stone. They decided to risk living better after that. Those who feel the energy in the stone believe it is protective and compassionate.

I love haunted house stories and can't get enough of them when my callers come in on open lines. Here's one from a contributor.

SMOKING IN BED

From a local newspaper ad I placed trying to find a home for our three cats, we were called by a couple who answered the ad. We brought the cats to their home, a lovely Victorian house that they mentioned they were trying to sell but they couldn't because there was a ghost in the house. They explained that if they were sorting pictures, for instance, and left the room, when they returned they'd find them all scattered about. Apparently there is a state law that if any house is haunted it must be revealed to any prospective buyer. I told them I had the ability to speak to spirits and asked if they'd like me to see what I could find. They anxiously pointed to a room at the top of the stairs where I should start.

When I entered that room I asked psychically if there was anyone there. A woman answered, saying she was afraid. She told me that she had been smoking in bed and woke up to the room engulfed in flames and couldn't get to the door. I told her she should look for a light, which would take her where she needed to go. She said, "Yes, I see it, I'm going now," and she left. There were no further instances of anything being disrupted. They were then able to sell their house.

Animal spirits are all around us, my listeners tell me. The communication between humans and animal spirits is so strong, you almost want to believe that it can be a teachable skill, even though some people nat-urally have that ability. This listener certainly has that.

THE CARDINAL

I had a very unusual experience about two months ago. I consider myself a very spiritual person and have had tons of intuitive expe-riences. I have always had a strong connection with animals and have saved a lot of them. I am also studying animal energy healing.

Anyway, about two months ago I was working at my drawing board up in my studio. I only have time to do my artwork on the weekends, so that's the only time I'm up there in that room.

While I was working, a female cardinal lighted on the win-dowsill and tapped on the glass with her beak. Then she peered intently at me. She did this about three times, each time just a "tap . . . tap." Then she flew off. This was not one of those in-stances where a bird sees its reflection in the glass and attacks it. This was very deliberate and the timing of the taps was always the same. And she looked straight at me. (My drawing board is only about four feet away from the window.)

She did this for three weekends in a row, and the only time she came to that window and tapped was when I was seated at my drawing board.

One afternoon I came home sick from work, which is very, very rare for me. I was lying on the couch in the living room and she came to the living room and tapped her tap . . . tap and looked in at me! I knew she was trying to give me a message, but had no idea in the world what it could be.

After the three weeks, she didn't come around anymore. So, about a week after she last visited, I was working at the small of-fice where I am the only one in there. A man walked through the door, introduced himself, and said he had been looking for me. He said he owned a publishing company and he had seen some of my work. He went to a lot of trouble to look me up.

After viewing his Web site and talking with him, I agreed to do some drawings for him. I asked him what he would like for me to draw for the first assignment, as the artwork on the Web site were moose, bears, wolves, and so on. He responded immediately, "I think I'll have you do a cardinal!"

This is only one of many, many experiences I have had of a supernormal nature. I've had dreams that have told me things before they've happened. I've seen departed loved ones. I had a ghost in my house for several years. (I think I persuaded him to go to the light, because he hasn't been back.) He was a good ghost, though, and warned me once of a problem with a gas leak in my basement that could have been dangerous.

Thanks for all the good work you do. I pray that I, too, can be a "worker in the light."

Here is one of the most charming ghost stories I have ever heard about love that crosses the boundary of death.

THREE CANS OF BEER

After being divorced for twelve years my wife and I got back together again. We pooled our money and bought land away from town. We both worked in town and bought produce and meat every day. We used a generator in the evenings to watch TV and listen to music, but we never used the refrigerator. We used it to store our mail and the blueprints for the house we were going to build. We had a large old metal washtub we had filled with ice for beer and soda.

My wife got sick and got cancer, so we didn't build the house. I have always been psychic, but she called it airy-fairy and just sloughed it off when I'd tell her things. She had cancer and we knew she was going to die and I kept asking what kind of a sign she was going to give me so I'd know she was alright. She would never say, so one day I said, "Well, it will have to do with beer because that's the thing you like."

About three weeks after her funeral I was alone in the house and I heard the refrigerator come on. I threw a pity party, crying, "Oh no, the battery is going to go dead and I don't know how to fix it."

I knew there was a button inside that said GAS OFF and ELECTRIC. I thought maybe my grandkids had switched it so I opened it up and, yep, there were three beers on the shelf. I cried and smiled, knowing it was my wife letting me know she was alright. And it never came on again!

A story of how a ghost in the house was an early precursor of a reader's spiritual awakening.

SOMETHING OF DARKNESS

Back in the day, Carla, my wife at that time, my two-year-old daughter, and I moved to our new home in Denver, Colorado. The house was a small, two-bedroom, older home owned by a student who was leaving the state for a few months. We rented the house with all her furnishings and moved in.

Everything seemed unobtrusive in the beginning weeks. We bought a single bed for my girl and made her her own bedroom/playroom in the front second bedroom, which was virtually devoid of furnishings. She wouldn't sleep in that room, however. We noticed she would play in there until dark and then want to be in the living room with us.

If we put her in that room while she slept, we would hear her crying in the night or on the couch the next morning. Finally, we just allowed her to sleep on the sofa. At this time, I had not awakened into my spiritual awareness as I am now, but I still had some knowledge of ghosts and the paranormal.

The wife came home a couple of months after we were there and announced she had been moved to the night shift. I was uneasy about this. As a small child, I was terrified of being alone and never understood why. Now, as an adult, some of that fear had subsided. Still . . .

The first week went well. Nothing scary in the house, nothing unusual. The second week Carla worked nights and on the second night of her shift, something strange happened.

My daughter had fallen asleep on the couch as usual. I started hearing a noise, which sounded like breathing. Realizing that it was probably just my baby's breathing echoing, I went back to what I was doing. But as I sat there, the breathing sound became louder and louder. I checked her on the couch and she was breathing quietly, but I noticed her breathing patterns did not match the other noise. Then I proceeded to go to each room to discern the origin. Nothing. It was as if the sound was coming from nowhere and everywhere. Finally it stopped. I was uneasy but decided not to mention this to Carla. It was probably just my imagination, anyway.

Each night the breathing sounds would come back. I thought about anything I knew about hauntings, but it was not much. I tried to investigate the house outside and in. One thing I did notice was the front bedroom was much colder than the other rooms. Finally, one night, the breathing became very loud. I walked to the opening of the archway of the front bedroom. It was distinctively coming from there, and the room was freezing. To make it worse, I got an impression it was a dark-clad female and definitely did not want anyone in there. Unfortunately, I had no one to talk to about this, so I kept it to myself. We had nowhere to go at nights as I had no family there, nor had I found any close friends, at least, no one I could trust with this. On it continued and I lived in fear. The one time I did get brave enough, I tried reading from the Bible to cast it out and it just got louder and madder.

Finally, one night about three weeks later when my wife was home, the sound started. She and I were both sitting in the living room and our daughter was playing. The sound had never been audible when Carla was home, although I had hoped for it. I needed someone to tell me I wasn't crazy!

"What's that noise?" she asked, looking up from the paper. I pretended I heard nothing as the breathing became louder. Finally she got up to investigate it, insisting I *must* hear it, too.

I allowed her to search around for a while and then sat her down and told her what had been happening. Both of us approached the front bedroom. She switched on the light and walked in. The room was an icebox, even though it was open to the rest of the house by an archway. She then reassured me this was not my imagination, but still it was unexplained. We had a ghost in our home that might want to harm us and we had no idea what to do! No wonder my daughter would not go in the room after dark! She was open enough to sense this thing from the beginning.

Carla was obviously shaken by this, but kept up a good front and her composure. Before admitting to anything supernatural, the next day she checked out everything in and around the house. She even examined pipes under the house and all the forced-air vents, including limbs blowing against the house and the roof. She decided it was unexplainable as well. Now we wondered about our next move. Ultimately, we decided nothing "bad" had happened. We were uneasy but unharmed. Waiting was our only option. If anything really started to manifest, then we would leave.

As time went on, we began to notice more unusual things. The room now became freezing cold, but only after six at night. In the daytime it was normal like the rest of the house. Just before six, my daughter would bring what toys she wanted to play with out of the room and she also started spending less and less time in there during the day. In the mornings, we started noticing the hardwood floor was damp, as if it were sweating. None of the other floors were that way. This would disappear quickly. Then it started to involve the walls. This moisture did not come down from the ceiling, but up from the floor until water was dripping from halfway down the walls. We asked a contractor to look at the house problem. He had no explanation. Carla and I called the landlord and told him we were moving out.

This was the first extreme paranormal experience I remember. I then knew that such things existed for certain. I have never solved this experience. As I said before, I was not knowledgeable in the paranormal at that time. I do believe that whatever this entity was, it was an evil force. Still this remains unknown.

A vision of death as a shadow person is a type of story that many of my listeners tell me about over the phone on open lines. This time I was glad that one of our readers sent this in as well.

SOUL-TAKER: A VISIT FROM THE SPIRIT OF DEATH

There is a being that few of us are privileged to see. I cannot deny having seen it. It was a wonderful experience when I saw the soul-taker. I saw this entity floating in my bedroom while I was para-lyzed, but yet noticed that a presence was definitely floating in the dark room. It woke me up to ask who I was. I spoke to it only with my mind. Then after my sleep ended, I had a vivid remembrance of it that morning.

The shape of the entity was like a dark cloud with jagged ends about six feet long and floating two feet off the bedroom floor. The cloudlike being was about a foot and a half in width. It was just floating there, conversing with me about who I was. I am not religious, nor do I have any hangups and beliefs, but ever since seeing this thing I have become an agnostic. There is no way that I will ever become an atheist. I can't fear death; in fact I look for-ward to the next phase in my existence.

I have seen what few were allowed to see. This happened back in the '60s. My sister was ill at the time in the next bedroom. She died a couple of days later. I conclude that I was awakened from sleep to converse mentally with a being that needed more certain information as to whom it was sent to take to who-knows-where. It must have been sent from a far distant place because it needed to ask me who I was, and it wasn't sure of its mission as to who to prepare for some future place. That same morning at breakfast I mentioned my dream to my dad.

Ever since that day my life has been in a continual peace with just about everything. In conclusion, I wish to say that I should not have remembered that night except my mind was awake, even though I was paralyzed, as I was mentally communicating to the entity. So you see that it is hard to be an agnostic after an experience like that.

There was a book I read a few years later about two boys seeing a dark cloud coming through a screen that then went back out through the same screen. This was seen in broad daylight. I have come to the conclusion that our lives are very short, which is a big reason that not much is known or proved. Nor do we have time to do positive and real, true stuff that can be made known. Man has not learned, nor is he allowed to learn a lot of things that have positive existence in other forms of life. As I said before, I can't become a blocked and nonthinking person. It's not my fault that I have this knowledge. I was allowed to have it in my permanent memory. I'm turning seventy next month and use my computers for watching old movies, listening to radio stations, playing a little crib, and keeping from getting stircrazy in this western town.

CHAPTER

2

ANGELS

Perhaps no subjects generate more interest among my listeners, and among our contributors, than angels and ghosts. Angels is an especially loaded subject because with it my listeners and contributors also talk about direct communication with the Creator. In fact, so many different people have so many different visions of what angels are and what they do, what the Creator looks like, and what the Divine wants of them, that you wonder why there are so many different manifestations.

Some say that in moments of dire physical or emotional stress people see what they want to see. Or, if there is an expectation that people have about what they will see, that expectation, in Heisenberg's terms, is exactly what they do see. It's easy, therefore, for people to argue that these events are actually self-fulfilling types of illusions. But I take the opposite approach. I believe very much that my listeners, my callers-in, and our contributors are actually seeing what they say they are seeing. Just a review of what people see and what they hear will convince you of that as well. Moreover, if you read carefully what our contributors say, there seems to be a process through which people can bring angels to them. Is this a form of prayer?

Take, for example, the story a friend of mine told me about a very mundane event at a local marina in Southern California. He said that he and his wife had just bought their first boat and then bought an outboard engine for it. Having no truck or SUV, however, they managed to stuff the outboard into the folded-down backseat of their car. With the engine all the way under the rear window, they drove into the marina where their new boat was waiting. But once there, these two people, neither of whom was into weightlifting, stared at the hundred-plus-pound engine in the rear of their car while they scratched their heads about how to get it out.

Nothing they did worked. No tugging, no hauling, no dragging, no amount of physical effort could budge the engine. Worse, they knew if they yanked too hard on the base of the engine the thing might slide out of the car and crash against the parking lot cement, thus ending their dreams of getting their boat under way until they got a new engine delivered.

As the heat of the California day increased with the height of the sun, they tried to strategize their next move, but it looked hopeless.

That was when an odd-looking stranger showed up. On a hot California day, he was wearing a flannel shirt and Farmer Jones overalls. He was more than friendly, in fact, too friendly for normally guarded Angelinos.

"Need some help?" he asked.

My friends just looked at him, speechless, as they contemplated what they wanted him to do. He didn't look particularly like he worked out at Gold's Gym. No bulging muscles like David Banner's Hulk were straining the seams of his flannel shirt. He looked just like he could jump inside a suit and drive to downtown L.A. for a day at the office in one of the bank buildings.

"You need me to get that for you?" he asked.

My friends were astonished.

"Here." He reached inside the car and in one movement lifted the engine out and hoisted it high in the air.

"Now, where do you want it?"

My friends meekly pointed to their boat all the way down at the end of the dock.

"On the transom?"

They nodded.

With the engine between his arms as if it were a rag doll, the stranger carried it down the gangplank and all the way to the very end of the floating dock. Then, seemingly without any strain at all, he lifted the engine over the sailboat's transom, braced it against the wooden mounting plate, and locked it into place.

"She's all ready to go," he said.

And he turned and started up the dock.

"But wait, thanks," my friend asked as he reached into his pocket.

The stranger held up his hand and waved him off.

"But who are you?" they asked.

He smiled and said, "Michael," as they nodded and turned around to look at the engine.

"Can we get you—" my friend said, as he turned back to the stranger, but broke off in midsentence.

Michael had disappeared. He hadn't run away or simply walked because the floating dock was too long for anyone to have moved that quickly. Worse, they couldn't see him walking along the boardwalk or in the parking lot. No, he hadn't simply walked back up to the shore. He, as my friends scratched their heads again in a knowing disbelief, had simply dematerialized.

Have you ever had the experience where you know something is a truth without ever having to express it? It's a thought that somehow gets laid into your consciousness as if it were a steel beam that supports a skyscraper. Who put it there? How did it get past your wall of disbelief, your skeptical mind? All you know is that it's there and once there, forever a part of your belief system. That was exactly the situation with my two friends from Los Angeles. Nobody had to tell them. No choir of a million voices supported by an orchestra of harps had to accompany their realization. It just suddenly materialized inside their brains at exactly the same moment as they looked at each other. It was the archangel, Michael.

Was he casually strolling down the harbor at Redondo Beach that day looking for someone to help? Had he looked down from heaven to see the predicament my friends were in and came down to give them an angelic hand? Had they summoned him in their own spirits to get them out of a jam because they had innocently gotten themselves into trouble?

I have my own thoughts on this, but I can prove nothing. However, this event, as nontragic as it was, mirrors the same kinds of events that my callers and contributors have reported. In moments of absolute confusion, complete helplessness, and a call to the universe for help—even they don't know they were calling out—help comes. A biblical phrase from Deuteronomy rings in my head, "Even before they call, I will answer." Indeed, sometimes we call even before we call, and the call is answered.

This is what I believe is the situation many of our contributors found themselves in. But, in order to call, one must submit to the fact that no amount of traditional human effort will save the day. On the other hand, do we have to wait for tragedy to strike us before we can experience the guidance of angels?

Of course, the answer is no. What many of our contributors have also written is that by their working in the light, reaching out to the larger universe, seeking truth not under the constraints of logic but in the revelation of insight at reaching a point beyond day-to-day human experience, they see divine intervention almost as a constant. They realize that we are in constant communication with the Divine every minute of every day. And this is the essential point of *Worker in the Light* as well. We are always in touch with the divine inspiration that informs the entire universe. We're in touch, in communication, but because we are so immersed in the logical overlay of our daily lives, we never realize that there's an open line to the universe. So we go on from day to day, toiling in our fields without the benefit of recognizing that we're not taking advantage of our higher sensory perceptivity.

I think of one of my contributors who writes about how her life was saved in a major collision by a bright light that illuminated her car just before impact, a light that saved her from going through the windshield by blocking the way. The truck driver that hit her was amazed at the image he saw in the glowing light, not by the bloody face that my contributor had after she hit the steering wheel. What was the nature of the light? Was it summoned or was it angelic intervention?

I also think about another story one of my contributors tells about her connection to the universe when she was a child. In her innocence, she had no reason to doubt that the voices she heard in her mind were angelic voices, coaching her, guiding her, and encouraging her. But the more she told her parents and her friends at school, the more people looked at her as if she were crazy. Even her parents kept asking her whether she was talking to imaginary friends. By the time she was a teenager, she had shut off the voices in her head, rejecting their reality for the reality of her friends. She wrote that she had tried drugs, had begun to drink, and was looking for relationships in all the wrong places. Then, after her marriage broke up and she was facing financial and personal ruin, she finally opened up her mind to the voices she had shut out.

The voices asked her where she'd been. They were always there, they said, always present, but she just wasn't listening. At last, she owned up to the relationship she had with her angels and, guided by them once again, she found her spiritual path and returned to the person she once had been. I like that story a lot because it tells me that we all have guardian angels who take care of us and with whom we can communicate if only we allow ourselves to do so. Our contributors who wrote to us about *Worker in the Light* told us that when they opened up to the universe we wrote about, they were able to experience a form of guidance that was all-inclusive, nondenominational, but tailored to the person's own belief system. We experience what we expect to experience even though the experience is the same.

When two lives cross at the point of life and death and one intervenes to save the other as it leaves this plane to become an angel, even if you didn't believe in an angelic presence, you would be almost forced to. This is the story here, a story my listeners tell me happens very often in families.

MY ANGELIC GRANDMOTHER

My eldest daughter is the subject of my story. When she was two years old, almost three, she was with her babysitter. On their way back home, the babysitter did not have her in a car seat, or a seatbelt. She entered an intersection and was "T-boned." The side door of the car was blown open, and my daughter was ejected and thrown thirty yards into a ditch. The car rolled several times and landed bottom side up on top of my daughter.

Two people who had seen the accident lifted the van off my daughter. Here is where the story gets strange. The person who hit the car is a person I grew up with; the men who lifted the car off my daughter were friends of mine! She was life-flighted to a children's hospital where she spent a week in a coma in intensive care. While this happened I was out of town on business. I got a call from my company to fly home now! There was an emergency.

When I flew in and got my rental car, I was not sure where I was to meet my husband, so I went home. When he was not there, I went to see my uncle who had just gotten home from cancer surgery. Hospice had set him up at home. When I sat down to visit with him, he had a glow in his eyes that said, *I am glad you're home.* He proceeded to tell me, "I'm glad you're home. I have been waiting for your daughter." We then sat and had a conversation about life, God, the road and where it divides. When he was finished with what he had to say, he told me to go be with my daughter, and that he and God were square.

I did not understand what he meant until early the following morning, when I was with my daughter. She awoke from her coma, and my uncle died. As I learned later that day, he died two minutes after my daughter woke up. She then spent another three weeks at the children's hospital recovering.

When she was sent home, she spent another four months bedridden, with external fixations on her legs and a partial body cast. When she was finally out of her cast and the fixators removed, she was sitting between her dad and me one weekend. She looked at me and stated, "Uncle Charles told me to tell you he loves you, he and God sent me home because I have work to do." I tell you, she never knew her uncle's real name (we always called him CJ), so I truly believe he was in God's hands! I believe CJ went to God in place of my daughter; that he gave his life for his favorite niece.

Is it possible that the eldest can ask God to take their lives, when a child is in need?

Sometimes encounters with angels are far more serious than just a helping hand. My listeners call in all the time with stories of how angels intervene in their lives in times of extreme crisis, just like in the following story.

AN ENCOUNTER WITH AN ANGELIC PRESENCE

It was a very cold morning in the winter of 1975. On this fateful morning the sun was shining through the frosty air as I drove down a familiar winding mountain road. As I approached a shadowed curve, my world was about to be changed forever. My car began to lose traction on the road. I had hit a large patch of black ice! With no warning, I found my car hurtling head-on into a large oncoming truck that was also in the grip of the ice. There was no seat-belt law in those days, so I was not belted, nor were there air bags. My car was sailing along at over fifty miles an hour, and there was nothing to come between me and tons of crashing metal. In that moment, I heard a calm, guiding voice speak to me: "Lay over on the seat and cover your face with your arms." I did this, but at the same time I was certain that I was witnessing the moment before my death. I saw no reasonable way to live through this, and though I sought in my mind for ways to escape this imminent doom, I was held in the inexorable flight of my car over ice. From the moment of recognition that it was the end of my life to the moment of collision seemed a small eternity of anticipation. Were the heavens deliberating and weighing the possible outcomes as I waited? Then came the impact, with a silence that followed. I wondered if I was still alive. Yes, and I became aware of a presence in the car. The thing that drew my attention was streaming light. Spectacular, the rays flowed in golden, crystaine patterns that subtly vibrated and radiated as if alive, filling the entire space. My car had been crushed right up to the driver's seat and my sternum had broken the steering wheel. Lying on the seat, I was bathed in a golden effulgence that seemed to contain a wealth of beauty and strength. I felt held by a loving intelligence. My experience of this golden light could be seen as sensory hallucination resulting from the trauma. Or it could have just been the sunlight. But then came the witness.

The driver of the truck opened the door of my car, dreading what he might find inside. Then I saw his face; it was full of wonder. I anticipated his words of concern, "Are you okay? Are you hurt badly?" Instead, he gasped, "You are so beautiful!" Because these words were so inappropriate to the situation—after all, I was disheveled and bleeding, pinned and unable to move within the framework of my crumpled car—I knew he must be experiencing the golden presence as well. I recall now Robert Johnson describing a similar light in his book, *Between Heaven and Earth.* His words described my own experience of the light filling my car that morning; it was "golden, radiant, luminous, ecstatically happy, perfectly beautiful, purely tranquil."

Days later, the experience continued to unfold. While still in the hospital, the X-rays revealed that I had torn ligaments in my neck. I realized then that the mirror had hit me under the chin, the blow causing a visible contusion on the skin under my chin the length of the mirror. Seven days later, still unable to lift my head from the pillow, I had a difficult night. The pain in my neck grew worse. Nevertheless, I sensed the presence of the light and because of that intangible presence, I wasn't disturbed. By morning, the pain had stopped and I could sit up again. I was able to lift my head, though the doctors assured me that I would need many months of therapy and neck braces. When the doctor examined me again and took new X-rays, he found the tendons of my neck were normal. He had no explanation for this except that the first X-rays must have been mislabeled, confused with someone else's. I went back to work the next day.

I understood much more about the magnitude of this miracle when my car insurance adjuster took me to see my car. I was rocked by the sight of the frame and sheet metal of the car accordioned right up to the small space that had held me. It was clear that I had broken the steering wheel with my sternum, and that my leg had been gashed under the wheel. The mirror was jammed upward after hitting me under the chin. But what was most surprising was the shattered glass of the windshield. I looked closely at this, and it did indeed look like a head or shoulder had impacted the glass. The glass had concentric circles of breakage as if something round had collided with it. Yet this had not been done by my body; my injuries were all accounted for. The adjuster was mystified as well. How did my body escape impact with the windshield? Something solid had to have taken the blow. Or was it that someone had taken the blow? Today I still sometimes feel the peace of angel wings like those that must have held me that unforgettable day in the golden light.

It is amazing how people see angels. They see them in panes of glass, in mirrors, or, as here, in clean wisps of smoke.

MY FATHER

My father died in 2004 after a lengthy illness. I was always close to him but not geographically. He lived in Massachusetts, I lived in Arizona. Most times we'd talk on the phone, if not every day then once or twice a week. I loved him deeply and I knew each time I spoke to him the time was getting shorter for him to be among us. I tried to always be upbeat with him, and to not use denial or avoidance.

I took a plane to Massachusetts when my sister called and said, "Dad has had a massive stroke, he is on a ventilator, I think you should come."

I got on the plane and flew to Boston, going directly to the hospital and to the intensive care unit. I found him alone, hooked up to a ventilator. He looked worn and tired and I didn't like the setting all too much. He wouldn't have, either. My sister came and we discussed things. "He wouldn't want this," I told her. "I know," she said in tears. "But don't expect me to stand there when they take it out; he might die right there."

I shook my head. "No, it's not like that; it will not be immediate, if at all; we'll see." The nurse came in after we told Dad, and turned the machine off. Dad actually reached up with his hand and pulled the tube out as soon as the tape was loosened. "Did you see that?" the nurse said, a little shaken. "He's something," I said. "I knew he wanted that out," my sister said. To our surprise he continued to breathe on his own, though the stroke had taken his ability to speak and possibly see. We thought he could hear us.

It took five days for him to finally win and go home to God. I was already home in Arizona and my sister called. "Dad's gone," she said, choking up. "It's okay, baby," I said, "I'll let everyone know." I went to the computer room and sat down. Before I could touch the keyboard my eyes were drawn to something to my right, just above the small speaker. I focused and watched what appeared to be a whiff of smoke curl and move ever so slowly, like it was made of dense, full material. It was pure white and it inched along but with grace, unaffected like smoke would be by mild currents of a breeze or airflow. It seemed to have its own mass, and bulk, and it was navigating on what must have been molecules.

I was shocked and awed by what I was seeing and couldn't pull my eyes away. "What is this?" I said under my breath. "What is this?" I watched it till it inched and curled its way into oblivion.

I don't know what explanation one might have for what it was. It was not smoke. It was not glare, and it was not my imagination. I believe it was either an angel or my father in his ectoplasmic form (spirit). I believe in life after death. All the holy books speak of it. However, we don't know what spirit looks like. Perhaps I got a glimpse of pure human spirit, and maybe, God forgive me, it was my dad being with me one last time.

Another serious topic on Coast *concerns how people talk to angels, or, even more important, what means angels use to communicate with us. I like to believe that you hear a still, small voice inside of you, and you know what you have to do.*

COMMUNICATING WITH ANGELS

I will now skip forward to the major transformation of my life. As God does, he guides you to where you need and desire to be. I was referred to a spiritual counselor, a pastor, who is such a beautiful being, you couldn't even imagine. After he learned about my heightened psychic abilities he introduced me to a process called "divine writing in dialogue." He explained that this meditation and writing will bring one closer to the heavens and divine ones, guiding you to walk in the light and walk the path with God and goodness. *That* is exactly what I desired, so I began communicating. I wrote every night before I went to sleep. It did take a few days to open the portal and get past the physical mind and thoughts, but once all the clutter was gone, I was at the place where I had open, daily communication guiding my life completely. I continue to communicate with all souls and spirits—those stuck in limbo, those needing resolution, those needing help crossing into the light. I have been presented with dark spirits, beings and energy appearing in an attempt to "snuff out my light," of which the sweet pastor taught me how to remove from my space. When they appeared, I simply smudged, and stated that I walk in the light and darkness cannot touch me. I commanded evil darkness be removed . . . and so they were. But I must add, you must feel and intend what you are stating.

I receive messages from angels and saints that pertained to me solely, messages relating to world events and ideas, the process of afterlife, misconceptions of worldviews, and so much more.

My spiritual position is "seeker for all"; I am to seek the truth of all. When the Divines tell me a person will come for my help, they do. When they tell me an event will happen, it does. Therefore, after having experience—so-called proof—of their messages, when they speak, I listen. We communicate just like you and I would, we analyze, argue, laugh, praise, compliment, and they warn me. I even get reprimanded in the most loving way you could ever imagine.

I communicate with Mary, Bernadette, Joseph, and many other special notable divine spirits. Most gratefully, I communicate with our maker, God, with Jesus at his side.

This daily communication is my life. I give them praise and gratitude for my entire life every day. I have never felt more grounded, at peace, and at one with the heavens!

And sometimes an angel will be drawn to you because you've made it a point to communicate. This is the whole point of Worker, *learning to communicate, just as this contributor did.*

COMMUNICATING WITH AN ANGEL

For six years I was a maintenance worker at a private resort. I worked at night by myself, maintaining the facilities, and it was during this period in my life that I increased my spiritual vibrations through diet, meditation, and diligent spiritual study. At the time I was studying the teachings of the Ascended Masters and as a result, I began having incredible metaphysical experiences such as increased psychic abilities, telepathic communication, visual phenomenon, and direct contact with spiritual beings.

I've had several spiritual experiences at work and one night, while buffing the lobby floor, I was listening to music by Sinead O'Connor.

As I was moving the buffer across the floor, there was a song playing that inspired me to think of God. In that very moment every time I was under a ceiling pot light, it would flicker. So I started walking in a circle of about ten feet in diameter, moving directly under each pot light to see what would happen. Every light flickered and flashed until I had several lights flickering and there was a light show going on in the middle of the lobby!

Needless to say, I was elated and excited but not surprised since I had had similar previous experiences. Little did I know, I was in for yet another special demonstration that night.

I would take breaks on the loading dock during the night where I enjoyed looking at the stars and watching satellites go by. The loading dock faced east and about fifty feet from the facility was a storage building. The building had windows on each floor, and on the main floor there was a ledge along the windows.

Besides the protected light on the loading dock, there was just enough light from the streetlights to see the window ledge on the storage facility. I went for a break just after midnight and about an hour later I came out again to cool off on this warm summer night. Only this time when I came outside I noticed something on the window ledge of the storage place that hadn't been there an hour earlier. I walked up to the window ledge and to my amazement, there was an old, beat-up painting about 8 by 10 inches of Archangel Michael! It was an oil painting and all it said on it was Archangel Michael in the bottom left-hand corner.

At first I thought it was a joke but suddenly I had the urge to say, "Archangel Michael, are you with me?" I got no response, then picked up the painting and took it over to the loading dock where I could see it in the light. The loading dock light was one of those orange-colored sodium lights so it gave off an orange glow and was very bright.

I then again had the feeling to test Archangel Michael to see if he was with me. I said, "Archangel Michael, if you are here show me by making the light go out." I repeated that several times and suddenly the light went out and came back on about twenty to thirty seconds later!

What's amazing is that I had been working there for several years and that light had never gone out on its own, let alone turn back on again.

I said, "Thank you, Archangel Michael, for bringing forth your radiance and being with me."

I went on with my night with a big grin on my face and ever since I've been working in the light!

We also discovered from our callers and readers that angelic visions and their presence can be accompanied by signs. This reader compares his sign to what Moses saw in the desert after he fled Egypt.

MY BURNING BUSH

I have had many what I call "burning bushes" put in my path, but you might find the two I'll share with you now of interest.

The first was a good friend of mine who got sick with pneumonia and was put into the hospital. Three days in he went into a coma. I was grief stricken; every night I would go to bed praying that this and that would happen, and finally I spoke with a spiritual advisor. I said I did not know how to pray for him; that I was praying as if I had a say in the matter. The spiritual advisor said to me, "Go home tonight and just pray for two things: that God's will be done and that you can accept God's will."

I did just that and the next morning I woke around four o'clock and immediately started sobbing as I had been doing each morning, waking and thinking about him, but this time I had just started sobbing when the next thing I knew I was enveloped in this peace, this total love and acceptance, this contentment that I have never felt before. At the same time I had this "knowing" I knew that Raphael was going to die and it was OK.

I went to work that morning a changed person. This was Thursday and he passed away the following Saturday. A coworker in the office said something to me about "when Ralph gets back . . ." and I looked at him and very plainly said "Ralph's not coming back." This man had watched me suffering since the moment Raphael went into a coma; so seeing me now very calmly, just about serenely, say that he wasn't coming back gave him the chills and he walked away without saying anything. After that

Saturday the coworker only looked at me strangely but never brought it up.

I have to add that before that Thursday morning I was the worst white-knuckle flier ever, and about two months later I was sitting in the airport getting ready to board a plane when I thought about that morning. I remembered that wonderful feeling I was given and I thought, "Oh, OK," and I have *loved* flying ever since. My life partner to this day can't understand it. The flight back home was horrendous; we were in a thunderstorm, bouncing up and down, and he always loved flying, but this night he was a bit worried while I sat at the window going, "Wow, look at that" and "Whoa, that was some dip, huh?" as if I were on a ride at an amusement park. I think what I realized before the flight out that day was that God is indeed always with me.

The second incident has to do with my granddad passing away from cancer. Many special things happened, the first being that I knew it a full year before he was diagnosed, so I was able to share special time with him. During his last two weeks on this earth I was with him when the doctor said there was nothing else to be done. After my granddad left the office I asked the doctor how long. He said two weeks. And it was two weeks to the day.

During the last week my grandma was hospitalized. She was vomiting blood but hiding it because of Granddad. Finally it got so bad that she went to the doctor and an ambulance was called to the doctor's office and she was asked if she could just hold out till Gramps passed away. Well, no, she couldn't, so I went down and stayed at my granddad's while she was in the hospital. I did not want him to be alone when he died. By the way, I was on autopilot the entire time—almost like a mantra over and over in my head. I just kept saying, "Don't think, don't think," because I would have told you I couldn't handle anything like I was about to beforehand.

Anyway, they fixed my grandma up and let her come home

early and I was stressing that I would not get her home in time before Gramps left. When I picked her up at the hospital that night I locked the keys in my car. I brought her down and went to open the door and my heart sank. I had a jeep, and whatever the police use to unlock a car does not work with jeeps, so a locksmith had to be called.

My grandma had left her cane up in her room, so I sat her down, told a security guard what was what, and went up to get her cane on the sixth floor. On the way up and then back down in the elevator I prayed so hard, "*Please*, just let me get her home in time, *please*." I got off the elevator, came around a corner, and there she was, sitting in my car. I looked over at the security guard and he said that "some guy" walked up and opened the door. Nothing was said, just some guy walked up to the car, opened the door as if it was never locked, and walked away. I could see that the guard was a bit shaken. That surely had to be a "worker in the light."

More things happened, including right before he passed when I saw two white orbs, two round lights yet not lights. I cannot completely explain what I saw but it was nothing like you see in the movies, though now I believe that what you do see in the movies comes from a kernel of truth. It was about 1:00 A.M. and Gramps was in a hospital bed in their living room and I was sitting in a chair next to him, combing his hair. He loved that, and he was maybe sleeping or going in and out of consciousness as he had been doing for the past two days. I was looking out the window when I saw these two orblike things, very faintly, and they seemed to be rolling toward the house. I sat up straight and thought I must be falling asleep.

It wasn't till later that I realized what I had witnessed because a few moments later Granddad out of a sleep said "Whhhattt?" He said it as if someone was bugging him and he finally said something. A moment later he opened his eyes and looked at me and said, "Get mother." I went and woke Grandma and he then asked for my brother also. Right after getting Grandma, I called another brother who lived next door. Grandma came to Grandpa's side and he said, "I have to go," and I could see she was confused. I whispered in her ear, "Tell him it's OK for him to go." Immediately she said, "Go, Brian, go see your mom and dad. I'll be OK. It's OK, you go," and he did. I bet that was my great-grandparents I saw coming toward the house. They were probably calling him, "Brian, Brian, come on, Brian," when he finally said, "whhhaat?" And for him to tell Grandma he had to go and for me to whisper what I did in her ear was all done through us, I believe.

Our Higher Power was supporting us fully. It was very peaceful, very spiritual. Two days earlier, Granddad collapsed while trying to walk to the bathroom, and everyone just about got hysterical, running in different directions. No one was calm. Now he's leaving and we are all with him and all very calm. I miss him so much, but in fact, he was so miserable that I kept praying, "Please take him now." So God takes him and I think, *Whoa, hey, I didn't mean* right *now!* Seriously, I didn't know what I was asking for, and not wanting it afterward I know now was a selfish feeling.

The day of his funeral the highway was backed up for miles. There was no way I would make it in time, so I closed my eyes and asked, "God, I know you have done so much for me lately but could you please just do this one more thing . . . ?" It was as if the road had never been jammed. All of a sudden the traffic just dissipated as it never had done before on this highway.

We all have guardian angels, who protect us. Seeing them isn't as hard as you think, as this contributor explains.

I BELIEVE IN ANGELS

I have always believed in angels and instinctively knew I had at least one guardian angel. I think all of us receive subconscious signals from our guardian angels from time to time. For example, did you ever find yourself sitting at a red light and, when the light turns green, have an overwhelming feeling *not* to go? Only to see a speeding car run the red light right in front of you a few seconds later? I know I have. Still, the idea of having an actual, face-to-face meeting with my guardian angels seemed a bit hard to believe—until it happened—one night before my thirty-fifth birthday.

It sounds funny now, but there was nothing funny about it at the time. Thirty-five sounded old. I had read somewhere that reaching the age of thirty-five was like reaching the top of a hill—the only way to go, mentally and physically, was down. The thought of it literally made me sick.

I went to bed that night thinking about my upcoming birthday and wishing that I could somehow postpone it another ten years or so. If only I could be nineteen again, everything would be all right.

I drifted off to sleep and found myself standing in the most beautiful landscape I had ever seen in my life. It was too beautiful to describe, as was the feeling of peace, tranquillity, and joy I felt at finding myself in such a place.

Close your eyes and image you are standing out in the countryside. It's a perfect spring day. The sun is shining and the temperature's about seventy-five degrees. You are standing among gently rolling hills, on grass so green and perfectly manicured it would be the envy of any golf course manager. Scattered among the landscape are cherry trees, each one in full bloom. The sky is a deep, rich blue, with a few white, puffy cumulus clouds floating by.

It's impossible to find words even remotely adequate to describe the elation I felt at finding myself in such a beautiful place. I could have stayed there forever. That elation, however, was about to be eclipsed by the presence of not one, but two guardian angels. The guardian angels suddenly appeared, walking over the crest of a nearby hill. One was male, one was female. They were walking toward me hand in hand. These guardian angels were wearing identical white robes. Each one radiated peace, compassion, love, and beauty—Michelangelo himself could not have imagined more perfect or perfectly beautiful human beings. I knew in my soul, as they approached, that these perfect beings were thirty-five-year-old guardian angels.

They didn't speak a word but telepathically let me know that age had no meaning and that I was as immortal and timeless as they. In that one moment, any fear, trepidation, or negative feelings I had ever felt toward anyone or anything vanished. I felt a sense of peace, serenity, and joy that cannot be described in words.

My guardian angels smiled and walked back over the hill, but before they left, they let me know that they would always be with me, watching over me—and that I had nothing to fear ever again.

Was it only a dream? I don't think so. I truly believe, with all my heart, that I really had a face-to-face encounter with my guardian angels in that wonderful place some call "the other side" or the place that I simply like to call "home."

When we are at our darkest moments, even then if we open up, look toward the light instead of the darkness, an angelic presence may come upon us to prevent us from hurting ourselves, or worse.

An Angelic Meeting

It was the mid-eighties. I was just recently divorced. My wife decided that because I would not go back with her she would hurt me through my children (whom I loved more than life itself). I considered myself a wonderful father and put my whole life into them. My wife fell into the trap of another man—closing the door on myself and my children—until she realized how important her home life really was to her.

I will get on to the despair that I went through. My wife, because of my refusal, wanted to punish me by taking my children away, and through money and material wealth, she did just that. I felt so alone and wished not to live anymore; therefore I planned my death. The pain was just too hard to bear; why live? This was pure hell for me. I thought that God had abandoned me and my thoughts were disorganized and without balance. I could not eat or drink, I was sick, spiritually tired, and at the end of the earthly road, or so I thought. I only knew one thing at this time and that was to not be joined with my broken heart, shattered into millions of pieces.

I am a hospice worker, so at this particular time I was planning to take all the narcotics from the cabinet, which is under safekeeping. I wrote a letter to my children and had a sense of relief at writing this letter, not to punish anyone but to alleviate the pain I was suffering so greatly. I also planned to leave or abandon the unit I was working once I had taken the drugs and to go where nobody would find me, to finish the job I intended.

With the letter beside me in the car I noted that the gas tank was on empty. I was thinking, *What a bother, now I have to go and get gas, I just want to be gone!*

When I pulled into the gas station nothing was too unusual, just a station. I had to go inside to pay first and found a man behind the counter who was just a worker for this company. There was also a man sitting on a stool gazing at me on the side one had to pay from, directly next to me. This man told me, "You will be alright, things will get better." I looked at him as if he was crazy, then glanced over to the man behind the counter, who shrugged. The man sitting on the stool stated, "You are hurting, you will be just fine, your kids will be coming back to you."

By this time I was starting to get annoyed at this person. I was thinking, *How do you know and why do you care?* Then I noticed that the man was very tall, he had a kindness that I had never seen before, his eyes were of fire, his hair white, and he appeared to be about sixty. He asked if he could come and speak with me at my car and I agreed. I really was not interested, but there was something different about this man that I had never seen before.

He came over to the car as I was filling up. He once again told me that I was going to be alright; that God loved me, and that my children would once again be with me. I was wondering why he knew about my condition and my children and thought this was *odd*, to say the least, but I continued to listen. I mostly was entranced by his eyes; they were blue—ice blue—but with red fire behind them.

He spoke of not giving up, that life has meaning. I was told that I would not have all the answers now but someday I would understand. He told me of a man that wanted to commit suicide who had cancer. He stated that he went to him, in fact several times. He told me the suicidal man was healed of his cancer and later became a light to others. I asked him, "Who are you?!" He smiled and stated that this was not important. I asked, "What do you do?" He told me he was someone that brings messages to others. He hugged me and told me to be strong and know that God loves me that I had purpose.

I seemed to not have anymore traces of wanting to do myself in. I felt happy and at peace for the first time in a year.

When I drove away I was looking in the rearview mirror as the man was walking away, and he disappeared—vanished. I cried and thanked God for all that was done for me. I do not know who this man was; I am sure that he is still traveling, and helping others.

I was healed from that instant. Yes indeed, my kids came back and we have the best relationship. I am their father, one who assists in guidance and love, and they in turn will do the same. I am so blessed that this white-haired man came to speak to me; without him I would be in darkness and so would my children.

Since that moment I have never had any suicidal thoughts. It seemed like a curtain of truth opened and I understood that some things just happen, to give strength and experience and to assist others.

As many of our callers on Coast *tell us, life on this plane is only one stage. Death is not really death, but a new stage. And, as this contributor tells us, angels are always at hand to guide us along the way.*

RESURRECTED

One day while at work, a coworker said her mother had "graduated" from a hospice. I could not believe her. One goes to a hospice to die. It is the end of the trail. One day this coworker brought her mother to work. The first thing I noticed about this woman was that she was surrounded by a white light. She was aglow. Days later this coworker told me her mother had been experimenting with auras. My belief is that this woman had been resurrected.

The truth is out there.

An angelic presence visits a recovery meeting and everyone there witnesses it. How many times have people had visions when they were alone, but wished to share them? At this recovery meeting, when everyone present had recognized the awesome nature of a higher power over which they had no control, something we acknowledge in Worker in the Light, *they were blessed by the vision of an angelic presence.*

A SPIRITUAL AWAKENING

I am a recovered alcoholic. When I was first sobering up with the help of AA, I was going through an absolutely miserable time. My mind was in a constant state of agony. It was like having a loud radio, which you have no control over, playing negative messages day and night about every aspect of your life. As you know an "alkie" typically suppresses any hurtful emotions, and through the course of one's life there can be many. If you are from a broken home, had many issues early in life—abandonment, sexual and verbal abuse—before you have any understanding or ability to properly deal with them, it is much worse.

In short, too often and too early in life I had experienced hurtful and damaging interactions with family and others and I turned, as my mother had, to alcohol to deal with every situation in life. I never went anywhere without drink or drugs. Let me say I loved my mom; even though she left us, she never hurt us intentionally.

One day I was complaining to a buddy that every time I asked God to help me (telling Him what I wanted Him to do), nothing happened. I was bitter. I was a mess. My good buddy suggested that the next time I was talking to God, maybe I should just ask Him what He wanted *me* to do.

I had never thought of that. I listened. My life changed dramatically. I started going to AA with my buddy, and I became willing to believe in a power greater than myself. I won't get into the principles of the AA program here but I found I had new power in my life; that God was actually and clearly working in my day-to-day affairs.

With healing comes tremendous emotional pain. You actually relive, emotionally, all the pain as it happened to you, and I believe at the emotional level and age that it was first experienced. It is very important, however, that you experience it, then move on.

Often the experiences others shared were felt deeply by all, and I know at least that alcoholics empathize strongly with one another.

One day at a packed meeting, maybe sixty or seventy people, there was a lot of pain in the room. People were crying as they were sharing and listening when, not so suddenly, there was something moving around the room. It's hard to describe since I could not see it, but I knew exactly where it was. It floated around the room. As it passed through me I felt pure love, comfort, relief, and rest. Everyone grew silent. I believe it was the Holy Spirit comforting us in our time of need. I don't think anyone spoke of it afterward, as though we knew without having to communicate what just happened.

Shortly thereafter, maybe a couple of years, I was at an AA gathering with people from all over the world coming to participate. I was at a prayer meeting and one of the founders' secretaries was there and a few others spoke, and I don't remember much about it except when they led out a blind girl to sing "Amazing Grace" at the end.

Wow, did she sing it, and when she was done . . . I saw the Holy Spirit coming again. It was sweeping through the crowds, and where it went people were crying, including myself when it passed through me. I was self-conscious, thinking people would see me crying (silly, I know), but when I looked around there wasn't a dry eye that I could see.

Never have I been so blessed, and I wish I could say my faith has been rock solid ever since, but I know what I have experienced and I'll end by saying I have been sober over twenty years now.

I have a beautiful family. I am truly blessed. I have not told this story often, obviously thinking people wouldn't believe it anyway . . . but there it is.

This contributor has an angelic vision that helped shape his future so that he could help others.

ANGELIC BEING

On Christmas Day, 1955, I announced that an angel lady had visited and urged me to be a writer. I taunted the brother who slept in my room and hadn't heard a thing with, "She told *me* secrets, not you."

My parents tried to convince me it was a dream about Santa Claus. No, I insisted, a beautiful lady bathed in white was standing by my bed when a light one hundred times brighter than any lamp awakened me.

Ignoring a pile of Christmas toys, I bragged about holding a magazine of the future with my photo on its cover and giggled, "It's not me; this person's old and wears glasses."

I told my family what the angel lady had disclosed: that the first half of my life would be fraught with personal illness and deaths. I'd begged her to go away, I explained, but she dried my tears and had me listen to why I should be a writer, how my story could help people. It's why she'd appeared, I said: to encourage me to learn my craft so I'd never give up the belief that I could indeed become everything she predicted. My parents gulped at this revelation, eyed each other the way parents do, and changed the subject. Repeatedly.

I improvised my first tale that Christmas morning with rapid-fire glee, but my thick-tongued rendition of "Let's Watch Lassie" came out as "Lekk Wakk Lakkee."

Two older brothers' mockery of my speech impediment did not deter me. I found another way to be a storyteller. Too young to know the ABCs, I smoothed out cast-off holiday wrapping paper, gripped a fat yellow pencil, and drew the epic tales that were playing like full-length Technicolor movies behind my eyes.

From that day on, I worked with such intensity that heavy pencil marks ripped the thin butcher paper my mother brought home. My right hand was perpetually blackened with graphite; the knuckles on my index and third finger hardened with what my father said were calluses from working a pencil all day, every day. My great delight was showing them off to anyone who'd look twice.

Write what you know. After two sisters burst upon the scene by my seventh birthday and upset my reign as the youngest, slotting me into the middle of five siblings, I knew I wanted to be an only child. Designing alternate realities where parents doted on sons who looked like me and wise dogs rescued kids from their misadventures was as easy as drawing the scenes. I devised mysteries for *The Hardy Boys*, detectives extraordinaire, and even included a few well-behaved girls in my growing collection of illustrated stories.

When my real parents refused to send me to a boarding school advertised in an *Archie* comic book, I sent myself through sheer imagination. What a glorious time I had riding bareback on a painted Indian horse through the desert! I illustrated stories every day for nine years, long after I'd learned to write. Sheets of thin, tan paper gave way to stacks of white drawing pads; nothing pleased me more than a new box of 64 Crayolas.

Two days before entering high school, at my brothers' advice that I'd be ridiculed if any teenager caught me holding onto such childish endeavors, I reluctantly put my practice aside.

My dream of becoming a writer receded as adulthood and all its responsibilities took center stage; I'd barely begun before illness dropped me to my knees. By 1979, I'd faced the deaths of my mom and young sister from breast cancer. My father was fighting the cancer that would take him in a few years, and no one could imagine my brother's death in 1992. All I knew at age twenty-five was I had to leave my baby son for over a month to risk brain surgery and an uncertain future.

I'm fifty-seven now and still can't prove this visitation, angelic or otherwise. Some may view my claim of prophesy as an excuse for thirty-three years of psychosomatic illness, although they'd be hard-pressed to challenge the neurologist who discovered the lemon-sized cyst on the right hemisphere of my brain. No one, however, can debate the fact that four out of seven family members died of disease, just as the beautiful woman bathed in brilliant light had predicted.

Sometimes, even unsummoned, angels can manifest themselves to save a human life. Here, one of our readers recounts just such a story and how his life was changed thereafter. He saw the light and was saved by it.

ANGELIC CHOIR

One Saturday I was rebuilding the front end of a Corvette, and I didn't have any radios on in the shop. I heard an angelic choir sound, holding a note for a long minute. I thought someone was driving up, and had a skipping CD. I crawled out from underneath the car and walked outside to see, and it was calm, slightly breezy for July. I didn't see a thing, and as soon as I had made it to the shop doors, there was no sound.

I turned around to walk back into the shop when I noticed my floor jack had backed way off, and that one of the two jack stands had fallen over due to worn concrete, and the only thing keeping me from a soon-to-be disastrous fate was an angelic choir. They saved my life that day.

Thank you, all that sang the life-saving note. I am truly blessed. I know we are being looked after. Thank you for it.

Children are innocent. Here, a reader tells us how an angel saved her innocent child's life. It was a miracle brought about by an angel who had a relationship with the child that our contributor would not find out about until years later.

A SHORT INSPIRATIONAL STORY

We had just moved into our new home about fifteen years ago. This was a builder's model home and for cosmetic reasons did not have screens on the windows. We had put all the children to bed and settled into our bed around 9:00 P.M. All bedrooms were on the second floor.

I was in that half-awake, half-asleep mode when I heard a frantic knock on my bedroom door. My nine-year-old son, Cody, announced that my four-year-old daughter, Bridget, had just fallen out her bedroom window. Remember, this is on the second floor.

I rushed downstairs, knowing that I would find my little girl seriously injured. I flung open the front door to find Bridget standing on the front porch with an odd look on her face.

We carried her inside and examined her completely. She did not have any injuries or scratches. Below her window were several rose bushes. We could not even find signs of mud or dirt from the planter containing the roses.

We took her to the local emergency room to be examined internally. The doctors also could not find any signs of injury.

Now, let's fast-forward about ten years.

We were all viewing some old family photo albums. I was showing the children pictures of themselves when they were younger. I turned to a page of photos of my grandfather and grandmother who had passed away before they had been born.

We had not really discussed my grandparents with them, so I decided to skip that page, not wanting to bore them. Bridget asked me to turn back to the skipped page. I did so. She pointed to a photo of my grandmother and announced, "That's the angel that caught me when I fell out the window. Her name was Marge. She set me down on the sidewalk and told me to go inside and to get back in bed."

I had never shown them the photos of my grandparents and never in my life referred to my grandmother as Marge. She was always Gramma.

EXPERIENCES

In my youth and as an adult, I have had a lot of unusual experiences. Under the category of prayers answered, I wound up at age fifteen going to a high school bazaar and losing all of my money at a booth where you put a quarter on a number and if the wheel lands on your number, you win a wrapped gift. I was crying when a husband and wife befriended me and came up to the booth and asked what was wrong. I told them that I had blown all of my money on that booth and had nothing to show for it, and that my mom was going to have a fit. They took pity on me and gave me a quarter. I put it down on a number. Just before the wheel turned, I said, "God, if you love me, let me win." The wheel landed on my number. I opened up the wrapped gift and found a plastic Snoopy statue playing the guitar. I must admit that I cried when I read what was written on the base of the statue. It said, "I can't stop loving you." I still have that statue and look at it when I need to remind myself and others that we are loved.

There was another time that I prayed and something similar happened. This time, my car broke down in a "no stopping at any time" zone. I was scared. I did not want to leave the car because I was sure that I was going to get hit if I did, or that my car would get ticketed. I sat in the car and was panicking. I began to cry a bit. I then prayed again, "God, if you love me, send me anyone, even an angel." I waited a while and then saw this man in a blue uniform driving his truck out of a nearby parking area. I called to him and asked him for help. He attempted to jump-start my car and when that would not work, told me to go across the street and call AAA for towing. He gave me the courage to leave my car and stayed with it until I returned. After I called AAA and found that they were on their way, I told him that he could leave and got in the car. He handed the battery cable back to me, and it was then that I noticed that his name was written in golden yellow lettering on his shirt. His name was "Angel."

This reader's story says it all, a life-saving angel. If I compiled all of the stories that my callers tell me about angels who have saved their lives, it would fill an entire book instead of a single chapter.

A LIFE-SAVING ANGEL

On a summer's night in 1998, I fell asleep on some tall, plush grass, which was located just off a hiking trail in a field. I woke up in the middle of the night, got up, and brushed myself off. I was about to make my way back to the trail when suddenly I noticed a bright light out of the corner of my eye. I believe that what I saw sent my brain into some kind of shock because I became frozen between fear and a readiness to react; however, I couldn't move because I was seeing something that I had never seen before, so I stood there, petrified.

The light first appeared approximately eight to ten feet away from me, and then seemed to move closer and grow larger in stages. Within a couple of stages, it was only about two to three feet from me. I stood frozen in fear, but continued looking and waiting for an exit from whatever potential harm that it would render unto me. I realized, however, that the light had a female form. She was actually very beautiful. In fact, I thought that she was the most beautiful vision that I had ever seen.

She smiled and extended what appeared to be her arm and hand. I also reached out my hand to her, and as soon as my finger touched what was her finger, I felt a very warm feeling come over me. I'm not sure, but I believe that I felt my fear melting. It was like taking a warm shower.

I don't know how long all of this transpired, but I watched her go the same way she came—in stages. When the light had completely disappeared, I looked at myself, still reaching out my arm, and heard myself begging her not to go.

Sometime during that moment I must have knelt down because I noticed that I was on my knees while I was reaching for her. I didn't remember going to my knees, but I stood up and brushed myself off again while looking around to see if anyone else had seen her. I was alone.

I decided to keep that incident to myself. I thought that

revealing it would lead to the question of my sanity. However, secretly I knew that there was more to the universe than I/we knew. I tried not to think about it.

About two years later I was driving along when I picked up a hitchhiker. I let her off not too far past my destination, but because I was in unfamiliar territory, I didn't realize that the two-lane road for the direction that I was going in suddenly became a curved, two-lane road for both directions of traffic. Not only that, the side of the road that I should have been on became cut off by a road-dividing wall as the road continued under an overpass. I was going the wrong way, and could neither see the oncoming traffic, stop, turn around, nor get back over to the right side of the road until I was completely through the curved underpass.

Well, I don't have to tell you that I was ready to soil my underwear. I'm sure that the surge of adrenaline had something to do with the shocking feeling that I felt during this moment, as well as in the previously mentioned incident. Whether that shock is a precursor to spiritual events and experiences I honestly couldn't say, nor do I want to digress.

I passed two cars very closely. The first car contained an elderly couple. I saw the shock and horror on their faces as we narrowly avoided hitting each other. I briefly took my eyes off the road to look back at them, but the shock returned as I realized that I made what could have been the fatal error of taking my eyes off the road.

Before I could return my attention back to the road ahead, I felt someone (or something) in the car reach across me. It caused the steering wheel to be jerked from my grip and it steered the car to the right. The hairs on my body stood up as I became covered in goose bumps at the alarming realization that there was another oncoming car, that I wasn't in the car alone, and that whatever was in the car with me had control of the wheel.

I regripped the wheel after very narrowly passing by the oncoming car. Judging from the look of horror on the guy's face as our cars passed each other, I would say that he probably did soil his underwear.

Fortunately, I got through the curved underpass without any more cars to negotiate. Consequently, the tunnel divider ended also, and I was able to cross over the small, raised median island and drive over to the right side of the road. Shortly after negotiating that, I had to stop for a red light. At that time, I realized that I had survived yet another near-death experience. This time I owed it to whomever/whatever was in the car with me. I slowly looked over into the passenger seat, and then the rear seat, but saw no one and nothing. I relaxed, but realized that although I didn't see it, I knew someone (or something), had just saved me from harm.

The light was still red as I had a flashback to all the other times that I had survived death and serious harm. There was the car accident at age three; many other car accidents as well as falls; the parachute collapse; the bombs that didn't go off in the military; and a couple of suicide attempts. It was then that I suddenly heard myself say, "Thank you, God. I know that I'm here for a reason." When I realized that those words actually came out of me, I knew that I was a believer. The traffic light changed from red to green, and I proceeded through that intersection as a different person.

My callers tell me that sometimes you can meet angels in the strangest places in our wonderful universe.

MEETING AN ANGEL ON THE ROAD

Several years ago my then wife, Amber, and I were driving from Texas to where I moved to in Oklahoma. I had been working all day and we left late in the evening. We decided to take the scenic route through a long, uphill, winding path.

It was getting into dawn and I was really tired. I had decided to stop as otherwise we might have crashed. When I found a spot to stop I pulled over. I noticed an older, light blue Chevy Suburban was parked just ahead with a female sitting in it. I decided to see if we could help this lady, so I got out and walked up to her door.

Her window was down and this lady was not only stunning looking but her blue eyes were such that I felt like I could see heaven. She looked at me and before I could say a word she asked if I was OK.

I answered yes and asked if she needed help. She answered that she was out of gas, so I offered to go get her some gasoline.

We headed a few miles into the next town and got a can of gas for her and returned. I put the gas into her tank and she had gotten out and walked over to my car, said hello to Amber, and then came back to her car.

She was tiny, and you would have thought that she would be intimidated by a strong-looking man, but she wasn't.

I got her car going and noticed that I felt as if I had just had eight hours of great sleep. She thanked me and offered to pay, which I declined. We pulled out and she pulled out right behind us.

There was a corner, and as we were between steep cliffs on either side we lost sight of her for a moment and should have seen her within a few seconds, but she was gone.

Amber had mentioned to me that she thought this lady was an angel because of her eyes and because we both felt rejuvenated.

We doubled back but never saw her again, and at that point we both realized that a guardian angel had been sent to protect us from having an accident.

The rest of the day I felt fine and when we got to my place in Oklahoma I worked the rest of the day and felt fine all day.

You can transform yourself into an extrasensitive like this contributor even if you were not born that way or were taught how to do it by a friend or relative. Working in the light is just such a transformation.

THE PURPLE ANGEL

Over the years I've had these sporadic psychic experiences so I know that I'm "extrasensitive." Therefore, it didn't surprise me so much when this happened. I bought an eight-by-eleven-inch canvas to paint with a solid color for feng shui purposes as I needed a bit of color on the white walls. While I am creative I am not an artist in the sense of being a painter. It was as if I was driven to purchase this canvas and paint.

When I got home from the store I opened the pot of purple paint, made the sign of the cross, and then completely covered the canvas in solid purple paint. Before the paint completely dried I wondered what the effect would be if I sprinkled the canvas with water, so I proceeded to use my hands to move the paint around, then finished it off with my brush—as if I was painting a wall, using an up-and-down motion.

I left the painting to dry in the bathroom for about an hour and a half. When I returned to view the painting and to see if it was dry I noticed an amazing thing. My painting was that of an archangel holding up a juvenile angel with its right hand; there is a human figure in the background walking forward. It was someone I recognized. When you turn the painting upside down that human figure becomes a little girl looking up at a flame.

There are some other really incredible symbolisms in this painting that have relevance in my life; others I don't understand. I am not a painter, and the technique of this painting is evidence of that—the images are created in varying degrees as a result of the absence of paint. I am what I consider to be spiritually evolving and view these incredible images as a reminder that I am surrounded with love and guidance from Father-Mother-God and my guardian angels.

I think the importance of this experience is to become more aware and mindful of daily life and thoughts, that we are indeed spiritual beings in human bodies with amazing capacities to create in this life. We just have to be open to the possibilities.

A reader describes how an angelic presence can intervene to overcome evil in the ongoing war between the manifestation of good and the force of the devil. Here is the essence of working in the light and being saved by the light.

A Battle with the Devil

The events I am going to detail happened many years ago, back when I was a teenager (I am almost forty-five now), and my memory is not as sharp as it once was. However, the outline of the experience is accurate, save for names, which I have removed on purpose, to protect the identity of others. In addition, I am going to be rather vague when it comes to certain aspects of the story, again, to protect the identity of others.

I've told very few people about the story, as most would simply choose to believe that I was making the story up or in need of mental care. I assure you that neither is the case. I am telling you the story for reasons that I can't quite fathom. I suppose the relative anonymity helps to some degree, but part of me wants others to be wary of the dangers inherent in any activity within the realm of the paranormal.

I grew up in the Midwest, in a small town of two thousand people. It was, and is, a rural area, with farming dominating the economy. Like most of my peers, I played sports and was very involved with the local baseball leagues. The teams typically held practice several times per week, and it was not uncommon for players to bring visiting family members with them to the practice.

One of my teammates brought his visiting cousin to practice with him and introduced the cousin to the team. When it came my turn to shake the newcomer's hand, I had this eerie sensation. I cannot explain it to this day, but I knew he was about to die. Of course I said nothing about my premonition, as I didn't wish to be ridiculed and had no means of offering evidence on my behalf. Needless to say, I was terrified and couldn't stop thinking about the very strong feelings I was having. Nothing like this had ever happened before.

Later that day, toward evening, I was notified that my teammate's cousin had been killed that afternoon in a motorcycle accident. I was mortified and filled with guilt. I was fourteen and had no idea what had occurred. It wasn't that I hadn't known anyone who had died—I had—but not after I had a premonition of them dying after just meeting them.

I became consumed with the aspect of ESP and began reading everything I could get my hands on that dealt with the matter. Over the next two years I studied the subject as much as I could, and I began really paying attention to any feelings of premonition I would have. Most of them came true, and I was convinced that I had a very special gift, a power that I believed mankind had lost due to its inability to control it emotionally.

I never discussed this newly found power with anyone. My family was Catholic, attended church regularly, and I went to catechism weekly. Somehow I knew this power was wrong, but I was convinced that, with time, I could control it and learn how to make this power work for me.

I practiced often to develop my power and continued reading books on the subject. In time I became convinced that I was chosen to have this power and that great things would come of it.

Time muddies events that happened in the past, but somewhere in this time line I was diagnosed with epilepsy and prescribed phenobarbital to combat it. I soon quit taking the medication, as I found that it made me very sluggish and hindered my ability to think effectively.

Somewhere around the age of sixteen I had a dream, only it wasn't a dream at all; it was real. In my "dream" I saw an evil entity attacking my best friend. I knew my friend would lose the battle, and I knew the evil entity was very, very powerful. Still, I was convinced that my power would protect me from harm and I was determined to save my friend.

I fought the evil entity. It wasn't the type of fight most would recognize, it was not a battle of fists and strength, and it wasn't really even a battle of wits or intelligence. It was a battle of power—sheer, crushing power—and I was defeated.

I recognized the evil entity as the devil himself. In our battle I became mentally and physically drained and I had nothing left; I couldn't fight any longer and I couldn't protect myself or my friend. I had lost everything.

The devil was every color of light there can be, and no color at all, just an overwhelming sense of brightness coupled with an all-encompassing power that crushes anything before it. I recall a sense of a deep, awful voice, not one that you physically hear, but a voice that vibrates through your body and makes itself known in a manner that spoken words never could.

The battle took place in space—at least I think it was space—with darkness surrounding me and soon enveloping me with an evil force. There was bright light and sheer darkness all at once, an unspoken voice that seemed to emanate from within my very soul, and the realization that I was but a mere twig in a vast, angry ocean of evil.

Not long after I lost the battle, I woke up early one morning with tears streaming down my face. I couldn't fight anymore, my strength was gone and in its place was something else—an unspoken voice telling me that I must die. I pleaded, I begged, and I cried, but all to no avail. My time had come; I had lost the battle and it was time for the victor to claim his spoils.

I walked upstairs and took two full bottles of phenobarbital.

It was done. I had succumbed to the evil force and would fight no more. I don't recall much that happened in the next several days, only brief dreamlike glimpses that seemed more like nightmares.

I remember large creatures attacking me, but somehow I'd miraculously get away and run for my life. But they'd always catch me and I'd escape yet again. This repeated itself over and over again. I recall being strapped to some bedlike contraption, breaking the straps, and having more of the large creatures attack me. I remember being all alone and I remember being very scared.

I woke up several days later. My head hurt and I was very dizzy. Family members and medical staff seemed to take turns scolding me, but not one of them would even listen to me when I attempted to explain that I hadn't wanted to kill myself. The doctor informed me that I should've been dead. He wasn't sure why I lived, as the barbiturates had all been absorbed into my body by the time I was taken to the hospital.

Later, my family filled in the missing pieces. I had gone to school and basically wandered from class to class. My teachers were convinced that I was a drug addict and had my sister take me home. When my parents came home, they took me to the hospital. Once there I broke away from them several times and fell down each time I attempted to run. The hospital staff strapped me to a bed and I broke the straps several times before I finally slipped into unconsciousness.

Nobody understood, and I couldn't explain it in a manner that fulfilled anybody's expectations. Former friends refused to have anything to do with me, and I was taunted once I went back to school. Rumors ran rampant that I was a drug addict, this despite the fact that I had never once tried drugs.

I spent a good part of my senior year in various mental institutions, as I had tried repeatedly to kill myself after that first attempt. I found the medical staff to be very similar to everyone else. Nobody listened and nobody really cared to listen. Not one bit of good was done. It was all wasted time and money. I still cried every time I was forced to make an attempt on my own life. I still begged and pleaded with the evil that was controlling me, and I still couldn't fight it.

Our foreign exchange student in my senior year was a girl from the Seychelles. She was a wonderful girl—bright, cheerful, and full of joy. Just being around her brought a smile to my face and laughter to my heart. Naturally, I wanted to say good-bye to her at the end of the year, as she'd be going back to her home and leaving us all for good.

I had made arrangements with her host family and went to their house for a final visit before she left. I knew the family relatively well, as we were members of the same church. Most of the evening went pretty well; we laughed and told stories and generally had a good time. As we were sitting at the kitchen table, their daughter, who was my age and a classmate, suddenly began to babble in gibberish and became very animated. I was confused and asked her mother what was going on. She explained that her daughter was speaking in tongues and that she was saying I was the antichrist. I was told to leave immediately and that I was never to return.

I was hurt and more than a little upset. I had always been a good kid. I got good grades in school, kept out of trouble for the most part, and obeyed the law. I worked hard and had held the same job since I was fourteen years old. But in the back of my mind I wondered, for I knew about the battle I had lost, and despite my attempts to explain the suicide attempts, I alone knew how impossible it was to deny what the devil mandated me to do.

Two days after I graduated from high school, my parents kicked me out of their house for drinking. I was now on my own and still facing the victor of the battle I had fought. I had been accepted to Texas A & M but dropped out under the naïve assumption that I wouldn't be able to go since I had been kicked out of my parents' house. Instead, I went to work in the real world, and soon moved out of the small town I grew up in.

I continued to have difficulties, but by this time had disavowed any connection to the "power" I once thought I had. I had recognized the danger and made every attempt to remove myself from it. At the same time I was relatively certain that the day would come when I would be forced into committing suicide and that I'd eventually be successful. I didn't want to die and I didn't like the negative attention such efforts garnered, but I couldn't stop it. I could not overcome the immense power that was forcing me to undertake actions that I didn't want to do.

I had long had the practice of talking to God just as I would speak to anybody. I usually speak out loud, and the conversation normally consists of asking God to help those I love. I had always refused to ask God to help myself. I somehow felt that doing so was wrong and unacceptable.

One day I was sitting in my pickup, very nearly overcome with the power of the devil telling me that I had to die, when it hit me. I don't recall if the idea was mine, or if somebody had suggested it to me, but I began to pray to Jesus directly and asked Him to help me. I told Jesus that this was bigger than I was and that without His help it would kill me. I asked Jesus to take this burden from me, and He did. It was as if the whole world's weight was lifted from my shoulders. Suddenly I was no longer alone. I didn't have to fight the devil. Jesus would do it for me.

That was roughly twenty-five years ago. I'd be lying if I said life has been easy for me since that time. It hasn't been; I've had many struggles and numerous disappointments, but I've not had to face the devil, all alone, since that day.

I still believe that the power is there; I just choose not to explore it. I've used it one time since that day in my pickup. That was in response to my wife's discovery of lumps in her uterus: she was extremely fearful that the lumps were cancerous. I assured her that they weren't, as I had made sure of it. I was willing to undertake the risk for my wife's benefit, but you can rest assured that I asked Jesus to help me in my endeavor.

Some people doubt God's existence; I am not one of them. I've been told twice that I should be dead: once as a young child when my parents were informed that I had mere months to live because of a brain tumor, and once when I attempted to take my own life. Yet I remain alive, though I realize the odds were not in favor of that had I continued fighting the devil by myself. I am alive only because of God's will.

I fear the power I once sought and while I have no doubt that I am capable of a great power, I am convinced that mere humans cannot cope with the emotional stress that comes with such power.

We said it in our first book and repeat it on Coast *almost every night: we receive signs from the supernatural all the time; guideposts to tell us where we are and that things are all right. This is just such a story from one of our listeners.*

A SIGN FROM MY FATHER: ANGELIC SURPRISE

My father passed away ten years ago. I cared for him at home along with my mother for the last three months of his life. It had been a long couple of years for him in the end-of-life process. My mom would go to work every day, mostly to avoid the sadness of watching someone she had loved for over fifty years slowly fade away. Taking that long road to the end with a loved one is the hardest thing you can do in your life, yet rewarding. We made sure he was comfortable and had everything he wanted and needed.

I tried to fill his days with something interesting to watch or eat, anything to help pass the time away. He went along with whatever, putting on a brave front, but I knew deep in my heart he was hoping the end would be soon.

I had been given a guardian angel pin from my boss a few years back. I thought if my father wore the pin, perhaps it would provide him with some spiritual comfort. I remember the smile on his face the first time I pinned it on him. He wore the pin every day until his death.

Every night for eight weeks after his death, I prayed that he made it to heaven. I also asked God for a sign, if He wasn't too busy. As a human being, I was looking for a bolt of lightning, a white dove, or a rainbow—something like that. But I really didn't think my prayer would be heard since it seemed like a selfish request. Two months later I received a sign I will never forget!

I had been awakened in the middle of the night with a runny nose. Knowing full well there weren't any antihistamines in the apartment, it was impossible to get comfortable. I was now wide awake and unable to fall back asleep. As I lay there, in my totally darkened bedroom, a bright glowing form appeared, starting from the bottom and going upward, until the form was complete. It was a solid, white, glowing entity that looked like an angel, but not the typical angel you see in books. It must have stood ten feet tall, had very large wings, a head that seemed too small for its body, no facial features, and no feet. It was very still and very peaceful. It didn't speak but it gave me a sense of love and peace. I rubbed my eyes, thinking I was seeing something. I even looked to another part of the room and returned my eyes back to where I had seen it, and it reappeared at the same place. At that moment I knew it was a sign directly from God that Father had arrived at his destination!

I don't know how long the angel stayed there, but it was so beautiful I couldn't take my eyes off it. The glow from the entity was incredible; it didn't even hurt my eyes. I went back to sleep and awoke the next morning without the sniffles, but I could clearly see the image of that angel in my head. Nine years later I can still see it as though it was a painting on my heart. It's really true, God does hear our prayers and He does send His angels to comfort us!

Another reader tells us of how an angel manifested itself to her to save her life at the point of having a terrible car accident.

ANGEL AT THE WHEEL

About four years ago, I was traveling home after visiting a boyfriend a few states away. I had had a fitful night's sleep the night before from allergies. As I was driving through New Jersey, I saw the sign for the exit I needed to take. The sign said the exit was in one mile.

I do not have any memory from the moment I read the sign until I came to traveling up the exit ramp. My little VW Bug and I were becoming sandwiched or bottlenecked between the guardrail and the trailer of a sixteen-wheeler. Simultaneously, as I came to and realized what was going on, a voice said to me, "Don't panic," as calm and peaceful as a lake at sunset. I didn't. I didn't slam on my breaks. I didn't try to avoid what I thought was inevitable.

I was not in control; somebody else was. I was looking into the rearview mirror of the truck at the same time the driver looked in the mirror back at me. Realizing what was taking place, he sped up so that he could get away from me, and I could get out of the situation I was in.

I can only say, there was an angel at the wheel keeping me safe for the mile I had lost, and it was angels who guided both the trucker and me out of what could have been a deadly turn of events.

TWO STORIES FROM THE HOLOCAUST

I'm including these stories here, without using names, because of respect for the victims and the survivors and the kinds of mystical insights both victims and survivors had during the terrible years of the Shoah. Here are two stories from Auschwitz about an angelic presence amid the horror of it all. I cannot explain, nor would I even attempt to, the meaning of these stories except to say that these are two lives that have been touched. When I hear these stories, I believe more fervently than I ever believed before that even in the darkest of nights, there is still one small point of light for those who can see it. The stories speak for themselves.

THE LINE

At Auschwitz, when the trains came in, there were two lines—one to the left and one to the right—and the *transportkommandos* would direct you to which line. Dr. Josef Mengele would stand there and look for those he wanted to examine: twins, people who looked odd to him, or even the very young. He would pass along the lines and stare at anyone that caught his interest. His *kommandos* would direct the others.

Those children who were too young to work and babies would go right to the chambers. Those who looked like they could work would go to the barracks.

I was on the line, not knowing who Mengele was or what he was doing. I was very young. And as the line moved I was, without my knowing it, sent to the line for the chambers. Then a man came up to me and ordered me to the other line. I just followed his order.

When a soldier came up to me and barked at me for being in this line, I told him that a man had ordered me here. He asked me to show him the man, but when I looked, he had disappeared. It was only a matter of seconds, but the man had disappeared. The soldier, not wanting to be bothered, simply pushed me with his rifle butt and walked away. I always wondered if the man who ordered me off the death line was an angel.

THE CHILD

I was in the Canada Barracks, a living hell because we were the *kommandos* working for Mengele. One awful night, as I could smell the odor of burning flesh, a stench I remembered at a hospital after the Nazis had occupied Poland, I decided that I was a part of it and decided to commit suicide. I ran outside the barracks to end it quickly, throw myself against the electrified wire fence, and burn myself in an instant.

I stood back and made a run for the fence when suddenly I fell. I found myself in a pit that I hadn't known was there. I was hurt but not crippled, so I tried again. This time I tried to hurl myself into the air, but my foot got caught in a root of some kind and I went sprawling to the ground, all muddy and bruised. I gave up.

Then, as the ash began to fall all around me, I went back inside the barracks and prayed as hard as I could. I remembered the words of a prayer from childhood, a prayer we chanted on the highest of the High Holy Days. At the center of that prayer, which asks, "who shall die by starvation, who shall die by strangulation, who shall die by drowning," I asked myself, *How shall I die?* and I prayed for a sign.

As I was praying and wishing for death, I heard the barking dogs and the orders, *"Raus, mach schnell!"* The guards were ordering us out to the train platform. Night trains were very rare at Auschwitz because most of the new prisoners arrived in the early morning. But this night there was a train, and we were ordered out to do our jobs: separate those who would die slowly from starvation and overwork from those who would die quickly in the chambers.

After we were sent back to the barracks and the burning stench started anew, I went to the latrine, where I heard a strange sound. It was someone moving, someone small.

I looked behind a toilet and there I found a small boy. He had somehow escaped the guards and the *kommandos* and made it to the barracks. He should have been dead by then, but he was alive. Was this the angel who had saved me from death?

INTUITION

Of all the calls I get on the air and the letters we've received, and with the sole exception of seeing angels and the spirits of the departed, nothing—not even UFO sightings—is more prevalent than personal tales of intuition and premonition. In fact, the consistency of stories I receive about people exercising their intuition and premonition is so great that I would come to believe, even if I've not had my own personal experiences in this regard; that this is a sense that all of us have and all of us can exercise at will. In *Worker in the Light*, we made it a point to train people in learning to exercise their intuition so as to receive premonitions of things that are about to befall them.

My belief in the immediacy of the future and our natural ability to determine it is so strong that even if there weren't years and years of real psychological testing—and I mean hard science—to support me in this, I would still bet on this as a reality. Simply stated, all of us have the ability to foretell our own future, even though in most of our daily comings and goings we negate what we feel because we're either too afraid to take responsibility for our own futures or because the reality of our having that ability is so overwhelming, we reject it and cast our fates to the wind.

In *Worker*, I said that if I could do anything to help people's lives, teach them what I know, it would be to help people see their own futures, which are all around them, and get them to take responsibility for inhabiting those futures. I am not original in this belief. For thousands of years, people have appeared, in ancient literature, in the Holy Bible, and in vast lore of the paranormal, who have been able to tell the future. Some tell it through the interpretation of dreams, like Joseph in Pharaoh's prison; some tell it through communication with spirit guides, like President Lincoln's medium, Nettie Coburn; some are astrologers, like Ronald and Nancy Reagan's Joan Quigley; and some simply go into a trance state to shut out their analytical overlay from daily life and then see the future very clearly, like President Woodrow Wilson's Edgar Cayce and President Franklin Roosevelt's Jean Dixon. Yes, American presidents, exactly like just about every political leader and the great kings in the Bible, took advice from those gifted with heightened intuition, seers, prognosticators, and even prophets. And what all of these gifted people with so-called "second sight" can do, my callers, our contributors, and I assure you, you can do yourself in your own life.

Do you think for even one moment that people get to the top by accident, that some of the great minds of industry and politics, that the world's greatest inventors and artists, make their incredible leaps just by chance or a throw of destiny's dice? I have said it on the air and I'll say it again here that there are no coincidences. I believe, and I know that I can demonstrate this, that people succeed in all their endeavors by intuiting the future, listening to that intuition exactly as if they were tuning a radio or television signal, and then acting on that intuition instead of denying it. Denial is defeat; embracing your intuition and your premonitions of the future are the keys to success. And this I can illustrate.

Among the key books that came out at the turn of the century was Napoleon Hill's *Think and Grow Rich*, a title far more inspirational than simply a manual for making money. Hill's philosophy, which you can still find promulgated on late-night infomercials today, was that becoming successful was not just a matter of birth, of luck, or of behavior, but of thinking that you could succeed and acting upon those thoughts so as to make them come true. Norman Vincent Peale picked up on this with his *Power of Positive*

Thinking in which he said, very simply, that thinking positively will make good things happen to you. And as we've all seen in the Law of Attraction literature, which has become so popular, this is their philosophy as well.

What they've said, we've said in *Worker in the Light,* and that's what our readers and contributors have said to us, that there are practical, basic ways to determine what is in your future. There are simple exercises to train yourself in listening to that intuitive signal that all of us receive every moment of our lives, even when we're fast asleep. These are practices that some of the world's largest corporations have adopted to train their executives in using intuition as well as bottom-line accounting to figure out what's best to do. Intuition has become so important in business that, a few years ago, when I read an article in the *Harvard Business Review* on trusting your intuition even when it seemed that you were paranoid, I know the world had changed for the better.

All this having been said, how can you learn to listen to your intuition, trust it, and become sensitive to premonitions, even if you're not going to be a precognitive seer? Are there any really simple exercises you can do—nonstressful ones that will train you to see just how powerful your intuition can be if you can only learn to separate that intuition from the negative, skeptical, judgmental thoughts that the world imposes upon you? Here are a few from *Worker in the Light* that our own contributors have used to guide them.

First step is to learn to connect with a universe in which all things exist and all time is one. If you can begin to see not only that what you do today creates the future tomorrow but that the future that exits tomorrow has already created the things you do today, you can begin to effect changes. Sounds paradoxical? Look at it this way: for there to be a past, there has to be a present and then a future. What if, rather than the past creating the future, it's the future that creates the past? How can you test this out?

We demonstrated both here and in *Worker* how one connects to the universe by choosing a mantra—a special phrase or word or prayer that only you know and has meaning and resonance for you—then practicing reciting that mantra to focus you and keep your mind from getting scattered all over the place. Then we illustrated what controlled and focused breathing was and how by practicing it you would learn how to energize and focus yourself at the same time. We also explained how reciting your mantra, over and over again, while you were doing your controlled breathing would begin the connection process. We then added the technique of casting off negative thoughts by imagining that they were leaves floating down the stream. A negative thought comes in? Float it away. Now your mind is free to encompass the universe. In this state, you have but to imagine someone, a face, a voice, a personality, and you will be able, after some practice, to hear that person speak to you in an unguarded way.

You see, your mind already encompasses much of what that person is, albeit things are in constant change. Much of what you believe true you simply deny because it is illogical to think that you can tune into a person's thoughts or personality. As illogical as that sounds, by practicing this simple breathing and visualization exercise, you will see that logic is its own illogic. This is only the first of many simple exercises, however.

Add to your breathing and visualization the practice of asking questions of the universe. Visualize your life years from now. Visualize the way you enter relationships or the ways you deal with your job or your children. Don't force these things but let them flow in such a way that around different thoughts, images will pop up. This is the universe talking to you. Once you see this, don't deny what you see.

You will read how one of our contributors was in exactly this same situation. He had the impression from the future that something was wrong with his ceiling and that it was about to fall down. Nothing the contractor could tell him about the soundness of the ceiling could convince him that his impressions were wrong. Very soon after his conversations with the contractor, which got him nowhere, the ceiling fell down.

Another one of our contributors writes about how she was having premonitions of violence. In particular, she says, she saw her girlfriend getting ready for her senior prom but saw a cloud over her face and had the feeling that violence would befall her. Sure enough, that evening her girlfriend was murdered. This contributor's grandmother said to her that her gift was something that the Romany gypsies, call "the veil of death."

Not all intuitive moments and premonitions have to be violent, however. And your inhabiting your future physically doesn't have to be the result of prolonged exercises. Many times you can practice intuition "lite" by throwing a question out there, inhabiting a space where that question can be answered for you, and by not considering the answer that you get very seriously as a particular future creating its own past.

For example, my friends were looking for an apartment in Manhattan. They scanned the newspaper for rent ads in the *Village Voice* and in the *New York Times* but found nothing they really liked. And everything was crazy expensive. Then a friend told them about an old brownstone apartment at the very northern end of the Chelsea neighborhood on the west side, so they made the trip in to take a look at it. On the one hand, it was perfect, something you'd never find in Manhattan: three bedrooms and a living room fireplace. On the other hand, my friend's wife pointed out that the entrance of the building looked weird, spooky—like a scene out of the silent movie, *The Cabinet of Dr. Caligari.* The walls seemed to come together near the ceiling, what should have been parallel walls meeting to form an enclosure. She shuddered at the thought of having to go in and out of this hallway many times a day. As they were leaving she told her husband that she had a vision she couldn't erase of an ambulance crew making their way through the lobby with him on a stretcher and her adult children coming to the apartment to pack her up. Sure, my friend contemplated the insanity of this remark, but he also knew that when his wife had a premonition that strong he should listen to it because it was always right.

How you can apply this kind of lesson to your own life? You do it by simply going to open houses, real estate showings, which are open to the public. Just look for them in the real estate section of your local newspaper. Even if you're not looking for a new place, try this out. Find ads for places in neighborhoods where you've always wanted to live. Then simply show up at those addresses and walk in as if you want to rent or buy the place. Once inside, tell yourself you're now living there: This is your kitchen, your bedroom, your bathroom. This is where you get dressed to go to work in the morning, where you park your car, where you plop down at night to watch TV or cruise the Internet. These are your closets.

Now ask yourself what kind of person lives there. Visualize the kind of family there and you're in that family. Is this a lifestyle you want? Can you inhabit that lifestyle? Now inhabit that lifestyle. You actually do live here. You're not a wannabe. You actually are what you visualize you are. Who are you?

If you go through this, what you find is that by inhabiting the future of living in this place, you are creating the present. You are letting the future determine the past, which, in fact, is the present. This is how it works. By being the person who lives in that house, you've made a number of choices, taken very clear steps to get yourself to inhabit that future. These are the steps you are laying out as you visualize yourself in the future. It is the Law of Attraction at work for you, and you didn't even have to buy the DVD or get philosophical about it. And you can try this any weekend you want to or feel you need to.

Our contributors have told us they can feel their premonitions come upon them at work, in their cars, or when they come upon various trigger moments, events that trigger a visceral response. The difference between our contributors and most other people is that our contributors now understand what it takes to shoulder the burden of having premonitions and becoming precognitive and take on that responsibility for their own lives. You can do that, too. And once you do, once you see your own future manifest itself before your own eyes, you will understand the very same power that others have seen for thousands of years before you. That's why these stories of people who have had premonitions or have used their intuitions to guide them are great examples of living and working in the light.

Intuition is not just a gift bestowed at birth upon certain people. It is something we all have and we all can be trained to use. In Worker in the Light, *we spent a lot of time showing readers how to tune into their intuition. It's not hard. It is, as our friend Paul Smith told us, just like learning to play "Chopsticks" on the piano. Start with something very simple and then gradually trust in your ability to listen to what that intuitive signal is telling you. You can do this, just like the many readers in this chapter can.*

How Intuition Can Run in Families

When I was twenty-two months old, I first read my mother's mind. She was delighted, as this goes back generations in her family. She said, "Oh, good, another one of us." I could always sense what the teachers in school wanted even though they could not articulate it. That, with a high IQ, got me through school successfully. In high school, I started doing weather work, changing the winds to get home safely when becalmed out on the water. To me this just seemed normal.

My father was a military officer, so we moved constantly, in a life of constant change, in multiple cultures and languages. I had many mystical experiences in Europe, knowing I had been there before. Turned out to be the perfect preparation for my purpose and career.

Despite my father disowning me for going to the Chica, as I was too smart for a girl, my intuition told me I must go, so I did, and had to work my way through what turned out to be four degrees. I was guided into economics, the major for my B.A., comparative economic systems—Russia, China, Japan, the U.S.—and how those systems influenced behavior. I could not afford to go to graduate school, so I went to work in staff and line management jobs.

Then I found out how badly people were treated at work and went back for my MBA, vowing to make a difference in organizations. During the MBA program at the U of C Graduate School of Business, I discovered the field of change leadership and a powerful three day white-light experience of complete joy clarified my purpose and my service to the planet: leadership and organizational change. I loved it and took many Ph.D. courses during my MBA.

Years later, the dean of students who signed all those course slips and made exception after exception for me asked: "What were all those behavioral science courses you were taking?" I was shocked and said, "You mean you signed all those slips for me without knowing what I was taking?" He laughed and said, "What's to know? You were happy, you were on the Dean's List every quarter, and the faculty thought you walked on water."

Mentors like that were placed in my path to help me, often only there for the time I was there.

My then husband was threatened by all of this, so I had to divorce him. He was brilliant but fear-based. I was not based in fear, and am not still. We are still in touch, decades later. Three years ago he told me I was into all this spiritual stuff so early and he wished he had listened to me.

Being raised to trust spiritual intuition and living by it, I never thought I was crazy. That turned out to be a huge blessing. So many suffer from that fear.

Being guided to Boston University for my Ph.D., I had serious problems with the model of change taught then by famous mentors who founded the field, but I could not quite put my finger on what was wrong.

One day I had an intuitive flash and the whole thing came clear. No appreciation! Change was all about finding out what was wrong with people and fixing it. Much pain, no gain!

Following my spiritual intuition, I started the field of positive change leadership, which is now much more accepted, thirty years ago as a kid in my twenties. I wrote my dissertation on appreciation when there was no research on it. As I was taking a stance 180 degrees from that of mentors, you can imagine how popular I was—a tall, blond, attractive, smart woman pioneering a new field! Not so easy.

Leadership's not sexy, you say? Think about it: Every problem on the planet goes back to weak, poor, or no leadership! Look around the world. We need better leaders.

I never doubted the work, trusting my intuition and spiritual studies in metaphysics. Clearly making change on our strengths, our best, was in alignment with Universal Law, as the Divine in us, our best, is our core.

"Duh." Strengths-based, positive leadership just seemed like common sense to me.

But here's the thing: Clients loved it and management teams were transformed so fast I could hardly believe it. They did not care that the academics laughed me out of the room. Adding my intuition made the work so helpful that many jobs, many good things were accomplished.

One client who had me peer into the inner workings of cells intuitively saved twenty million dollars in false starts in research, another did a better job of cleaning up the Valdez oil spill, and another started the Human Genome Project earlier than it would have begun otherwise.

All that work on positive leadership systems transformed me. I just kept walking my talk and, lo and behold, my joy and strength kept increasing as I was so blessed to help leaders make a difference.

And of course, I also still did weather work and other planetary healing work metaphysically.

At a college reunion, a former beau talked to me and said, "You have remade yourself, haven't you?"

After twenty-five years of positive leadership and change work, my intuition guided me into a very challenging and upending series of experiences and groups, which made it clear that I needed to step up and serve at a higher level. Books and training systems poured out of me.

Looking back at my entire career, I saw that all my predictions had been accurate: The fall of Russian Communism, the fields of social accounting, behavioral economics, behavioral finance, the shift from authoritarian to collaborative power, the positive leadership work, intuition for executives, and more. I started my Master Intuition System in the early 1980s. I had always been a leadership futurist, I just did not think of the label.

Now I know. My intuition guided me to write another book, on the future of leadership power, *The Power Shift from Old Power to New Power*. Old Power countries with centuries of brutal warlords imprinted in their psyches want domination. Period. In the United States we are naïve about that, as we want power for the money, and do not understand the entrenched power psychology of China, Russia, and the Middle East. This puts us at a disadvantage.

Heavy stuff. Going to print now. It gives me an umbrella for the positive and intuitive leadership systems. Imagine the value to a company's leaders to be able to see the future. Without these skills, leaders will not be able to take our companies forward fast enough for the Idea Economy and we will not be safe economically.

Old Power countries control our access to oil, and the higher price of oil weakens us. Petrodollars from the Middle East are already purchasing major U.S. assets. China wants power over us and holds enough of our debt to have it now. This is a national security issue receiving far too little attention.

Bottom line: Incredibly rewarding life as planetary world server, making a difference. Manifesting positive things for clients and me for all these years is great fun. Knowing my purpose and staying faithful to it for my entire adult life strengthened me hugely. The actual purpose, the leadership work, has helped thousands of people.

© Linne Bourget, M.B.A., Ph.D. Used with permission.

My listeners and readers tell me that intuition can start as a very small voice that simply won't go away, no matter how you try to silence it. You ignore it, and it pops into your mind. You deny it, and its insistence forces you to reconsider it. Finally you give in, and when you do, you discover that it was right all along. My readers tell me, "Trust that intuition." And my intuition tells me they are right.

MEMORIES OF INTUITION

My earliest memories included "a familiar voice . . . a thought not originating from me." It began after being hospitalized as a young toddler for pneumonia. I was in the hospital in an oxygen tent for days. I wasn't afraid, and every time I was left alone, I wasn't afraid, though other children around me would cry hysterically from fear, a reassuring voice would resonate things like, "It will be OK."

When I was five I was devastated by a loss. A cousin, a young mother, her infant son, and her husband were asphyxiated in their home. She was someone I loved deeply and intensely for such a young girl. Call it a prayer, call it a wish, all I know is that I asked to "know" before something bad happened so I could make myself strong to endure it. Since that time, I've known when something bad was going to happen. Seldom specifics, but nevertheless, my first discovery that I got my wish was when my aunt asked me to beat the dust out of some pillows that were on a couch in a mud room. She wanted me to take them outside and beat them. Before I reached for the first pillow, a thought and a vision simultaneously entered my mind: "There's a rat under that pillow."

So I said, "Auntie, there's a rat under that pillow, I don't want to do it cuz it's going to jump out and get me."

She said, "Child that is nonsense, see?" As she "demonstrated" a giant rat leapt out from the couch onto her shoulder and she went nuts! The following day, she asked me to gather the eggs in the henhouse, and as I walked obediently toward the house with my basket in hand I could "see" a giant snake as I reached for the eggs. I turned around, and when quizzed about the empty basket, I told her, "There's a snake in there, I don't want to go get it."

Without hesitation, she called, "Papa, go get the eggs and take a hoe with you. There's a snake."

While these events may not be too terribly frightening, I've always been intuitive about bad things happening. When I was seventeen and almost a senior in high school, I felt an urgent need to "turn around and get home at once. Your mother needs you." My heart raced all the way home. I was on the way to see a movie with a friend, and I had to turn the car around it was so bad. I didn't know what my friend was going to think, but oh well, I had to go.

When I arrived, there was an ambulance in front of the house and inside they were working on my father's attempted suicide in the front seat of his car in our driveway. My mother and father were separated. I had to clean the blood and move the car, so my mother wouldn't have to see it.

And if you listen to that intuitive voice, it just may save your life.

A LIFE-SAVING INTUITION

My husband and I vacation twice a year—the same weeks every year. We always vacation at a beach with a wild horse sanctuary so we can watch the wild horses run on the beach. It also still has a small-town feel and is not very crowded.

In the summer of 2004 we decided to go the last week in June and stay at a different section of the beach. I told my husband I thought something was going to happen this week, but I did not know what.

All week nothing happened, and every day we drove to the beach. The last day before we had to go home we decided not to drive to the same beach but to one farther from our hotel. We took our stuff to the beach, but I forgot the camera so I ran back to the car. Just as I got back and sat down in my beach chair a little girl about seven years old in a big hat was running along the beach with her family behind her. Beside them we were the only ones on the beach for some distance. It was a red-flag day as there was a storm offshore making the waves very rough, and there was an unbelievable undertow. No one was supposed to be in the water on a red flag. The outer banks are known for rough surf and undertow on a good day, but today was the worst I had seen in ten years.

Just at that moment a huge wave crashed on the shore and a deep, hard swash swept across the beach. It knocked the little girl down and sucked her into the waves pounding the shore. Her father without thinking dived in after her and the very next wave knocked him off his feet, but he did manage to get ahold of the little girl's arm. They both were just getting churned in the waves pounding the beach, slowly getting sucked out farther. This happened in a split second. I could not believe how the ocean just swallowed them right off the beach.

My husband and I looked at each other and ran to the water. My husband does not swim well so he only went in up to his waist. I went after him, trying to time the waves so I did not get knocked off my feet. I say my feet because there was no swimming in that water. I had to bury my feet in the sand and walk to them. I like to think I am kind of strong, but the ocean is more than anyone can challenge.

I grabbed the man and his little girl and slowly tried walking backward out of the water between pounding waves. We slowly made it. My husband tried to grab the little girl, but her dad was starting to go into shock and was slow to let her go. Just then we knew the little girl was alright, as she started crying very loudly. Her father could not stand on his own, so I just held him until his legs could hold him up. I guess it was at least ten minutes before he could speak. The grandmother was about to panic, just repeating over and over, "I can't swim. I couldn't help."

Not until then did anyone from the beach farther down arrive to see if everyone was okay. No one saw them get swept in to the ocean, only us pulling them out.

The father and grandmother thanked us and the little girl really was not even upset, just mad she had lost her favorite hat. She did not realize she almost drowned and could get another hat.

We just started to think about it: If we had gone our usual week and stayed on the hotel beach, would they have drowned? We had almost gone to that beach initially that morning. We went on vacation at the right beach at the right time and sat down at the right time to be there to save the man and his girl. The man was already going into shock and had a death grip on the little girl and would have taken her down with him. We were the only ones around. It almost sends chills down your back, at least it did us.

I could not stop thinking about it for weeks and felt just energized afterward for weeks as well. For a moment when I was running to the beach, I swear it felt as if I was leaving my body, as if
something else was going to take over, but I remember saying in
my head, *I have to do this*, and I was never more clear-minded in
my life. I guess this is why I felt so energized, that maybe I was
allowed to be used by the universe for something more, a higher
purpose.

If you've followed the simple course of practice in Worker, *you will be
able to exercise your intuition the way this reader did and possibly prevent a disaster.*

A FIRE

Back in the early eighties, I would drive my son, Kwame, back and
forth for tutoring a couple of towns over from ours twice a week.
The routine was, drive him after school, drive back home to start
dinner, and then back to the tutor to pick him up.

It was on one of these return trips when I began to notice the
smell of burning leaves. The windshield became a "viewing" window, showing my middle child, Lynnette, engulfed in flames.

Although Kwame was waiting to be picked up, I turned the
car around and drove back. I headed for the home of Lynnette's
friend, Taiwo.

Taiwo's dad is deaf. I rang the doorbell and lights flashed on
and off within the house. Taiwo's dad did not see the flashing lights
right away, so I began to go around the house, jumping up and
down in front of windows, trying to get his attention. My anxiety
mounting, he finally saw me.

The smell of burning leaves was now overpowering. When
he came outside I asked where our children were and whether he
smelled smoke. He did not know where they were nor detected
smoke—or anything else for that matter. Getting into the car, I

instinctively drove to the street across from the woods, next to their school. I got out of the car and looked up the hill. There I saw a young teenager walking his bike across the ridge of the knoll. I yelled up and asked if she saw a fire. I called up again and asked if she saw anyone. The answer was no to both questions.

Back into the car and home. My husband had just gotten home from work. I went into the house, yelling that Lynnette was in a fire and he had to come with me. He dropped everything and asked where she was as he moved toward the front door.

I told him I wasn't sure. He stopped dead in his tracks and just looked at me. He asked me how I was so certain. My response, "I 'saw' it as I was driving to pick up Kwame."

He gave a look—not exactly rolling his eyes—but a look of "You've got to be out of your mind!" With tears streaming down my face, I began pleading with him to come with me. Reluctantly, he followed me to the car, got in, and asked where we were going. I told him I wasn't sure, but again, I instinctively drove back to the same spot as before, the woods next to the school.

As we arrived, we saw fire engines up the block. I parked the car and as we got out, Lynnette and her friend Taiwo came riding over the top and down the hill in front of us. The shock on Lynnette's face was palpable as she stopped, her shirt wet and blackened.

Without asking a question, I told her to keep riding and go straight to Taiwo's up the road.

Her father and I got back in the car, turned around, and followed.

We put Lynnette's bike in the back of the car and took her home. We asked her what had happened. It turned out these two little girls decided to make a blowtorch, like the one they saw on TV. They used an aerosol can and matches. When they saw they had ignited the dry leaves, they ran to the stream, used their shirts to sop up water, and ran back to try to put out the fire. We never did find out who reported the fire or called the fire department.

I continually experience these types of events. There are usually only two people who can verify the experience, myself and the person I warn, whether it's the waitress who I suggested go see a podiatrist (this was a few weeks ago), to tracking down a friend in a hospital minutes before his emergency surgery.

Although I've had this talent my entire life, I didn't "come out" and start sharing it with people until I was a teenager. I have had hundreds of these experiences; most of them can be attested to by at least one other person, usually several who can corroborate the details. Most incidents have been of an intervention nature.

It doesn't matter where I am or what I'm doing—asleep or awake—I will be able to "connect." I personally feel this is an intuitive sixth, seventh, and eighth sense, something we all are capable of tapping into. It may be that I'm able to feel and interpret electrical impulses—as in reading minds. I can look at a situation as if past, present and future are all "now." My most difficult challenge is in knowing when a situation has, is, or will occur. Sixth sense (the five senses), seventh sense (time), eighth sense (people): Each time I receive feedback or verification, my talent becomes stronger.

4

PROPHETIC DREAMS AND LUCID DREAMING

I n *Worker in the Light,* I talked about my many guests on *Coast* who had experienced prophetic dreaming and mastered the art of lucid dreaming.

Lucid dreaming itself sounds like a paradox. How can you be consciously aware of being in a dream when you're supposedly sound asleep? As strange as it seems, that's exactly the case. Of course you're asleep, but that doesn't mean your mind is not active. In fact, the dream state is so important to mental health that depriving someone of dreams is considered a form of torture.

Lucid dreaming is a state in which the dreamer is fully aware that he or she is dreaming. Rather than be controlled by the illogic of a dream and simply go along with the story line of the dream, the dreamer realizes that he or she is inside a dream and suddenly exerts control over the dream itself. I am reminded, for example, of my friend who lived on a boat and in his dream looked outside of the cabin to see that the boat was on a railroad flatbed rolling along a track. Instead of accepting that as a logical reality, my friend said to himself, *Wait a minute, my boat is in the water.* He realized that for him to be seeing his boat on a railroad train, he had to be dreaming. At that point, instead of fighting it or telling himself to wake up, he told himself that if he were dreaming, he should be able to fly. So he turned and jumped off the ladder into the cabin and moved his head and his dream-flying eyebrows to fly through the air. He was successful. He was flying. This is the power of lucid dreaming. Because you are aware that you're dreaming, you can make anything possible. The issue then becomes, how do you lucid-dream and what can you do in it? I say, you can accomplish just about anything because of the nature of the dream state itself.

Lucid-dream researchers explain that the dream state is a psychic experience. In some religions, a dream is considered an alternate state of waking. They say we function in a dream world with different rules of engagement. We awaken from dream states still vibrating with emotions, as if we were actually reliving various experiences in our dreams.

Is there a physiological component to this? We do experience physical reactions to our dreams. We feel fright, we feel joy, we feel sadness, and, at least in my case, I have awakened from some dreams in an state of absolute terror. People have told me that they have the sense upon awakening that they feel they have been truly wrenched from the dream world into this world, but that the dream world they inhabited was just as meaningful or even more meaningful than the world they returned to upon awakening. I admit that I find these kinds of stories fascinating because I'm just the person to believe that there is an alternate reality, a dream state, which not only might be as real as a waking state, but one that informs the waking state about realities the dreamer must be alerted to.

If we give just a little bit of credence to the possibility that the dream state is an alternate reality, then we arrive at the potential of deriving something meaningful from the dream state. For example, even in traditional psychotherapy—Freudian as well as Jungian—the dream state is considered a place where the mind can experience things that are too threatening to the conscious mind. The subconscious can pump up all kinds of repressed memories that lie like silt along the very bottom of our subconscious—feelings, emotions, forbidden loves, and taboos that would shock our conscious minds into cerebral arrhythmia. Stored away in our subconscious minds, these thoughts are like monsters in the basement behind locked doors. Except when we dream. At that point they are allowed to turn into Dracula-like mists and drift through the bottom of the locked doors into our dream state where our powerful minds can cope with the threats they present. We may wake up in terror from these dreams or feel vaguely disquieted about memories long lost to consciousness, but we have dealt with them in a safe way. By analyzing these dreams, psychotherapists can apply some form of medical logic to what is crazily illogical.

But what if, as some of my guests on *Coast to Coast AM* have said, we have the ability to navigate through some of the most menacing dreams? What if the very illogic of those dreams shocks us—while still deep in sleep—into realizing that we must be dreaming? In *Worker in the Light*, we report on research conducted by people such as Dr. Stephen LaBerge, one of the most prolific lucid-dreaming scholars, who has explained how lucid dreaming can enhance one's life. We described in *Worker* how lucid dreaming works and laid out Dr. LaBerge's plan for how to learn to lucid-dream.

We said that lucid dreaming works because the dreamer—once the person realizes that he or she is in a dream—does not automatically wake up but actually tries to navigate through the dream. In a lucid dream state, because you understand that you are in a dream, you understand that your mind controls it rather than it controlling you. This is also a form of spirit-walking in which your spirit, now freed from the corporeal demands of your body, is free to roam about and even encounter danger because the body is safely tucked between the blankets and out of harm's way.

As powerful as Dr. LaBerge says lucid dreaming is, the trick is to stay in that lucid dream state after you recognize you're dreaming. In other words, you have to stay awake in your dream without waking up: awake and asleep at the same time. At first glance, that's a toughie, but it's something that spirit walkers, shamans, medicine men, and prophets like Edgar Cayce had mastered in order for them to wield the power of lucid dreaming. With surprisingly little effort, most of us can accomplish it.

Lucid dreaming is almost like keeping yourself within that out-of-body experience even after you've seen your own body in front of you and know that you're out of it. Your first reaction is not to know what to do, and the realization of where you are so challenges your reality that your logical mind kicks in, tells you that this is impossible, and you snap back into traditional reality. It's just like the late Christopher Reeve's Richard Collier character in the film, *Somewhere in Time,* who has out-of-bodied himself back eighty or so years to the early twentieth century, where he falls in love. When he sees a modern penny in his pocket however, reality collapses in around him and he snaps back to the present. This is very much like what happens when you realize you're dreaming in a dream state and can't control your emotions. You suddenly snap awake, realizing that you just had enormous power within your grasp but let it slip away.

How can you keep this from happening? How can you, at the point of wielding this power to navigate through your dream world, remain asleep and in your dream while your waking mind has actually taken control of the dream? These are the questions that Dr. LaBerge and I discussed on the air and we wrote about in *Worker in the Light.*

> First key point is training yourself to enter a lucid dreaming state. Most of our contributors, whether from childhood experience when no one knew any better, or simply on their own, already took the first step. They invested—a positive and volitional act—themselves with the belief that such a dream state is not only possible, but it's doable. Having done that, the reality of being in a waking dream was not so stunning as to throw them out of it from the start.

LaBerge explained to us in *Worker in the Light* that once you've accepted the premise that lucid dreams can happen, you have to first learn how to enter a lucid-dream state, then how to stay there once in. At that point, just like someone from Krypton, you can begin to explore your superpowers in ways that many of our contributors have. In lucid dreams not only can you fly or navigate underwater as if you were a marine animal, but you can communicate with other people, travel back and forth in time, and even penetrate the minds and thoughts of others. You can communicate with the departed, join your spirit with the spirits of your long-gone ancestors, and try to send messages to those you perceive are in danger.

Our contributors who lucid-dream can do so consciously, for the most part. They have learned to follow the steps that LaBerge sets out and we explain in *Worker*. They, and you, can begin by practicing finding a mental key to trigger your awareness that you're dreaming. We suggested wearing a watch to sleep and conditioning yourself to think of that watch just as you go to sleep. Doing that may place an autosuggestion in your mind that in a dream you will look at that watch. It will remind you that you are dreaming. When you realize you are dreaming, do something out of the ordinary by controlling your environment in the dream. One way is simply to take off. Tell yourself you can fly and, guess what, you can. One of my friends simply jumped off a ladder, telling himself that not only would he float down, but that his eyebrows would direct his flight. He did and they did.

Other methods to get into a lucid-dreaming awareness state involve counting yourself into a dream. You think of a number, say, eleven, and as you focus on your hand you think of the number eleven. You associate that number with your right or left hand and in a dream, when you think of your hand, you think of number eleven and remember that it triggers you to think: *Alert, dreaming.* Then enjoy the state you're in. Don't be disappointed if you wake right up. Once you've begun the process, you can do it again and again until you can spend significant time in a dream state. Is this what Edgar Cayce did? It would be fun to experiment with that the way our contributors are doing.

Many of our contributors have reported dream visions of people visiting them in dreams, communicating information, warning them of the future, or even providing them with certain premonitions. In fact, dream premonitions are so prevalent in many of the stories that our contributors sent us, it's probably a good thing to explain that they are quite common and that you can train yourself to experience these dream premonitions as well. In *Worker*, for example, we suggest that one of the last acts you perform as you're heading off to sleep for the night, is to repeat your mantra as you do your breathing exercise. As you do this, reach out to the universe so as to make that spiritual connection. Doing so will actually put you in contact with a vast storehouse of information shared by the human collective. You will be able to retrieve this information, see shared images and use your connection as a kind of psychic Worldwide Web. This, of course, was C. G. Jung's concept of the collective unconscious. He said that human beings didn't just sink into their own subconscious minds during a dream state, the way Freud argued, but that they reached out to a vast source of shared information. In so doing, they partook of common images and shared common ideas. In his own way, Jung was describing something that Plato described when he talked about a world of forms that was unchanging and gave meaning to things in our three-dimensional space.

If you reach out into this collective, I believe, images will come to you from that collective—images that not only represent different places but times as well. This is the model behind predictive dreams, dream premonitions, and even prophetic dreams. I cannot tell you the countless number of people have written to us, telling us stories of the dream prophecies they have received. Many of these stories are prophetic manifestations along traditional religious lines. People talk to angels in their dreams, see images of Jesus, and see things about to happen or are told about them by relatives who appear in dreams to give them warning. It's easy to dismiss some of this as wishful thinking, but in a large number of these reports, the predictions and premonitions actually come true. Is there a statistical measure of significance? I don't know, but I focus on the stories of people who write me about things that have come true.

What I do know from experience is that the exercises that can put you in touch with the larger universe and the human collective do, indeed, work. I perform them myself, and, at the very least, those exercises give me feelings of peace and solace in a high-pressure, deadline-driven, and often confrontational world. You can perform them to see how they work for you and see whether the experiences you have are similar to the experiences our contributors have told us about. Who knows, like them, you may very well be able to communicate with the departed or become sensitive in your waking state to dreams that give you premonitions of the future. It's exciting even to think about such things, but even more exciting to read about the experiences of others who've been there and peered into possibilities of what dream working in the light can do for people.

I am constantly reminded of how Edgar Cayce at first rejected his ability to decipher prophetic messages in his dreams. But eventually, as does this dreamer, he accepted the messages from the future that he was receiving. In Worker, *we explain that prophetic dreams are not scary in themselves, even though sometimes the future they foretell is unpleasant. If you learn to accept the prophetic nature of dreams in the knowledge that the future can be changed, you will experience a great sense of empowerment.*

PROPHETIC DREAMING

Here is a dream I had at my home in Vancouver at the exact moment Princess Diana was dying from an auto accident. I was working in my home and suddenly became sleepy to the point that I had to sit back on my bed. It was afternoon and I dreamt I was speeding after a big black vehicle and we went into a tunnel. This is part of the dream. Hours later I learned I was dreaming at precisely the moment Diana was experiencing this.

I once had a dream, or so it seemed, except I was wide awake. I dreamt of the Kobe earthquake. Two days later I saw the exact same images on TV that I had experienced in my dream. It was as if I watched the TV article two days in advance in my subconscious. This dream was also detailed.

I have also had a benevolent voice that talks to me at certain times and actually once saved me from being injured in an auto accident. When I was getting a breath of fresh air once in the middle of the night, this voice told me to close the window because Death was passing by. I have been forewarned by this voice many times, so I always obey it as it has always helped me. I am also the seventh child of a seventh child and I was born with a veil over my face.

When I read about dreams foretelling disaster and chaos, I think about the young woman that Joel Martin writes about in his Haunting of America, *who had dreams predicting the collapse of the World Trade Towers. Many of my listeners call in with such dreams of disaster, and I always give them the same advice. If these are events you can control, make the changes now to change the future. If these events are out of your hands, then consider them warnings to you to prepare for hard times. This is the kind of dream that this reader has experienced. But we have to ask, "Who was the figure in his dream?"*

A DREAM OF THE FUTURE

When I was an adolescent I had a very vivid dream. On a warm summer morning I saw myself leaving my family home. The neighborhood where we lived was made up of suburban homes on acre-or-so lots, with some of the lots not yet developed. I saw the house, yard, and surrounding area as it actually was in an early morning light. There was a being there guiding me, without any words spoken. The being was much like those depicted in the *Cocoon* movies, but this was in 1964.

We walked through an adjacent empty lot, across the road, and to another vacant lot where there was a chromelike structure or vehicle. It was a smooth, shiny, capsule-shaped structure, which resembled an Airstream trailer. We entered this structure, where my guide indicated that I look at two screens that resembled television screens embedded in a counter. They portrayed scenes of social conflict and chaos. One set of images I watched showed crowds of people fleeing military equipment, fires, and explosions. It was communicated to me that this could be the future, here in North America, but that it could be prevented.

In this story, our contributor experiences a combination of a prophetic dream and a synchronicity of events. This is not uncommon, but it always reinforces my belief that there are no coincidences.

PROPHETIC DREAMS

Six years ago I found myself dreaming a lot—very intuitively. A certain loved one who had passed away years ago came to me in a dream. First, I moved back to the family's old ranch area with my children and my wife at the time. My wife and I were not in the same path and did not get along. The dreams lasted about two winter months.

I first had a dream that we were driving in separate cars and there was an accident on the highway near our house. Two weeks later there was an accident. We arrived at the scene about fifteen to twenty minutes later and there was a death from the accident. When we were driving home there was a truck weaving in and out of lanes on the highway about fifteen minutes away from our exit off the highway. When we got to the accident the same truck had caused the accident. This story always has made me know that I saw this before it happened and if at that time I realized I had this foresight I would have done something about it. Two weeks after the accident my ex-wife was stopped for a DUI.

I had another dream that my grandmother came to me and told me she would take care of my children for me. She told me not to worry and that everything would be okay. I jumped out of my bed and bawled for a very long time that night. The dream was eerie and very real.

After that dream my wife at the time and I had a very upsetting night. It was around Thanksgiving and I was not able to be there for my kids, but I know my grandmother was there for them (like she said she would be). A couple of weeks later I divorced my wife. I knew it was meant to happen, and this dream foretold the future.

All my life I have had very strong and vivid dreams, which now I know were there to tell me the future. The dreams that winter were meant to help and predict what I needed help with. I still think about the series of dreams I had that season and know that it was my inner power preparing me for the upcoming events through these dreams along with other beings I may have let into my dream life. By the way, the divorce papers were signed and finalized on the day my grandmother died.

Here's a story that sounded to me very much like President Abraham Lincoln's dream that foretold his own death by assassination. Sometimes it pays to listen to a message in a dream even though every one around you might think you're simply being suspicious, paranoid, or given to fantasies.

MY SISTER'S DREAM

My sister had a dream one night when she was in high school that she found extremely strange. She dreamed that there were five caskets waiting for someone but one casket was not going to be used. The next morning she decided not to ride with her friends to school. She usually was picked up each day by her neighborhood friend. That morning four girls that were in the car were hit by a truck a mile from school and killed. My sister was the one who didn't need the casket. The family found this dream very strange and curious.

I became friends with a psychic as a result of some of my dreams, and he told me to write all my dreams down and watch the news and such.

Many of my listeners describe events that make me think that some of them are clairvoyant in their dreams. A number of readers and listeners seem to have this gift of clairvoyance. Some find it disturbing while others have learned to live with it and even use it to help others. The following stories illustrate all of these possibilities.

TWO DREAMS ABOUT DISASTER

I recently dreamt I was watching an airplane in the sky. It was a small passenger plane, red on the top and white on the bottom, and it was circling. All of a sudden it fell out of the sky and crashed on its belly with a great thud in a field adjacent to where I was standing. I ran to the wreckage and the two men inside were dead. A few days later I read in the newspaper that an experimental plane crashed in a field in a bordering town. A farmer was watching as it crashed in an adjacent field, and it was red on the top and white on the bottom. Both men inside were killed in the crash. In the picture in the paper the plane was sitting on its belly.

Last week I dreamt I was watching a house that was on fire. I was watching it burn on one side when all of a sudden it exploded through the roof in a ball of flames and I knew that a woman was trapped inside and had perished. The dream was very vivid. The very next morning while reading the CNN news on the computer I saw the headline for an apartment building fire that caught a church next to it on fire. Also, there was one woman trapped inside the church, and when they were getting ready to go in and rescue her the fire exploded through the roof and engulfed the church in flames and the woman perished, just like in the dream.

LUCID DREAMING

Lucid dreaming is a skill that can be easily learned. I'm glad I did learn it. I have discovered realities that I never considered. After I lost my daughter I have had many experiences and even contact with her in other realities. In one reality she was at college and talking to me on the campus pay phone. I knew she was dead in my reality but she was quite real in this one. I was kind of experimenting with this experience so I asked her if she still wanted to be a pirate and she responded that that had been a childhood dream like being an astronaut. In her lifetime here she did indeed work on a ship.

In another lucid experience I was drawn to a large building that turned out to be a bowling alley and I was floating about five feet above her head and to the left. I was the ghost. She was about nine or ten at this time and a woman came up to her and they started to walk away. She seemed oddly familiar, and it occurred to me that she was the girl's mother in this life.

In addition to prophetic dreams, other listeners either have discovered their gift of lucid dreaming—exerting control of their dream state once they're aware they're dreaming—or they have successfully learned how to lucid-dream.

LUCID DREAMING

I have had an abundance of experiences in lucid dreaming, which I have had since I was a kid. I'm in my thirties now.

I am science-and-logic minded, with no college. I have read and studied about 2012, lucid dreaming, dreams, and other realities, such as the Mayan. I am very much into this stuff, and *Coast to Coast AM* is among the top on my list. Here is my story:

Once I started lucid-dreaming when I was little I really started to question things. Where did we come from? Where are we heading? Why is it that when I stop and look around in my dreams I can feel without actually touching, smell without actually using my nose, see without using my eyes, and hear without being conscious of anything in everyday reality? And yet this dream world is so very vivid and colorful, almost flawless to its core.

Of course, at first the lucid dreaming came and went and they were not very long, it was even hard to stay in my dreams because you know you're dreaming and that proves quite difficult. But once I started to get the hang of it, it was a blast. I could do anything, walk anywhere, move things with my mind, and make buildings into mountainous landscapes without even blinking an eye. I can fly through the clouds and feel the breeze.

Here comes the good part. When I stop to look around, I think. I think very deeply, asking as many questions as my mind can fathom, and when I look around I can feel, see, and hear no real difference between the dream world and ours. The only difference is that I'm not just going through the motions; I know I'm dreaming. I know that everything around me is me. And if I slow my thought pattern down enough, I can almost hear how to make it happen . . . but that's where I always get stuck. I feel an awakening . . . I feel as if any day I can wake up and just know something . . . like the knowing when you realize, "OMG I'm dreaming," that overwhelming feeling of knowing and power, not greed power but unbiased power. It feels like pure being. Pure at its absoluteness.

I've even faced death in my dreams—inescapable even while lucid and being godlike. I faced what I later found out was me. Long story short: In my dream I said this to myself, "In the end of all things there is only truth."

When we dream, do we actually enter a different universe or are we only processing thoughts from our waking hours? Some dreams are simply too real to be anything other than reality, albeit an alternate reality.

PROPHETIC DREAMS OF MULTIPLE UNIVERSES

I mentioned this to an alien abductee friend who told me that he believes we exist in several dimensions and/or time lines because our brains are not designed to take in everything from the one we are in.

Several years ago, I often had the experience of having a dream and then awakening to experience what happened in my dream in real time. I had dreams that came true, and *exactly* the way I dreamed they would. Then a good friend of my mine died. She was an elderly woman who headed an abductee support group in my state. I had come in contact with her and her group and also several other "metaphysical" people here.

One night while sleeping, I dreamed I was visiting her in a house in a place I somehow knew was Arkansas! Now, as sure as I knew it was Arkansas, I also knew this was somehow a different Arkansas in an alternate universe. She showed us around her house and the neighborhood, and everything looked very spiffy and middle class—unless you looked closer and you could find things like rotting foundations, carpet falling apart, mold, and mildew. The message I got was this: be careful because how things look are not necessarily how they are! This dream would always come to me before I made any major move such as taking a new job. Sure enough, if I dreamed of the alternate universe, I was often let down—or, on occasion—pleasantly surprised! Then, a few years later, things changed. I no longer see our dead friend in the alternate universe. I see me living another life on another time line. In fact, a psychic friend once told me I am living in seven different time lines! In these time lines, I have different wives, children, and friends. I am always being rushed to learn something new or accomplish an impossible task.

Last night I was categorizing papers and putting them into manila envelopes in time for someone to arrive and take them. Some believe that people who are involved with the UFO situation have a second life going on when they sleep at night. From what I can tell, this makes sense!

Anyhow, one morning when I was waking from a trip to the alternate universe, I was in a state between sleep and consciousness. At that time a strange-looking little gray alien was standing over my bed and shaking an index finger at me as if scolding or reprimanding me for something. I noticed—for some odd reason—that he had horns on his head. This scared me so much that I screamed and sat up in bed! I have some Catholic sacramentals that I placed on my nightstand and I opened a Bible to the Twenty-third Psalm and since then the little horned gray alien has never returned! I don't know if he was a fluke or what. Anyhow, are we all having our "other selves" prepare us for something coming up very soon in the future? And is this something that we will understand on a soul level? I'd be curious to know if one of these other time lines is our "escape hatch" or our "rapture."

A CHILLING DREAM

I was thirty years old when I first had a foretelling dream that I took seriously. My oldest daughter's birthday was the next day. Her grandfather, Bart, was all set to leave the next day for his first vacation in Hawaii. He had always wanted to visit there and see all the different flowers they had growing on the islands. He was a botanist and was in awe of plants and flowers.

Anyway, that night I had a dream I was in a coffin. I was saying, *This can't be me. I can't be in that coffin.* I told myself, *You have to look and make sure that it is you.* When I got up the courage to look in the coffin, it was Bart lying there. I woke up crying. My wife asked me, "What's wrong?" I said, "Dad died." She said, "No, it's just a dream. He's going to Hawaii tomorrow, go back to sleep."

I didn't rest well the rest of the night. I was afraid of what else I might see. So, at the light of day I told myself it was just a nightmare and not real, until my brother stopped by our house in late morning to tell us Dad had passed in the middle of the night. It seems he had had a reaction to a flu shot he had taken a couple of days earlier, because he didn't want anything to stop his trip.

My daughter says that was her worst birthday ever. She is now close to giving birth to her first child, a little boy named Bart.

My Daughter Kristen

My husband and I were a very happy couple with a perfect family: a beautiful daughter, Anne, and a handsome son named Todd. We were done having kids, so we thought. A boy and a girl. Life was good, what more could we ask for? We were in our late thirties, and one night in a semidream state I was taken into a pure white room. There was a man in a pure white robe with a long white beard. He held out two baby bottles, one close to his body and one stretched out away from him. They had dates on them. One date read the third on the bottle closest to his body and the nineteenth on the other. No words were spoken, but I was informed I'm to have a daughter born in September between these two dates. I immediately sat up in bed, woke my husband up at 3:00 A.M., and said, "Honey, I'm pregnant, it's a girl, and she will be born in September."

He said, "You're not pregnant, go back to sleep."

I went to work in the morning and told all my friends at work, "I'm pregnant."

My husband followed me around the house for about a week asking, "Honey, how ya feeling?" after telling him about my dream.

After about a week I finally turned to him and said in a loud voice, "I know my body and I'm pregnant." So I left him alone for at least another week. I went to the doctor who confirmed it. Finally, my husband asked me how I had known that one random night and I told him.

On September 8, 2001, I had the most beautiful girl named Kristen. On September 11, 2001, after getting my two older kids off to school, my husband was getting ready to pick me and new baby Kristen up to bring us home from the hospital for good. With the TV on as he was ready to leave the house to go to the hospital, he witnessed the whole 9/11 event live on CNN.

All my kids go to Catholic school, and four years later on a Friday, September 8, my day off and Kristen's fourth birthday I dropped all three kids off at school. Kristen was in pre-school at the time so I walked her to class. As I was leaving the classroom it was time for morning announcements over the intercom, and I froze to listen. The school made their morning prayer, pledge of allegiance, morning announcements, then said we would like to wish a couple of happy birthdays, like they always do: "Today we have two special birthdays. First it is Kristen's fourth birthday, and the other birthday is, as you all know, our blessed Mary's birthday." It sent shivers down my spine.

Today Kristen is six years old, adorable, articulate, active, and smart. She is everything I ever dreamed she might be. Although we hover over her like helicopters, she manages to get away and has had three terrible accidents, at ages two, three, and four. Twice she fell two stories onto rocks, and both times the doctor could not find a single scratch on her. Then her brother accidentally clubbed her in the eye with a golf ball. It should have killed her, but it healed quickly. All our kids are special, but we often stop and scratch our heads and wonder about Kristen.

In addition to prophetic and lucid dreams, our listeners also experience dreams in which they are visited by a loved one, angels, or even a kindly spirit. This is just such an example.

A DREAM VISITATION

The dream started out with me feeling a strong love. I have never had a dream with such a profound feeling. I went into this all-white room where there were people milling around. As people parted, there stood a little girl who had died about a month before. She was my daughter's best friend. She was looking healthier and thinner than she had been in life. I remember she was wearing a plaid shirt. I remember the colors were reds and browns. She "told" me (somehow), "Tell everybody that I am doing okay."

She also showed me that she was protecting her younger brother who was born right before she died. She showed me by putting her arms around his shoulders. This dream was about eighteen years ago and I still remember and feel it so vividly.

And the spirits can sometimes manifest themselves as animals or even lost pets.

THE BIG BLACK DOG

For many years I dreamt of a black dog. It almost always was in the form of a black Lab—sometimes a different breed, but usually a Lab.

Sometimes I would dream of the dog several nights in a row or, other times, maybe not for weeks. The dreams were always good ones. Whatever I was doing in the dream, the dog was there beside me, doing nothing especially exciting. It was just comforting to have it there. I came to believe that the dog was a guide because this went on for years.

Last June I was very depressed and grieving over an incident that had happened in my life. One morning I decided to look at a deck of angel cards that I keep for inspiration. I don't look at the deck like a Tarot reading or anything of that nature—I was just looking for comfort. I picked a card that said "Signs." It indicated that I should look for signs that angels were watching over me. I was very, very despondent, as I mentioned. I then went downstairs and headed out the back door, late for a doctor's appointment. When I walked out the door a big black Lab dog came running up to me. It had a red collar. I was stunned. My yard has a six-foot privacy fence around it and both gates were locked. There was no way for the dog to get in the yard, and it was way too big to crawl under the fence. I have lived there for twenty-four years. I have never seen a black dog in my neighborhood in all that time, and never that particular dog, and never had a stray dog in my yard—lots of cats—but no dogs.

I came back from my appointment and the dog was gone. I have never seen it again. It was not my imagination. It happened. At the risk of sounding crazy I believe that the dog was sent by an angel. I have no other explanation.

LUCID DREAMING

I once found myself waking up from a dream that was somehow more real than what I woke up to. In this "dream" I found that I had no body, no sense of time, no name, no sense of myself as an individual.(This sentence shows up some of the limitations of language when describing such a situation: how can "I" have no sense of identity?) I was just awareness. I was aware of everything that was going on around me. If I thought about Japan, I would be in

Japan; if I thought about the moon, I was on the moon. I could feel everything that went on everywhere.

I felt the sensation of trees, tickled by the wind. I could feel the sensation of the wind, shredded by the trees. I knew what it felt like to be the mouse in the jaws of the cat, lovingly surrendering. I knew what it felt like to be the cat gratefully killing the mouse.

I realized every life had a story, and it was a story of struggle and error, and all these stories were told to me by the creatures (man, woman, animal, and plant) that lived them. Their stories all became a part of my experience, and it was all okay. This sensory overload was somehow not overwhelming to me. I took all of it in and it became part of me, and it was okay.

Then I began to develop a sense of apartness; some sense of individuality was returning to me. I found myself in a place that was no place in particular, and there were other beings around. I can't describe them; I guess I didn't think their appearance was that important to me at the time.

I was made to carry (maybe wear would be a better word) something that I thought resembled some sort of wiring harness that branched off in four directions from the main stem, which was topped with some sort of knob. Then I had to crawl into a bag of some sort. (Later when I thought about the meaning of this part of my experience, I realized that I was being fitted with a brain and spinal column, and the "bag" was my skin.)

At that point I opened my eyes and woke up. I was in my bed, looking up at the ceiling of my little apartment. I looked down and saw my feet sticking up under the covers. It took several seconds for me to remember who, what, and where I was, and when I did remember it all, I was overwhelmed with a feeling of disappointment at being me, back here again.

Here is a lucid dreamer, who, driven by desperation, took the time to learn the skill that we teach in Worker in the Light.

LEARNING TO LUCID-DREAM

When I was twenty-seven, I had a horrible awakening. I had all these symptoms—headaches, neck aches. I became allergic to everything—cigarettes, food—it just was unbearable. Everything that could go wrong, did. My asthma got worse, I gained a lot of weight, I lost friends, I felt lonely, I lost my job, my relationship with my girlfriend was going down the tubes, I was a miserable mess, and everyday breathing was a struggle. I felt Like God was giving me a big butt-kicking. I had no choice but to be spiritual in this matter, to reach out, so I got online and looked around for things that could change my life, I was searching and searching.

I chatted with a lot of online folks when Yahoo Chat had user-made rooms. I would go in there asking for advice. Many would suggest Reiki, or praying, or lighting white candles—nothing I understood—as this was all very new to me.

One day my father and I went into a bookstore and I came across this book about harnessing and awakening your psychic abilities. He bought me the book hoping to cheer me up, having no clue how this book would open up a whole new world for me (thanks, Dad). There is an exercise in the book where you pull energy into your chakras and activate them. After doing so you would have a lucid/vivid dream indicating you have opened doors in your spiritual life.

Skeptical and very desperate to escape the hell I was facing, I did the chakra exercises every night until one night I had a vivid dream where I was running through doors and flying through windows, and in the middle of this hallway was a white tiger walking toward me. I felt fear, then realized it was my spiritual self I was being introduced to that I was so afraid of meeting. I had become open.

This was surely the most vivid dream I had *ever* had. I tried remembering if I had any dreams like this before, and I could not.

Life for me changed quickly. I searched out Reiki masters in the area, knowing they would be hard to find, but was amazed to find one that lived out in the country. He was elderly and retired from attuning people. I begged him and something about me, my eagerness, changed his mind and I was attuned to Reiki level one.

The first twenty-one days of clearing were horrible. My hands were burning up like overcooked hotdogs; they cracked open and bled. My Reiki teacher was perplexed by this rare condition. My asthma improved and so did my relationships. I noticed people could tolerate me better. I became healthier in many ways. I finally started to feel happiness. It had changed my whole way of thinking. It wasn't hard shedding old skin; I was welcoming it.

I started lucid-dreaming around the same time I became open, and it felt like I had two lives. I remembered I knew I could fly anywhere if I wanted to, but as soon as I would take off to go visit someone, I would wake up. I remember the way it felt—the surging, zooming energy, the bold colors, the serene, incredible feeling.

I hated waking up from these wonderful dreams. I would also get dreams that had a lot of symbolic meanings and clues. I realized I could get a lot of my answers in my dreams if I asked for them to appear. Also, in the early mornings I would be awakened with information about my daily concerns, just a strong knowing that everything would be OK. Then, just as quickly as it came, it went away, along with that beautiful surging energy that I love to feel and I would be back to sleep. I always had trouble remembering why I was awakened the night before, so I wrote my dream down so I wouldn't forget it later on in the day.

I had a dream about my mother's death, and the hospital room that she would die in, and knew from that dream she would die soon. She was in the hospital for a kidney transplant and had fallen in the bathroom. They did some scans to check her out and found that she had blood in the brain. At the time they assumed she had gotten it from falling, but she had originally fallen because of two brain anuerysms. She was taken into surgery. They went in and tried to coil the two anuerysms, but did not see the third one. It was too late, she had too much blood on the brain, and that caused her to be brain dead.

We decided as a family to pull the plug, and six days later she passed away in the very same hospital room I dreamt about. No one in my family had a clue she would die after surgery, but I did. I was prepared. I had the experience that other people have had when someone close to them dies or is going to die; I had only heard about this connnection but never experienced it until then. I felt totally special to have this happen to me. I felt like it got me ready for the biggest heartbreak of my life.

I got my third degree in Reiki and my life has changed for the better. I am happy-go-lucky and nothing keeps me down. I see everything as a learning lesson and a blessing. I trust my intuition: Everything that happens has its purpose even if it doesn't make sense to me now. I work at a hospice where I use my Reiki to try to heal or make passings easier. I truly feel I am one of the workers of the light and I couldn't have made it here if I did not have my awakening.

Angelic visitations also take place in dreams that heal the dreamer or make the dreamer aware of his or her special soul.

ANGELIC AWAKENING

In the late '80s my father developed a precancerous bladder condition. It was treated and he seemed to be OK.

A few years later he was checked and it was back—only this time it wasn't precancerous. The treatment was more radical this time. His bladder was removed and a new one was constructed out of part of his large intestine. It was a new procedure at the time, and not perfect (he had to empty the pouch several times a day using a tube), but it was better than the alternative of wearing a bag for the rest of his life. He had some chemotherapy that went very well and things got back to normal.

In the meantime, Dad started going back to church. That was fine, as long as he didn't try to get me to go. He knew better. He eventually developed a spot on one of his lungs. He had surgery and had that lobe removed. He joked and said that he would do just fine with three-fourths of his lungs. Again he seemed to be doing just fine for a while before the cancer came back—this time with a vengeance! It was in his lungs again, and this time it was inoperable. He died in early November 1995.

I was angry! Angry at everybody, especially God. I may not have believed in Dad's religion but I did believe in God and I raged at Him. My main mantra became that he was only sixty-three, and as soon as God knew He had my dad back in the fold He just let him die.

About a month after his death I had a dream. I know I must dream; everybody does, but I seldom remember my dreams, but this particular dream is as clear right now as when I dreamt it.

I was standing in a meadow. It was a beautiful, mild summer day. The sun was bright, but not glary, squinty bright; there was a softness to it. The grass in the meadow was about midthigh to waist high, and it was soft and fragrant. There was a light breeze and I could hear crickets and insects in the grass and see butterflies and small birds flitting around. Off in the distance on the other side of the meadow was a group of trees, all big, shade tree types. I was standing near but not under another tree of the same type that was by itself in the middle of the meadow.

As I stood there taking in the lovely scenery, I noticed someone walking toward me from the area of the trees. As that person got closer I could see it was a man, and when he got about twenty-five feet from me I saw that it was my father, but he appeared as he had when he was about thirty to thirty-five years old. One thing that was a little amusing was that he was wearing a jacket (I couldn't see lower than his waist so I don't know if he had on pants or shorts) that was cut like the old Nehru jackets that people wore in the '60s. The jacket was made out of a slightly shiny material like satin, and it was exactly the color of a car we had bought in 1968. He loved that color and he loved that car. It had been the first new car we had ever owned.

But to get back to the story, he didn't come any closer than about ten feet from me, and he didn't say anything and neither did I. He just stood there and smiled at me and nodded and then I woke up. I felt so much better after that dream and I quit being angry at God because I knew everything was OK.

Since the dream I have learned a few things. Many people who either dream of dead loved ones, or who have had near-death experiences of their own, describe the exact same place. The Spiritualist Movement actually calls it Summerland, I believe. And it is a perfect name for it.

I feel that the reason that he just stood there nodding at me was to let me know that I had been right when we had argued about religion, and that there is no hell and that the only judgment is when we judge ourselves.

Prophetic dreams can also be apocalyptic, my listeners tell me, and I have heard so many apocalyptic dreams, I am now a believer.

A TIME-TRAVEL DREAM TO 2012

I have had three very significant and somewhat jarring experiences of this type. One dream occurred in the late 1980s. Though I have had a longstanding interest in mystical experiences, I had never thought of or nor investigated UFOs prior to this dream.

It was during the middle of the night when a craft landed outside my home—the one I really lived in at the time in New Mexico—in the late 1980s. It was a very small vehicle, with one seat in the front and two seats in the back. I and someone else who knew me were picked up, without any incident, and walked as if by invitation into the craft. The craft was silent.

In fact, the craft was almost invisible until we were inside it. The driver, whom I only seemed to catch a glimpse of, had a large head with no hair, long, thin arms, and was somewhat translucent. There was a greenish tint within the craft.

As the craft had landed in my driveway, there was no rhapsodic runway. Much as it must have landed, the craft took off by rising straight in the air and heading toward, it seemed to me, the northern part of the globe. I could feel the northeastern motion of the flight as we swiftly catapulted toward the North Pole, then took a southeasterly turn and went toward what seemed from a distance to be the eastern seaboard of the United States.

We landed when it was still dark at a place that looked like a state park, with vegetation that reminded me of coastal Virginia. We landed by dropping down on a spot, vertically, just as we had taken off.

We were escorted on foot from our landing spot into a large, one-story old-timey building with many rooms. The building could have been built during the 1930s, if not earlier. The driver of the craft, who must have been just our chauffeur, took us to the door of the building and then disappeared. Not once during the flight did the driver speak to us.

The building was an old house, well-lit and full of people. The house was filled with stuffed, comfortable, and inviting chairs and couches. Everyone was dressed, it seemed, in the time of a particular period in U.S. history, though the earliest time was likely the late 1800s. It was like a family reunion, though I didn't recognize anyone from my life on this planet in the twentieth century. It seemed like I had, however, been invited to this reunion because everyone was so kind, so polite, and willing to welcome me into the enclave.

I walked from room to room taking in vibrations of love and understanding. At one point, there appeared to be a lot of activity going on in a room adjacent to where I was standing. I waited patiently until I could walk through the doorway to get into that room. A gentleman came up to me and asked, "Why are you waiting to go through that doorway? All you have to do is walk through the wall to get where you want to be." My consciousness was rocked a bit by that advice, but it did seem to ring true, so I walked through the wall with no adverse consequences, and was amazed to see what was on the other side.

The next room was very crowded. People were grouped together, talking about and staring at five people on the other side of the room. All five of the onstage people were related and all were women. Each was the child of the female to her right. None of them was a child or an adolescent. The oldest would have had to be, in our time track, more than a hundred years old, yet she looked much younger, maybe in her late sixties. Each of the females was dressed in the style of her time. I was shocked by these women. It seemed an impossibility in our time. My shock was not shared by the other watchers in the room. They were enjoying the clothes these women were wearing.

So by that time, I had been flown from one part of the United States to another in an "alien" craft, dropped down in the middle of a "family" reunion in some unknown place and time, walked through a wall without flinching, and seen five generations of parent-child, adult women enjoying the attention they were getting from others. I was, though, not prepared for what was to come.

I left the women to their audience and went back to the adjacent room, through the doorway this time, though. The room was filled, and people were walking about as well as sitting on those inviting couches. The one I chose to sit on was covered in red velvet. But before sitting down, I noticed a newspaper lying on an end table that was covered with lace and lit by a lamp with a decorative, off-white shade. The newspaper was very old and worn, colored yellow the way such paper gets when it ages for years. The year on that paper was unmistakable. It said "2012." I reeled, realizing in the dream itself that I was a time traveler.

I'm rocking. I know I'm a time traveler. I've just got to sit down. The room starts to swirl. Where am I? Where is home? I stumble toward that red velvet couch. I begin to recover from my swoon as I become captivated by the conversation of the two folks who are sitting on either side of me on the couch. One of my new friends, well, I can't keep my eyes off him. He is undoubtedly the most beautiful man I have ever seen. He speaks perfect English. He seems perfectly at home in these surroundings. People enjoy conversing with him. There's only one twist. This man has the face of a large dog, somewhat like a German shepherd.

Here is a dreamer talking about the physicality of her dream experience. This is not abnormal, of course; people have physical symptoms that intrude into the dream state and are interpreted by the mind as part of the dream. But this experience is very special, as you will see.

THE PHYSICALITY OF DREAMS

In the mid-nineties I started having bad dreams, the ones that wake you up gasping for air in the middle of the night. The dreams were about me dying when I turned thirty-five years old. I could see myself in a casket at my funeral. I also could see myself standing next to the casket looking at myself inside.

These dreams increased later that year when I was in the hospital with a deadly bout of meningitis that put me in a coma for four days. The only thing I remember was those dreams. When I turned thirty-five the dreams stopped. I was worried! Well, that year my mom died. I stood alongside her casket. The dreams were not about me dying; they were about my mom. People say that my mom and I are twins . . . we look alike! That's why I saw myself in the casket or I thought I saw myself. So I think I saw the future. God helped me see the future.

A dream can also urge the dreamer to do something to avoid a disastrous future just like the experience this reader had.

A DREAM VISION WARNING

"Only you know how to save my mommy" was the message in my dreams. I would find it scratched on a chalkboard and the binders of books on bookshelves. I even heard it from an old woman with a little girl's voice. This dream continued for a few days.

About five years later I was working at a new job. On a sad day when my supervisor had been seriously injured, I quickly ran to her and began performing the first aid techniques I had learned as a child, which saved her life. I was to find out later that I was the only person who was trained and quick-minded enough to perform the task. When I later met her family I was told her son said in the emergency room that only I knew how to save his mommy. Even the people who helped me until the EMT crew arrived said that only I knew what to do. I don't want the credit of being a hero but I do believe that in my dreams I was told I would do this.

Dreams can be a healing experience, too, as this reader discovered amid some of his darker moments.

HOW DREAMS CAN HEAL

I had the most wonderful experience about ten years ago. I was married and had two young children at the time.

I had been abused mentally and physically since I was a child. Well anyway, I found out my husband was cheating on me. I was already depressed because deep down I knew, but when I found out for sure, I went into a deep depression and wanted to kill myself. But I had two kids that I love very much, so I spent most of my time in bed when the kids were at school. Then I got up and proceeded as a mother.

They knew I was sad. They drew a picture for me that said, "I hope you feel better," and signed their names to it. After they went to bed that first night I did also and slept way on the left side of my bed away from my husband at the time.

I was awakened during the night. I sat straight up as I looked at the tall dresser where a picture was hanging. I saw a child I thought was my son. I called his name and told him to go back to bed, but there was no response. The child had his arms crossed and was staring at the picture. Then I thought to myself, *That's not him. He's stocky but not that short.* Then I said, "Kimmers, what are you doing? Go back to bed," figuring it had to be my daughter. Still no response. I was scared at first. Then I thought maybe I was dreaming. Then for some reason the fear left.

The next night I was crying and wanted to die but didn't want to leave my children. I was so tense as I tried to sleep, when all of a sudden I heard someone call my name very softly. I can't say if it was a woman or a man. Then I heard the voice say, "It's going to be OK."

Thinking I was losing my mind, I closed my eyes and a minute later I felt like someone was circling a hand around the top of my head without touching it. I opened my eyes. There was no one there. The hand above my head felt so good; it was like heat and energy flowing from the top of my head down through my whole body. It lasted about five minutes and my body and mind were so relaxed I fell asleep. When I woke that next morning I felt so great mentally and physically, and my depression and anger were gone. It was like a brand-new world to me from that day on.

The third night, same thing. I heard my name being called and the voice that said it's OK. And at the bottom of my feet I felt the same thing, like someone's hand was there going in a circular motion without touching me. I felt so much energy enter my body, from my feet to the top of my head. I still yearn for that feeling again. It was the greatest experience I ever had. When I came out of the depression I felt so strong that I told my husband I would divorce him and never look back. It took a few years, but I have done it.

I have had intuitive experiences throughout my life and still do. I'm very spiritual today and look at the world and people in a different way.

These are dreams of a parallel universe or of a different reality. If you learn to lucid-dream and continue the practice, you will be able to create your own universe in your dreams—a universe of personal spiritual enlightenment where you may even have superpowers, the way this dreamer has. I have discovered that if your life is difficult, indeed a waking hell, then the dreams themselves become the life and the waking state only a kind of shell. This dreamer's experience is enlightening as well as descriptive of a reversal of life and dreaming, when lucid dreaming becomes life.

Dreams Can Create Reality

I have always been a lucid dreamer. I use the word "dream" because of its understood meaning in the common consciousness. For me, however, I just cross over to the place where I exist, unencumbered by the human burden.

I have *always* known exactly who I was in my dreams. My dreams have always been of being and doing—of *living* in a world other than this one. I am in a parallel world where there are people I know, both from this one and not.

There are places I would frequently visit. There is a huge old house with different entrances, filled with many mysterious rooms and wondrous things. There is the land of the volcanoes, the gorge of winds where the flying is awesome. The field where the ship used to land is also there—so many wondrous places to visit and adventures to be had there.

I am a flier. I taught myself how at a very early age and have progressed from needing a device of some sort—usually a piece of fabric to fill in my wings, pretty much the way the superman character flies in the movies.

I have never experienced what people would call a nightmare in this place. All my nightmares were experienced on the human plane.

Writing all this down both saddens and encourages me. I haven't visited these places much in the past decade. I miss them—and how I felt when I was there.

I used to drink for one reason—to pass out. I drank to kill the pain of having to live in this hell where I was trapped, this place where I had been dumped with a defective operating system and just enough of the faintest recollection of who I was to torment me.

When I was very young and the physical torture began, I had the dream world and all of its wonder and mystery to escape to. It was where I really lived, and this world was the nightmare I had to endure. I was *awake* in my dream world and a sleepwalking meat puppet here in my waking state.

I discovered drink as a preteen. A marvelous thing, this drink took away the pain I carried in this world without having to be asleep. I took to it like a duck to water. I believe this choice coincided with my inability to look into the light of the sphere on the ship.

When my march along the path of destruction of my ego was completed, and I survived, I was given a second opportunity with the light. To quote a fellow traveler, a chance "to remember the face of my Father." And when I did, and turned around, there he was, not as a three dimensional figure, however, but as a presence that was overwhelmingly felt.

Our dreams can open paths for us, paths of learning and paths to enlightenment. If we can understand the meanings expressed in our dreams and learn not to be afraid of the paths that are laid out for us, our dreams can be productive and prophetic as well as self-empowering.

THE LODGE

My professional career had been cut short by an inoperable heart valve problem. The doctors told me to get my affairs in order, as I had only six months of life left. Since the traditional medical system could not help me, I turned to Edgar Cayce books, did healing meditations, and joined a "Search For God" study group (the Edgar Cayce Foundation's Association for Research and Enlightenment, A.R.E.) that met weekly. Our focus was on Bible passages, consciousness evolution, meditation, dream work, and alternative healing. Psychic events began to occur during the meetings.

Years later, I experienced a very vivid dream in which my wife, our four adult children, and I were sitting in the waiting room of a very old, lodge-type building with typical dark, heavy woodwork. When the French doors opened, a young man said, "David, it's your turn now." I got up and followed him down a long, wide, dark hallway to a room where I was surprised to see many very unusual looking "beings" gathered around a very bright white light in the center of the room.

Chairs were placed around the walls in a circular pattern, and to my immediate right sat a petite young woman whose dark hair was cut in a "Dutch bob"—popular around 1944. She was holding a black box about five-by-seven inches in her lap, bending over it and writing on a paper lying on top of the box. She looked up at me as I entered, said hello, and smiled warmly. I said hello and smiled back.

Then the beings in the center of the room began moving apart as the light in their midst began to slowly move toward me. I was amazed to see that although most of them appeared basically human, many had animal or "creature" type heads, and some had fur, horns or lizardlike skin. What sort of a place was this? I became rather apprehensive. The lighted figure was hard to make out. Although he had a huge, lionlike head, his light was so very bright the glare made it hard to see any details.

As he moved toward me, I got a feeling of incredible love and intelligence, and he said, "Braxton, I'm so happy to see you again."

I was shocked. I didn't recall ever meeting anyone like him, and why did he think my name was Braxton? . . . Who was that? He gave me a big hug and told me I was to return down the hallway, and I would discover something for me across the hall in the room with an "open door." He stressed those last two words.

I followed his instructions and found a dimly lit room with nothing inside except a book lying on an old wooden table. It seemed to be spotlit by a light from above. As I came closer, I noticed the cover of the book was dark blue, very smooth, and rather shiny. About one inch in from the spine of the book was a thin, white vertical line running from the top to the bottom of the cover. However, there were no words, no title or author, anywhere on the cover, back, or spine of that book. I flipped open the page to read what was inside, but to my surprise, the pages were all blank!

Puzzled, I left the book on the table and returned to the waiting room, where my wife and children were still waiting, and as we left the lodge, I awoke. I was so impressed with this dream, that I immediately wrote it down in my journal and tried to understand its meaning.

Was I to find some book and read it? Or was it a sketchbook awaiting my drawings? Or did it refer to the personal journals I'd been keeping since joining the study group? I had no clear answers, even though I asked frequently in meditation and tried further dreamworking.

In June that year, my friend, Danny, and I decided we'd take one of the A.R.E. "You Are Your Own Psychic" workshops to be held in July. We registered and sent in our fees.

One week before the workshop was ready to begin, I received a pamphlet in the mail about a three-month-long schedule of various metaphysical and spiritual classes, taught by some very well-known people near our home. One class, held as a series of workshops throughout the year, was taught by two experts on energy and crystal healing.

It turned out I used to babysit the daughter of one of the instructors and the other was a classmate and good friend of mine growing up! The synchronicities were startling. I sure wanted to take those classes, but I'd spent all my money for the A.R.E. class, and I didn't want to disappoint Danny by dropping out at the last moment.

A few hours later, Danny showed up at my door, the pamphlet in hand. I held up mine as we both said, "Would you consider going to this other workshop?" We laughed and called the A.R.E. people, who graciously refunded our full fees. We had enough to take the healing classes and called to register immediately.

At the workshop, I met a woman with whom I connected so well, we both felt we'd met somewhere before. In a few minutes, we realized it was in the "Lodge." She'd had the same dream! She was the dark-haired young woman sitting near the door, and in the real-life classes, she sat with us in chairs arranged in a semi-circle while the lectures and techniques went on. The "black box" was her audio tape recorder, and she placed paper on it to write down info during the classes. We decided the Being of Light was the teacher of this workshop for whom I babysat, as his high forehead radiated light and love constantly. We could often see light beings dancing with joy about the ceiling of the classroom. I was taught to heal my heart valve myself, and the very next day, I climbed a mountain with the group—yes, I was slow and clumsy, but I did it! And the next day, there were no sore muscles, either!

(Three years later, when we had moved to another state, I spent a week in the hospital trying to find the source of my hypertension. I had a clean bill of health, and the doctors said, "We can't find any trouble with your heart valve, and we don't think you ever really had one. Must have been a misdiagnosis!")

The workshop was superb, and I wanted to take the August class also, but was short on funds. Two weeks later, our tax refund arrived, and my wife and I split it between us. My share was just enough to take the August classes. The September seminars were only two weeks after that, and again the money problem was present, but a nice check arrived from one of my galleries—again, the exact amount needed for that month's classes.

I had amazing paranormal and spiritual experiences throughout my life, which increased significantly after the crystal classes. I began teaching workshops on painting, meditation, astrology, and energetic healing.

The practical techniques of one of these seminars could be taught in only a few days, but to raise the students' awareness to a point where they could understand and use the Higher Creativity Techniques required at least a week.

The book I'd seen in the "Lodge" turned out to be one I began writing in 1998. It was originally planned as a prerequisite booklet for enrollment in those seminars. It included insights gleaned as a teacher, astrological counselor, and alternative healer, open to people's most private thoughts, feelings, and spiritual yearnings. I did not have to seek out or research anything—information arrived from many different sources, demanding to be part of the book. Skills and knowledge from both ancient mystery schools and meditations concerning mankind's future were presented. Artistic, scientific, psychological, and spiritual research by professional and knowledgeable people documented the book's unique concepts. Writing the book became a journey that greatly expanded the subject matter and uncovered an astonishing concept about the End Times—mentioned in the Bible and most other spiritual texts—that demanded to be shared worldwide.

Yes, it did become a sort of "textbook on healing," but it proved to be about healing far more than the human body. My love for the earth and all her life forms expanded to a love for all life everywhere, and that's what the book has now become.

This reader's dream speaks for itself in that it is a prophetic dream, which, because the dreamer followed it, her life was saved.

A DREAM THAT SAVED MY LIFE

I had been going for mammographies every year for at least ten years. There was no cancer in my family at all and everything had been fine, so I decided that I would just skip a year and do it the following year. The night of the day that I made that decision I was visited by my grandmother in my dreams. (She passed away over forty years ago.) She told me to go for a mammography. She said I had to. The next morning I was quite shaken, but called and made the appointment. The doctors found an early stage breast cancer and we took care of it, so I am still here to tell the tale. I was told that had I not found it then, the ending to the story would have been quite different.

Here is one reader's short instruction course in enlightened dreaming, not just being lucid in your dreams, but knowing the directions your dreams take you. This contributor was lost in her own beliefs of scientific determinism. But, following her path to enlightenment with the same kind of process we laid out in Worker in the Light, *this contributor found how lucid dreaming was able to help her clear away preconceived notions about the world and open her mind to a reality that ultimately saved her from near suicidal despair.*

How to Dream with Your Eyes Open

I fall asleep . . .

As I strayed from my original Christian upbringing I began to lose faith and trust in God. Not the God of the Bible per se—or of any religion for that matter—but the God who is creator of all things.

You know, when you lose faith, hope, and trust in the Source, you lose everything. It may sound simple and commonplace to come to a point in life where you challenge certain religious or theological beliefs, but anyone who has ever experienced it to the degree I have knows that when you take away one's ultimate beliefs about life after death, salvation, and spirituality, you take away one's sense of security. This almost always has a profound, negative effect on the mind of mankind.

Our minds are truly delicate, and those beliefs we hold most sacred and irrefutable are the very illusions we rely on to shelter us from uncertainty. Humanity's deepest fear is uncertainty because uncertainty breeds fear. It's cyclical. It's the unknown that elicits fear in the mind of mankind. This is why listeners of *Coast to Coast AM* are so mystified and thrilled, yet fearful at the same time, to hear about paranormal activities, UFOs, government conspiracies, biological and nuclear warfare, clairvoyants, and so forth. We always want to know what is going to happen, what we have to look forward to, where we're going to be X number of years down the road. People can't live with peace of mind when they have the perpetuation of life after death lurking in the depths of their consciousness, terrorizing their psyche.

This is precisely where I was last August and September. I found myself completely lost and without hope. Without faith. I had lost my trust in God, in the Creator. I had lost my ability (and desire) to take the spiritual realm seriously. I no longer believed in it. I began to delve deeper and deeper into the mysteries of biology, trying desperately to uncover the truth in genetic research and quantum mechanics that religion had failed to expose to me.

I began to immerse myself in the popular books on psychology and brain science, genetics and physics, which all told of the power of the human brain to create its own realities. I studied the published research of neurobiologists and psychiatrists who had performed multiple tests on subjects and found conclusive evidence that suggested all of our spiritual and religious experiences lie only within neuronal processes and abnormal brain functions and nothing more.

I discovered all the foundational principles of neural science and how different experiences, such as speaking in tongues, like my fellow church members and I did when I was younger, or becoming "filled with the Holy Ghost" were abnormal biological experiences induced by a deep state of altered consciousness. Nonetheless, it was a reality constructed by the human brain. So far as I was concerned, that's all there was to it. A primary principle of neural science says, whatever the human brain can truly believe about life and reality—deep down inside—ultimately becomes true in physical subjective reality. Beliefs manifest themselves in physical reality so far as the observer is concerned. Whatever we believe and however we see the world, we project that onto our human experience and in turn, the world confirms our beliefs back to us. This is where the saying, "Truth is in the eye of the beholder," comes from. Even for medical science this sounded a bit hokey to me; I knew, however, that scientific determinism was solid and produced excellent results. At least far better results than religious theory could ever provide us with.

I embraced science and reveled in its discoveries. Those discoveries that proved we are simply genetic machines, unable to control our vast and mysterious physiology were the ones that thrilled me most, yet were going to work on my subconscious at the same time. I also began to discover how the aforementioned truth behind the operating principles of the brain directly affect our quality of life. From my boundless research into the human mind and brain, I discovered one very important principle that guides neuroscience. The ultimate truth behind the brain is simply this: *the human brain cannot tell the difference from an experience that actually happens in objective reality or from an experience that is vividly imagined.* This Supreme Secret later came to my aid and rescue!

Fortunately, scientific determinism began to take away all my illusions about life and spirituality. Unfortunately, I began to see a world without a God, at least a world where I didn't need a God. I was faithless and hopeless. I lost my sense of security and didn't realize it. Not until it really began to affect me detrimentally . . .

During my time of faithlessness and hopelessness, I began to spiral downward psychologically. I became addicted to narcotics, experienced panic attacks that bordered along pure insanity, and had sensations of downright dread encompassing my mind frequently and consistently throughout the day. At night, I had to overdose on Vicodin or Oxycontin just to fall asleep. And that was on top of the prescription Cymbalta I was using (under physician recommendation and guidance).

I had thoughts that were not a part of who I knew I was; yet they compulsively and spontaneously took control of my mind. These thoughts were as irrational and nonsensical as they could possibly be. They were thoughts that triggered fear and panic in a single instant, like, "What if I'm feeling panic and anxiety because there is something truly, deeply wrong in my body or, worse yet, my brain?" "What if my brain is going to shut down and stop functioning properly?" "What is going to happen if I die?" "Who will take care of my son?"

My frequent trips to the doctor's office didn't help matters. They only made them worse. As soon as I began to get control of my narcotics addiction, my doctor told me that I might have done irreversible damage to my liver due to my abusiveness with the opiate drugs. Blood tests showed my liver-enzyme levels to be dangerously high.

Great! Another reason to panic! And panic I did. A lot. I got worse when I found out my liver may be irrevocably damaged. I went into deeper panic and anxiety, dreadfully anticipating how I would relay the bad news to my family if the up-and-coming blood tests did indeed confirm I was at risk of dying. What would they think of me, knowing their own daughter and sister killed herself in downright stupidity and weakness, like a junkie? What would my son think of me—then only five years old—when he grew up and heard the truth as to why his mother died? It was protracted suicide. I was killing myself, slowly but surely.

THE AWAKENING . . .

Just before I had began to immerse myself in scientific determinism and lost my hope and faith, I studied and practiced different forms of meditation and guided visualizations because of the positive, supportive scientific evidence that surrounded them. The benefits of hypnotism, lucid dreaming, guided visualization, Buddhist meditation, and even ancient Japanese Ninjutsu mind-control exercises had all been a part of my spiritual experiences and practices in times past.

I knew their effectiveness firsthand and from the numerous studies reported by alternative physicians and researchers. I toyed with the idea of lucid dreaming and meditation again but I couldn't bring myself to face my dreams due to my high state of fear and anxiety. Likewise, my experience with meditation and physical exercise was similar. I could cause a panic attack if I excited my mind or body too much, so I didn't want to try that.

I was completely out of control and lost. There's not much worse than feeling hopeless and faithless. I broke down one day when I was all alone and I prayed. I prayed to the God I had forsaken, to the Creator I lost my trust and faith in. I asked for guidance and clarity. I asked for peace of mind. I asked that my life be spared and I be given the chance to make something of myself. Intuition told me I was meant for something more. My doctor told me otherwise. I believe intuition (and God) had the final word . . .

The following night, after my prebedtime reading, I went to bed as usual and fell asleep pretty quickly. The medication I was on made me very tired, so sleep came easily. Now, for the record, most nights I didn't remember a single dream. I had terrible dream recall. The Cymbalta not only knocked me out all night through, but it may as well have given me amnesia as well!

However, this night was very different. In spite of the poor dream recollection, I managed to have a very vivid, *lucid dream*. Several times over the years, I have had this dream. It is always the same. I am walking alone, in the cold. It appears to be wintertime and there's a dark, gray mist surrounding me, possibly heavy snow and winds. I'm naked, exposed. Little do I know it, but I'm walking on ice, covered by thick snow. I fall through it. Submerged under the water, I can't see. There's only darkness all around. Despite the small amount of sunlight I know is above the surface, I fail to see it. I hope to see it for guidance, to lead me back to the surface from whence I fell through.

Try as I may, struggling with all my might, I can't make my way back up. I can't find the place where I fell through. It's as if the hole that was made when I fell into the ice-cold water disappeared once I was submerged. Despite my best efforts, I failed to save myself. Dark, cold, alone, and fearful, I'd wake up from my dream in a state of confusion, dread, and panic.

This night, however, was very different indeed. At the start of my dream, I realized I was dreaming. The dream was lucid and I was very well aware of it. Instead of trying to fight it and wake myself up, I allowed it to continue, confident I could guide it to my avail.

I recognized every last detail of the dream. The place was a continent unknown to mainland U.S.A. It was evidently a solid sheet of ice as far as the eye could see all around me. Now just before I fell through the ice, I knew it was coming. But I let it happen anyway. As I sunk down into the dark, cold water, I didn't panic. Not this time. Instead, I felt calm, serene. I could breathe. I could think clearly. I knew then and there I had complete control over my mind.

In that moment of unexpected bliss, I had a truly sudden revelation. An awakening. My eyes were closed! Don't you see? My eyes had been closed every time I fell under the water, in every other dream! I had them closed! Hence, the darkness, the inability to find my way out. It wasn't any external circumstances controlling my ability to find my way out of the disposition; it was *me* and me alone that hindered my progress. *I had made the choice to close my eyes to the truth.*

When I made the choice to open my eyes to the truth once again, I found my way. I found my Self. I found hope, faith, and peace of mind unlike I'd ever known before. Most important, I found God within me. I found my way out of the dark and cold, back into the light.

This lucid dream was an epiphany for me. For as much as I've learned about scientific and genetic determinism, evolutionary theory, so on and so forth, I have learned one great truth that both science and spirit confirm together, as one coalesced whole. Napoleon Hill sums it up best in his book, *Grow Rich! With Peace of Mind*, when he says, "Anything the human mind can believe, the human mind can achieve."

Is this not the same as the neurobiological principle that proclaims, "The human brain cannot tell the difference between a real experience—one that actually happens—and one that is vividly imagined?"

Indeed, I believe scientism and spiritualism shall one day meet as one. It may be quite far off, but it is inevitable. Modern physics and even epigenetic research is beginning to confirm the Supreme Secret that Napoleon Hill talked about in his book. It's that coveted secret that Rhonda Byrne touched on in her book, *The Secret*. But it goes so much deeper than we may realize.

My experiences with lucid dreaming and my research into self-improvement and personal growth have led me to a greater understanding than either religion or science, in all their glory, could ever possibly reveal to me: We as humans—if we so choose—are indeed the masters of our fates and the captains of our souls.

Another prophetic dream can bring riches to those who believe that dreams are real.

DREAMING OF A LAS VEGAS WIN

I had a dream to prove to my friend that there is more to my dreams than just lots of weird stuff. I was shown in my dream that I should go to the Trump Casino the next day here in Las Vegas and play this one particular Wheel of Fortune machine, and I was shown it paying out 250 dollars in quarters.

Upon waking I told my friend about the dream and I proceeded to go that night to the casino where I played that machine and, yes, it paid 250 dollars in quarters, and I also won fifteen on

Keno, which I never win at. I had the cashier write down that I did win on that machine and I brought it home to show my friend that it did really happen and my dreams were more than just dreams.

I knew that I was going to win not for me but to show this other person that they needed to really look into things being more than the rational explanation that they always come up with.

I was very happy to have the help from the other side and it also made me feel that I am really having these dreams for a reason (which reason is still to be determined).

Because a lucid dreamer enters a universe of things in which all time is compressed into a single time, past, present, and future merge. Therefore, a lucid-dreamer has the ability to change things that happen in one universe, but are not predetermined. This is what one dreamer discovered as he took steps to save his own life.

THE PROWLER

My name is Rodney. I am a seventy-year-old man who doesn't claim to be psychic. However, I sometimes have very lucid dreams that have proven to be prophetic. Here is one such dream that occurred many moons ago.

Late one night, I fell asleep in the chair in front of the TV. I began dreaming that I hadn't checked the three entrances of my home to make sure they were secure. In my dream, I went to the patio door, and the front entry and found them locked. I then proceeded to the kitchen/garage door. I noticed the door was ajar!

I walked over to close and lock it, but instead of just pushing it closed, I grabbed the doorknob, twisted it, and pulled it open wide, as if to slam it shut! When I pulled the door open, I saw a very large, menacing young man in a red T-shirt with the number "42" written across the front, standing there in the doorway! It startled and terrified me so much, I awoke from my dream.

The next day, a friend called and invited me to his home to play canasta. While there, he remembered that earlier in the day, he had helped his neighbor across the street clean her house, because she was moving. He had promised the neighbor to return later to the house and secure the windows, which had been left open to help dry the floors he had mopped.

It was getting late in the afternoon and before going home, he asked if I would go with him across the street to help him lock up the house. We walked up the front porch and I impulsively rang the doorbell. My friend laughed and asked why I had done that. I jokingly said that if a prowler were in the house, I wanted to warn him we were on the way in! He laughed, unlocked the front door, and we entered.

After closing the windows and checking the kitchen, living room, and dining room, we went to check the bedrooms. As we entered the long hallway, he said, "You check the bedrooms on that side and I will check the master bedroom in the back." As he disappeared around the corner of the hall, I noted the first bedroom door was the only door closed. The other two doors stood open. I hesitated. My dream came back to me. I just knew someone was standing behind that closed door! Feeling foolish, not following my intuition, I decided to look into the room. I reached out to turn the doorknob, but the knob would not budge. I tried to turn it to the left and then to the right, but it would not turn! As I stood there with my hand on the knob, I could then feel the strong heavy presence of someone standing right in front of me, just on the other side of the door! I knew someone was tightly holding that knob, so I could not open the door! I let go just as my friend entered the hall and asked if I had checked all the bedroom windows. I calmly told him that yes, I had closed all the windows in the room.

I walked slowly down the hall with him to the front entry of the house. Just before leaving, he remembered the windows off the back porch. He began walking back to close those windows, but I calmly told him I had already closed them. (I really had not!) We then slowly and calmly walked out the front door. Once he had turned and locked the door behind us, I told him, "Let's get out of here. Someone is in that house." He didn't even question me, but immediately let out a yelp and we both ran!

Once back at his home, we called the woman who owned the house and told her of our experience. She came and went through the house. But, of course, no one was there at that time. I asked her about the bedroom door . . . if it was difficult to open, and she told me it was not. I went back to the house with her and tried the door to that bedroom. It opened easily!

Evidently the intruder had fled through the bedroom window and escaped through the backyard. Had my dream saved me from some unknown tragedy? I don't know!

Many of my callers talk about how their dreams contain images of the future. Here is another one of them.

MY DREAM OF DEATH

When I was a little boy I had a nightmare that there were stacks of brown snakes writhing around my bed. When I woke I jumped and ran, crawled into the foot of my parents' bed and slept there till morning.

A few days later my mother died.

The dreams have continued throughout my life.

Many people tell me they can communicate with loved ones through dreams. Here is one story, which strikes me as how two people spiritually close to one another communicate even when they are asleep.

COMMUNICATION WITH A LOVED ONE THROUGH DREAMS

My lover was sent overseas by his management firm, and I was going to join him in a few weeks. Frankly, I was very excited and making all my preparation for the trip.

One night as I was sleeping I was startled to hear my name being called out loud and clear. It was his voice. I sat up in bed and looked around, I called out to him, but got no reply. I then got up and went through the house, and no one was there. It gave me a cold chill as I returned to bed.

I became concerned because I thought he was in some kind of trouble. I wanted to call him then and there, but the time difference made it difficult and I didn't know his office number.

I called him the next day at his hotel, and when he answered the phone, my first question was, "Are you alright?" There was silence for a second and he said, "Not really." He then told me he did not go to work that day because he had some difficult heart palpitations and thought he was having a heart attack. I asked him what time it was when that happened and he said about "2:30 A.M. Eastern Standard Time." *Wow*, that really blew me away, because that was the time I woke up hearing my name.

By the way, he did not have a heart attack, but it was the beginning of his heart problems that would take him not too many years later. I did get to go on my trip and had a great time.

During our many years together we had many incidents that were strange. We could send each other messages when something urgent was pending. We each could literally hear them in our heads. Those were the days when there were no cell phones available, and it seems he and I didn't need cell phones. However, getting his message from overseas really seemed like a stretch.

VISIONS AND VOICES

When your job is to listen to voices all night long, voices of the awestruck, the bereaved, the thrilled, and those in disbelief, you get to appreciate voices. Many of my callers talk about the voices they've heard and the visions they've seen. They talk about the angels who have sat beside them or visited them in dreams. They talk about the departed, who appear to them in visions, and they talk about the visions themselves.

Visions, be they dream visions or simple glimpses of things that seem more real than not, have been a part of human existence for thousands of years. We can go back to the Bible and read about Moses's vision of the burning bush, Abraham's vision of the angel Zadkiel staying his hand from slaying Isaac, or the poets' visions of deities from the Greek or Hindu pantheon.

It's no surprise to me, therefore, that our listeners are vision-enabled. They see all kinds of visions and are thrilled when the visions they have prove to be accurate.

If you look at the great visionaries of the past—people like Joan of Arc, Nostradamus, and Edgar Cayce—you see people who are not afraid to speak up about what they saw. But after they spoke up, after they revealed what they saw, they were then forced to defend that vision either against the Church or the religion of scientists demanding to see proof that they had actually seen something.

Our readers and callers many times face the same dilemma and ask me if I think they are delusional or actually reality-challenged. I tell them that no matter how strange their vision seems, they have to go with the belief that they actually saw something. I tell them that people have seen visions way before them and will see visions for as long as human beings reside on this sphere. And if people have seen visions for as long as there have been people, then who's to say that they haven't seen visions as well.

Having said all of this, we have to look at our contributors' visions to understand both the breadth and magnitude of the human visionary experience. People are on individual and collective quests to understand what they have seen and what it means. Here are just a few of the kinds of magnificent experiences our listeners have sent us in response to our call for sharing stories of spiritual awakening.

People have told me over and over that when they sit by a loved one who is near death, the person sometimes sits right up, as alert as can be and seems to be either talking to some invisible entity or is aware of something or someone in the room that only he or she can see. I say that when this is happening, the person near death is being welcomed by angels or loved ones. I know this because I have heard many stories of people near death saying that a parent, spouse, or dear friend is waiting to guide the soul to a better place. This was the experience this reader had, and it warms my heart to know that death is not the end and we will all be reunited someday.

A Deathbed Vision

Over ten years ago I witnessed something when my brother was in the hospital dying from cancer. My brother was not a religious man by any stretch of the imagination. The last three nights of his time on earth I spent with him in the hospital, from sunset to sunrise. I was worried about him dying in the night and being all alone when he died.

One night while I was with him, he voiced regrets that he was not a good husband. You see, he was a terrible alcoholic and his home life was very dysfunctional. In fact, even I really wasn't that close to him at all. As I searched my brain for any positive memory, which was quite the struggle for me, he quietly told me, "I will bless you." That was definitely not something my brother would ever say, especially to me.

On his last night he had been unconscious for about twenty-four hours. I sat at his bedside in complete darkness. I didn't want to disturb him with the light, if by chance he woke up, since he had suffered with a lot of pain. It was around midnight and all of a sudden he sat straight up in bed. He was looking to his right, and I was sitting to his left. It was funny, he didn't look sick anymore. He didn't look like he was in pain anymore. He looked humbled and in awe. He continued to look to his right and kept nodding his head, as if someone was talking to him.

He seemed to be intently listening to someone whom I could not see. There was a bright light in his eyes, yet the room was very dark. I looked around the room and tried to figure out the source of this light that must surely be reflecting in his eyes. I could not find any. I believed it was the light of his spirit and he was communicating with the spirits on the other side. I felt a strong urging not to speak, not to interrupt.

As he continued to "listen" to whoever was speaking to him, he turned his head and looked at me. I'll never forget the look of regret in his eyes and the concern he had for me. Yet, he looked like a child, listening to someone very important to him. I actually thought at the time that "they" were telling him that it was time to go.

He looked at me for a moment, then looked back to his right and nodded once again. Then he doubled over in pain, lay back down, and died. It was an experience I'll never forget. Whenever life gets me down and I think that this is all there is, I remember that time and it gives me hope that there's more to life than our time on this earth. I'm not a religious person, just like my brother, but I truly believe that there is life after death.

On a side note, shortly after he died, my wife and I received a little bit of money from a relative. It was enough to buy our first computer. The computer changed our lives and we now both have good paying government jobs. I'm not sure if that is the "blessing" my brother promised, or if I will receive something more in the future. I think about the future of this planet all the time, and I hope that he will help me get through the terrible days that are surely just around the corner.

Where do visions come from? Are they visions from within or visions from the outside, of this earth or from another reality? These two visions, one out of mythology and another of a demon spirit, ask those questions.

A VISITATION

I had one experience of sleep paralysis, but with a difference that I haven't heard discussed.

As a young woman I was lying in bed, falling asleep. I opened my eyes and saw a being standing to the right of the foot of my bed. It was feminine, dressed in an embroidered toga, helmet, holding a lance or staff, with an owl on her right shoulder. I consider this to be a vision of Athena. The owl's eyes burned a bright orange. The room was bathed in a soft gray light.

At first I was fearful, more of the paralysis than the presence. I gradually gained composure and consciously calmed my breathing. Then I was able to tap my left leg with my finger. I thought to myself, *I'm definitely awake, now, and I can still see her!* I spoke, "What can I do for you?" With that she disappeared and the light took a few moments to fade. It took me some time to get back to sleep as I pondered the experience.

So, I was definitely awake while still having the vision of her and her bird and still seeing the soft light. What would the psychiatrist say to that? I relaxed to the point of being able to shake off the paralysis. I moved. I audibly spoke. I was awake. I had trouble getting back to sleep! I was not in some incredibly lucid dream sleep (unless all life is a dream). Rather, I was awake in an objectively existing dream place or dimension.

In my own experience of my life, I was visited. And it was a very positive and enriching experience.

And now the demon visitation.

A Wicca Vision

Early in my wicca training, we were to each develop our own "Strawberry Fields" by going to the same comfortable place through repeated meditations. My place is a lakeshore at twilight, surrounded by wooded hills.

Once I was confronted by a being there that was very frightful. He was seven to eight feet tall, had an elongated bald head, and was wearing a long black cape. I saw him as vampirelike, capable of using victims and taking advantage of people. Over the next couple of years he reappeared to my inner experience in different environments and landscapes. Each time he seemed less threatening, yet still powerful. I came to see him as representing power that I have, but feared. As I grew to recognize my own power and feel secure in my own motivations—as coming from my guiding spirit, rather than as ego-based—I came to know this being as a part of my own spiritual guidance system.

This is a case of a perceived polarity of positive and negative being resolved in unity through higher awareness. The polarity of good and bad decreases as the chakra level of the interaction rises. The opposite ends of the base of the triangle close in on each other as it reaches up. The eighties band Shriekback has a song that expresses this concept very well. Check it out. It is called, "Everything That Rises Must Converge."

This prophetic vision reminds me of the story of the Mothman prophecies that accompanied many UFO sightings in West Virginia.

A BRIDGE COLLAPSE

I was driving south over a long bridge when a female voice in the car said, "This bridge will collapse."

Of course I looked around my car, but I was alone. When I heard the voice, I was driving over the top of the bridge. A feeling of falling came over me, but only lasted a few seconds.

Some days later—but at the exact time to the minute of my hearing that voice—a commercial vessel collided with the bridge. During this terrible accident, a good number of automobiles fell hundreds of feet, killing many people.

On that morning, I happened to be looking south and saw one big, black cloud in the sky, not knowing it was over the bridge. A few years later, I met an officer from the ship that hit the bridge. He told me as it was heading toward the bridge, he saw a big, black cloud over the bridge. As he steered under the bridge, he felt like the freighter was being pushed, something he could not explain.

Since then, I have met many people who were supposed to be on that bridge that morning, but for some reason, they were delayed.

Visions of peace are also one of the many types of experiences my listeners report. Here is a beautiful one of self-fulfillment.

VISIONS OF DOVES

One early morning on the freeway going to work, I saw two white doves crisscross in front of my windshield. Then they flew up.

Another time, about 2:00 A.M., something made me open my eyes only to see a huge white "Pegasus" from the floor to the ceiling with its wings wide open. This was a spirit Pegasus because I saw it until it disappeared.

Another time I woke up early in the morning (still in my bed) and about thousands of tiny white balls of light came straight at me at the speed of light. This gravity was so powerful that my left arm felt as if it was going to explode, because it had stopped circulation.

I've seen a spirit lady sitting at the edge of my bed just looking at me. I call her the lady in gold, because she looked to be pure gold. Another time, I was at work, and all of a sudden I felt pure peace, pure love, so great that I couldn't stand up. I heard my boss calling me over and over again, but I couldn't move. It was so beautiful. Finally, my boss came down to see me and asked me if I was OK. He then told me to take a break. When I went to the restroom, my hands, face, parts of my body were a glowing bright red and pink. The girls thought I'd been drinking, since I did work at a bar. After about ten minutes, I was back to normal.

I hear when great spiritual things like this happen, they only happen once. I only see good things. I don't even think about bad or evil things. Don't fear it! Don't feed it!

And then there are visions of extraterrestrials. I ask myself, are these only visions or are they actual visitations?

VISIONS OF ET?

No matter what has happened to me, I remain a skeptic when it comes to the unseen world. I mean, about the only thing that has *not* happened to me is being abducted by aliens, and frankly, at times I wonder about that. I know I have had dreams about talking to aliens.

Today I was all stressed out, sitting in a dentist's office, when

I remembered the time I was sitting in a wheelchair, in an operating room, waiting to get my appendix removed, *completely* stressed out. A bright, shiny thing, which I couldn't see with my eyes but somehow I could see, came into the room. It hovered over me, around me, and at once I felt completely at ease. I calmed down, totally centered, truly at ease, at peace. A bed was wheeled in. I got onto it, went into a deep meditative state, and was wheeled into the operating room. The doctor that was to operate on me after a while walked into the room and casually asked, "Is he already sedated?" To which I responded, "No, I was meditating until you disturbed me."

Then there was the time I saw my grandfather at my aunt's funeral. He was having a good laugh and enjoying himself. Now granted, by itself that is weird, but considering he had been dead for nine years and was only about a foot tall, it was really weird. I swear he was real.

These are just a couple of my trips into the unseen. Where does this leave me? Still a skeptic.

What in us doesn't allow most of us to believe what we see because it is not the dominate thought model? Just a passing question.

But, hey, maybe I am just crazy.

How many people had strange visions foretelling of a disaster not just in their lives but in the lives of people in their communities? There have been many such visions, especially in the lives of the victims of Hurricane Katrina.

I LIVE IN MISSISSIPPI

We have never, ever evacuated for a storm. Right before Hurricane Katrina came onshore, I was gathering up my important papers and a vision popped in my head. I saw my home full of water right to the ceiling. I knew we had to leave, no way about it, and we did, thankfully. My home was flooded with ten feet of water.

I have always had these insights. Things just either pop into my mind or I can hear the messages. I also sensed my mother's cancer through my hands, before it was confirmed with a CAT scan. I scanned her body with my hands and I felt it through my hands.

Visions of loved ones' visitations are also among the many experiences my callers have. Most of them have to do with a relative's believing that this was not a vision from within, but an actual visitation of the loved one's spirit. I tend to believe that, too.

THE SPIRIT OF MY FATHER

I had a strange experience while my father was a few weeks from death, and some similar episodes since then. Keep in mind, my father and I had a somewhat rocky relationship, but we still loved and cared for each other. I saw to it that all his needs were met right up to the moment that he died.

One night, as he lay slowly dying in a hospital, I was home trying to sleep. Suddenly, I became very restless and it was as if his spirit was actually *in* me. I felt I had become him and took on his pain and torment. It was not a good feeling. It was quite disturbing, as if he was telling me he was trapped in his body and wanted out. It was like he was making me experience the intensity of what he was feeling. I had literally become him, physically and emotionally.

I had similar episodes after that, but on a smaller scale. One day, I finally told him in my prayers that it was time for him to leave me alone, make peace in the spirit world, and go to a better place. I began to wonder if I had some type of psychological phenomenon as a way to deal with the emotions of his death. I've tossed out that idea, however, as it truly felt spiritual. I'm generally a normal, intelligent, and rather conservative person, but with a strong respect for the supernatural world. My father and I were always highly intuitive, so this experience seems reasonable to me.

This is a similar type of experience. Is it a ghostly visit or a true vision of a spirit?

Visions of the Departed

One night I was closing my refrigerator door and turned around to go back into the other room, totally unprepared to see what was before me. There were three illuminated columns, lit from floor to the ceiling. In the center column stood my sister Jocelyn, looking like a hologram. The other two columns, one on each side of her and just slightly behind her, were both empty. That sight just really startled me, but I felt no fear.

I told my older siblings about this experience when I talked with each of them over the phone. They both gave me their totally different opinions. It frightened one and struck interest with the other. I also told my family here about my vision.

Two days after my vision, my oldest brother passed away. Just five hours later my other brother passed away. This was six months to the date of my sister having passed. There were totally separate causes of death for each of them and both passed in their own homes.

Were the empty columns I saw here in my home just two days before they passed connected? It wasn't making any sense to me before, but I can now think it does.

Visions can sometimes be the inspiration for a spiritual renewal or awakening, as it is in this reader's experience.

My Spiritual Awakening

My spiritual awakening came after the death of my dad. Life was predictable for me: I was married with two great kids, a home, and pretty much an easy-go-lucky life. The death of my dad came as no surprise for me. He had suffered with a long illness. I was grateful that he was no longer in pain, although with the loss of a parent it's a feeling of emptiness. No longer could I rely on that truth, the trust, the love of a father's touch.

As I now reflect back on my earlier life, I carefully admit to some of the signs I was noticing, shadows moving back and forth down the hallway, toys going off on their own with no batteries in them. Something bothered me but I could not put my finger on it; something was different, and I was noticing it.

A couple of weeks had passed after his death and I was adjusting. The calls of sorrow from family and friends had finally ended. I noticed how uneasy I became about everything. I was sensitive to sight and sound. Even the news on the television bothered me. The plants appeared greener, the noise around me was louder, and I felt as if I could feel the pain of others. The shadows I had seen as a child seemed to have more of a formation to them. Something had changed; the energy around me had changed. Months passed, and my uneasiness increased as if something unseen was with me.

Late one evening as I sat at the kitchen table, I was preoccupied with wrapping some gifts for my kids after what seemed to be an never-ending day, and I was pretty tired.

Something I could not explain touched my shoulder—so strong it felt like a hand—yet the kids were asleep and my wife was out of the house. I stopped what I was doing and just sat there without moving. As I turned, nothing was there. I recall rubbing my eyes as this white mist swirled in front of me. Sparks of light began shooting from it as if it was a Fourth of July sparkler. I stood in a trance, my feet would not move, nor would sound come from my mouth. There was no fear, just the unknowing. I felt as if something just took a key and unlocked the burdens I had carried for most of my life, released them, and they melted away from my body. All I heard was that I was going to help those into the light: "Do not fear . . . many will come to you for help."

Two days passed, and I still had no idea if I had imagined the experience that I had earlier, or if it was real. I could not dismiss it from my mind. Once in a while, to entertain myself, I would go into the Internet chat rooms. A woman came into the room that I was in, and I found myself asking her some questions about a red car. Did she own one?

She replied, "No." "Do you have someone you know with a red car?" and she said no. The next words out of my mouth were, "Whatever you do, no matter what, do not get into a red car that is around you. I do not know why, but there is danger around this car." I found myself repeating this over and over again to this stranger. After all, I did not know her, and she did not know me. I could not let go of the fact there was danger around this woman; that a feeling of death was surrounding her.

I did not return to the chat room for a week. When I did, it only took a few seconds before the woman whom I had told about the red car began to speak. "I have been waiting for a week for you to come back! The red car you told me not to get into belonged to a friend who had stopped by the next day to take me to lunch. All I heard was your voice over and over again warning me about getting into the red car, so I decided to decline the invitation. For some reason, I felt you were very serious about this warning," she said.

I was not prepared to hear what was coming next from this woman's story. She began to tell me how later on that same night, her sister called to tell her the girl in the red car had been killed in a car accident. I dropped to my knees in disbelief. Is this what the spirit who approached me meant about helping others?

It has not been easy learning how to communicate with the other side. Not all of it has been pretty. It is truly a gift of sight to see spirits, to hear them, to feel them. The journey has been long and frustrating. Each day that I am approached by a spirit, somebody's loved one who has died and crossed to the other side, I wonder why there is a need for them to not move on, to come back for that one last message. Yet I am privileged to see the effects it has on the loved ones left here on earth, knowing their loved ones are OK, happy and healthier than before, and that one message helped them to accept the death of their relative, friend, or loved one.

I am truly thankful that I have an amazing family who has sacrificed the time I spend passing on the messages from the dead, and for understanding my work within the light. My final thought is: You really don't need a psychic or medium to hear messages from the ones who have died. Open your heart to all possibilities; seeing is believing . . . believing is seeing.

Sometimes the vision itself is accompanied by a newfound ability or a newly discovered sense that the experiencer has. In this case, a religious vision or visitation was accompanied by my listener's ability to speak in tongues.

SPEAKING IN TONGUES

A friend and I were walking home from school. One day we passed by this little church where people I could only describe as "disciples right out of the Bible," dressed in linen robes, were chanting and praying. What was odd is that I had walked by that church a thousand times, but it was always dark and empty. However, on this occasion there were people inside.

When we stopped to look, I believe we were actually derisive, calling them freaks. One of them came out, one who looked like me, and invited us in. My pal and I were laughing until we got inside, then everything turned real serious. They started chanting and laying hands on us, then one of them touched my forehead and said, "I give you the gift of tongues." Just as he touched my forehead I let out a phrase. I'm not sure what it actually means although I have an inner idea and I can only describe it phonetically: *Ada shun bada kum.*

The same thing happened to my friend, although I don't remember what he uttered.

When this happened an overwhelming feeling, like a warm shiver, immediately came over my entire body, head to feet! A feeling I can now only describe as the holy spirit.

That phrase is as clear to me today as it was back then. For whatever reason I rarely saw my friend again, and if we did bump into each other we never spoke of the incident.

The oddest twist to this story is that as many times as I was drawn to that place and walked or drove by it even as I got older, it was always empty. I never saw anyone in the building again. Even a few days after the event initially happened, no one was there.

Later on in life when I was about thirty, I joined a church. It was there when I was baptized that I felt that same feeling like a warm shiver come over me. I know there is something to it!

Until recently I kept those words or phrases I uttered back when I was a teen in the back of my mind. About six months ago while searching on the Internet I started looking into ancient languages. I came across something similar but not identical. I'm not sure but I believe it was in one of the ancient Sumerian dialects that there was a translation for the beginning two sounds, which translated into something like "the life-flowing river." The hairs stood up on my neck.

I'll search till the day I die to find the meaning of those words or sounds. If there is an actual translation it could only prove one thing to me—the existence of God, Jesus Christ. I've had many strange experiences since that time that I can't explain but seem to understand.

Many people, myself included, believe our planet is alive, a being in and of itself. Can our planet send us visions? One of our listeners says it can and does.

Visions of the Planet

I was always a very spiritual person. I explored various religions and philosophies but found them all lacking in different aspects. More and more I explored my native heritage and beliefs.

Right around my thirtieth birthday I had a very profound spiritual awakening. I was living with a farmer near a riverbank. I felt very uneasy and uncomfortable with his use of chemicals on his land and crops. One day, when I was planting row upon row of tomatoes, my hands started tingling. I felt the pulse of the earth. I removed my hands and the tingling lessened, and as I placed another plant in the earth it returned and got stronger. I knew of a surety at that moment that the earth was alive and I was connected to Her and to all things in the natural world.

A few evenings later my roommate brought in a crystal heart that the plow had turned up. I no longer have the piece of crystal, but I can tell you this: it was formed by knapping as one does flint.

The next afternoon I looked out across the fields toward the tree line and I saw a robed figure outlined against the trees. The figure was in a dark robe much like the classic grim reaper. Then my vision went into zoom mode and it was like I was close up. Mind you, the field was a full acre.

The figure removed a hood and I beheld a beautiful man with a ruddy complexion and reddish gold hair, and upon his head was a golden crown. He had a full, well-trimmed beard and mustache. But the eyes were what held my attention. They were a liquid brown and full of such love and joy. I will not say it was Yeshua of Nazareth (Jesus), but it sure was a visit from someone. The next moment my child was saying something and distracted me and when I looked back the figure was gone. All I know is from then on I have had visions and have the ability of psychometry.

I can run my fingertips over a surface and get impressions. I had some psychic abilities before, but after being connected to Mother Earth they increased dramatically. I know of a surety that all of life is interconnected and the energy of the divine source flows through all things—be it a rock or a human being or a tree or an alien from another planet or dimension. All things with the life energy have consciousness.

I know that all religions are valid to a degree, and it does not matter what path I follow as long as it leads me home.

Thank you. Peace and Love to all. May you all find that connectedness.

Here is a vision of a loved one whose spouse was in distress.

MY MOTHER'S STROKE

My parents have been divorced for over twenty years. Back in early February my father had a TIA, a small stroke. The doctors determined that his pacemaker needed its batteries replaced, went in, and replaced them. He came home to my house a week later, on a Friday, for rest and care. The following Friday, he and my daughter were watching a movie during which he fell asleep.

He woke up screaming at my daughter *"Help her, help your grandma. She's having a stroke!"* At 4:00 A.M. the next morning, my phone rings. It's my stepfather. My mom had had a stroke. It may have started the afternoon before, but my mom wouldn't let him call an ambulance at that time.

Here, a mother's visitation from a guardian spirit is the motivation not to listen to a doctor's advice, but to take things into her own hands. My psychiatrist friends will say that the person is actually speaking to herself, telling herself what has to be done. But my spiritual friends say that's not the case, that a real entity is speaking to the person having the vision. Here, you have to be the judge.

SAVING A CHILD

My son was a very healthy, happy baby. However, one Friday afternoon he began to sneeze and cough and became very ill. I called the physician who normally looked after the family and she was unavailable till Monday. His condition worsened and as the evening progressed I could hear water gurgling deep in his chest.

I called the emergency hospital and the person who answered the phone advised me not to bring such a young baby into the emergency room because many patients had the flu, and that I should wait until Monday to see a personal physician.

I was convinced by some inner knowing that my baby was developing serious pneumonia, and as I picked him up and held him I heard a very loud commanding voice from somewhere "out there" or somewhere inside me, saying, "Put him in the car and drive," which I did. As I drove my car through the dark city around me, not knowing where I was going, this commanding voice gave me clear directions to enter a highway, and later on to exit and continue.

This was a strange part of town where I had never been before. I can remember trying to see street signs through my tears. "Turn right and then turn left," the voice commanded me, and very soon I arrived in front of a small but beautiful building that had a large, fully lighted sign that read OSTEOPATHIC HOSPITAL.

I had never heard of an osteopathic anything, much less a hospital, but the commanding voice said, "Stop your car and take your baby into this hospital." Minutes later I found myself and my baby in a beautiful lighted hallway with a number of concerned nurses and one very delightful and welcoming physician. I could see when he took my baby from me that he must have had a lot of practice caring for small children. He was immediately comforting and loving toward my child. In minutes the nurses constructed an oxygen-aided, moisturized tent in which they placed my baby. His crib was set close to the door to his room, and as I sat with him while the doctor examined his chest, I noticed that the nurses going by would smile and make some gesture toward him that was both welcoming and healing. As it turned out he remained in this hospital for two weeks, fully recovering to his wonderful healthy life, as it is today.

The point of this story is obvious, of course, that the power within or without that commands us in times of emergency or just in times of everyday life is not one to put aside as unworthy of modern science. I might add, to strengthen this proposition, that the newspaper headlines on the Monday morning after I took my baby to the hospital read that five infants died from pulmonary complications over the weekend.

Just as voices can be healing or commanding, some give very direct warnings that must be adhered to or disaster strikes.

A WARNING VOICE

In the mid-seventies I was at a friend's house when another friend, Jay, came over with Jeff and Corey in tow. Handsome Jeff and I hit it off immediately, right from a certain electricity that passed between us at first glance. I know it's strange, but the energy was so powerful I ducked my head and couldn't look at him for a time. We spent the afternoon hanging out.

Corey had just shaved his head and wasn't sure he looked good that way. He and Jeff were musicians and were playing a gig the next day.

Jeff paid special attention to me, even ad-libbing a song to me on my friend's guitar. They had several young men, like me, traveling with them. They ran errands and generally hung around and looked good, and were paid well. Maybe I'd be interested.

I was about twenty-two and my looks were compared to a number of famous actresses. Indeed, when a fashion rag printed Meryl Streep's age, height, weight, and measurements, I could have been a body double. I was also a basically down-to-earth gal, didn't do drugs, and was quite naïve.

That evening they all took off to hit the nightspots. I had a date, but Jeff took my hand and kissed it, saying he was really glad to meet me. He asked if it were at all possible I could meet them later, and told me where they were headed.

I went home full of thoughts of Jeff, and when my date wasn't there within fifteen minutes I walked into my room to dress for the nightspots. My room overlooked the ocean and had no curtains. When I turned on the light and caught my reflection in the glass, something said, "Don't go." I said out loud, "What do you mean, don't go? Of course I'm going to go." I turned to get something out of my closet and when I turned around and caught my reflection again, I heard in my head, "*Don't go,*" this time with such authority and finality that I responded weakly and aloud, "Don't go? OK, I won't go." And I went to bed.

The next morning I found Jay right away, hoping that Jeff and Corey were still around. They had hung out all night talking and doing lines, but the guys had gone early that morning. As we chatted, Jay was leafing through a rock magazine and suddenly let out a shriek. There was a picture of Jeff, who had his own band and was finally breaking into the mainstream. Then we all shrieked.

I was beside myself, going over the previous events. It seemed I had missed out on an opportunity of a lifetime. From time to time I would relate the story to others, and one cosmopolitan Brit said, "Bloody lucky!" To my surprise he began to tell how the rock groups and their ilk lived in the fast lane full of drugs and sex. He said they just used people up, and more than one body went out the back door of hotels they stayed in, but the media kept it quiet and protected them from scrutiny. Little by little I began to see, wistfully, that had I fallen in love with Jeff, which was nearly a sure thing that I couldn't predict what I might have put up with to be with him.

I have never had an electric first glance like that again.

Some people see ghosts who are ghosts because they don't know where to go after they died. Some murder victims are just like that, spirits who are trapped on this plane because they were not steered to the path that death opens up. This listener tells us that he sees murder victims, just such spirits who remain in this plane.

Seeing Murder Victims

My life has changed forever because of a visitation from the spirit of a murder victim.

At my computer one day, the spirit of a murder victim appeared in front of my eyes. She showed me the details of her murder. I called the police and told them what I had seen. They thought I was part of the murder and started to investigate me.

After knowing specific details about the murder and showing them locations of where her body parts were found, they trusted me enough to work with me on the case.

Within a week of this visitation I began to see other spirits at work, in my car, and gathering around others at the mall.

Everything I believed about life and death changed forever. Within six months I became a professional psychic medium on the radio, have helped thousands of people make spirit connections with their loved ones, and taught hundreds to do this work. I quit my hundred-thousand-dollars-a-year job and do this full time. I have worked with several police departments on murder and missing persons cases. I love this work and my mission is to reach as many people as possible to make the connection to the afterlife.

Thanks for having such a great show. You help bring awareness to the world.

Here, a very prophetic vision helps our listener tune in to an environmental problem that could have affected the lives of many children. It was not only the vision, but the physical presence of something that made the vision more intense.

AN ENVIRONMENTAL VISION

After checking out the theater where I was to perform in the Los Angeles west side the following week, I was driving home when I started to sneeze. I sneezed all the way home, which was a two-hour drive. I had never sneezed more than three or four times at any given time in my life so, needless to say, not only was I scared because it is very difficult to sneeze and drive, but I was afraid I was going to go into the *Guinness Book of World Records.* No joke. It was that bad.

When I arrived home and opened the van door, the sneezing stopped immediately, but I was left with a stuffed head that pounded for days. While at my day job later in the week I was told by a schoolteacher that the school was thinking about closing because attendance in all the classes was extremely low. In a class of twenty she had three students that day.

After our last performance two weeks later, I was again driving home with some props stored (in zipped plastic bags I had saved when I bought new comforters) in the back of the van. At the area on the expressway where the sneezing fit began I started to think about what the teacher had said. *There must be something in the air that is making all the children sick,* I thought.

The next thing I knew I was on another highway. It wasn't lit like the expressway. It was very dark, and no cars were coming from the other direction or on my side of the road. I felt a hand patting me on my left shoulder and heard, "Calm down, you are meant to see something." It was at that point I saw a sign, which told me there was a fee booth ahead. I had seen toll signs before but never a fee sign. I began to wonder if I was even in the United States.

I looked at the clock and realized I had been driving for thirty minutes without awareness. I had also spent every cent on our celebration dinner and bridge toll and had no money to pay any fee. *I will just have to tell them this when I reach the fee booth and ask if I can turn around,* I thought.

When I reached the fee booths—there were three—they were closed and not a soul was around, but there was an exit. I took the exit, planning on stopping at the first place I came across to ask, "Where am I?"

I drove for another fifteen minutes on a heavily treed road with no home or business until I came to a stop sign. I had to turn left or right. There seemed to be more light from the right, so that is the direction I turned and drove into the back of a recycling center. There was a fifteen-foot fence with barbed wire along its top surrounding a building to my right and a sea of open trailers with plastic bottles in them to my left. The van began to ping as if someone was throwing rocks at it and the plastic bags in the back began to crinkle and crawl. I looked up at the tall smokestack on the building and saw smoke coming from it and I knew: This is what I was to see. This is why the children are sick. I couldn't turn the van around fast enough. I then remembered the compass that had been in front of me the whole time. I headed south and east until I was again on the expressway.

The very next day there was an article in the newspaper comparing a survey on toxins emitted into the air and water with one from a few years earlier. In the article it said government and state agencies were exempt from the survey.

What was happening a man in the Southwest told me, was they did not have a chemist on duty and they were burning two plastics together that produced something that would make the metal ping and the plastics crawl. He then related the following: In the eighties they dumped this particular chemical over Niagara Falls just to see what would happen and they found that within a ten-mile radius every woman wearing pantyhose had them disintegrate on her legs. They then put out in the news that a bad batch of pantyhose had been sent to stores around that area.

What to do with the information I was given that night? I tell as many people as I can. Knowing others told that chemist the same story makes it even scarier. I was enlightened.

A battle vision that shows that even in some of the worst and most violent places on earth, one can still see a vision of hope.

A Vision of Peace in the Presence of Death

I was on my way to Afghanistan as a member of the U.S. Marine Corps. I was terrified of dying in combat, although I never admitted it to anyone in my platoon, but I really had trouble with this fear. After arriving in Afghanistan, it was on my third night that I had the most powerful dream of my life. To this day I believe it was more than a dream. I had two grandfathers who both served in World War II, both who had already passed on some years before my deployment.

I was still scared of becoming a casualty over there and my faith in God was at a low point in my life. I remember how hot and miserable I was when I went to bed that night thinking about how much I hated being there and how bad life sucked. I finally fell asleep and I remember this like it was yesterday because this dream was so powerful I could never forget it:

I found myself alone on a plain of green grass with this thick fog or mist surrounding me. I remember a lot of gray and a lot of green. I saw a man in a brown robe from far away coming toward me. It was weird because as he came closer the details of his face were blurred so I never did get a good look at him, but I was able to make out a beard. I'm not sure this was supposed to be Jesus. I didn't have the feeling it was Him but I had the feeling that whoever he was he knew Jesus.

The man instructed me that I had to come with him because

"there were people who wanted to see me." I couldn't speak; all I could do was follow, but I felt so secure in his presence that it was like I didn't even care where he took me because I had a feeling of unconditional trust in him, and yet I didn't even know him. We walked through the fog or mist into another opening containing another grassy plain, pretty much just like the first one I was in, but this one contained a table with two figures seated at it. The man in the robe was gone before I realized he had left, but my attention was now focused on moving toward the two individuals seated at this table.

I soon made out who they were—my grandfathers! I stood there in front of them, just stared at them for a while, and never said a word; all I could do was look. I felt like a child in their presence, very humbled and almost embarrassed over what I had become since they had last seen me. That feeling soon left me and an overwhelming sense of acceptance and love came over me. I had the distinct feeling that they were proud of me. I sat down in front of them and heard them speak but without sound or voices.

I cannot describe the way I communicated with them. All I remember was staring at them and feeling an understanding between us. The best way I can describe it was that every time I was about to speak or say anything to them, their response had entered my mind before my words left my mouth. And despite the fact I was on the opposite side of the table from them I always had the feeling of being embraced by them.

I didn't want to leave, but soon the man in the brown robe returned to get me and my grandfathers vanished into the mist. I woke up crying but with a calm and ease that had come over me. I was not afraid! The fear of dying had left me and I just felt peace in my heart. It was amazing.

From that night on I knew no fear of death. I had my moments where I missed my family and wanted to see them, but I knew that something else, something big, was in control and whatever was to be would be and that it was a plan already set in motion. This dream really opened me back up to God. I look back on it and think it is responsible for keeping me safe over there and for me keeping my senses. So this was my experience that I have wanted to share and tell people about. It is 100 percent accurate to the best of my memory. I hope you enjoyed it.

In this personal story, a listener tells the story of how a vision saved him from an accident when he had a dangerous job. There are so many versions of stories like this experience, I often wonder why people still deny that visions are real.

SAVED FROM DEATH

I had a job delivering materials to warehouses and factories. On one particular day, I had a skid of welding wire in the back of my truck. It was pushed in far enough that the forklift could not get the forks under it, pull it back, and lift it off. I was up on the truck putting a chain around the skid so that a driver in the forklift could pull the skid back to the edge and lift it off. The skid was pulled back near the edge where the forklift stopped while I unhooked the chain.

The driver of the lift had an uncle that also worked at the same place, and they were talking about something. As I unhooked the chain I stood up with my back to the lift. Suddenly I heard a voice that was (dare I say) inside my head that forcefully said, "Move!"

I stood there for an instant trying to process what had just happened when the voice again shouted, "*Move!*" and I swear something pushed me to the side. In a split second as I moved or was moved, the forklift lunged forward and one of the forks rammed the wire and went into the spools about a foot. Two guys had been goofing around and the one on the ground pushed the other's foot off the clutch pedal. The fork would have entered my back through the spine at about mid-chest height.

This is but one of a number of experiences throughout my life, but to me it is one of the most important experiences that I could ever have had, which let me know that there is either or both a higher self that can see somewhat into the future or a guardian angel/guide.

There have only been a few people that I have told this to, because some will call you crazy and not believe you, and it is also a very personal experience. Throughout my life this and other experiences have changed my belief in nothing after death to that of becoming spiritual. I have had to learn the hard way that what one may experience personally will be another's path to ridicule and laughter.

This is another beautiful vision of how a special place on earth spoke to one of our readers.

THE LAND CALLED TO ME

My parents used to own a piece of land. It was like our summer getaway, and it was heaven to us. Then my mother sold her share of it about twenty-two years ago to my aunt. She had done so in order to dissolve a rocky business relationship with her. My brother and I were mad at this decision. We had a strong attachment to the land.

Up until a decade ago I would "visit" the land regularly. In retrospect, I would go to honor it, to pay my respects. I was the only one of us that had done so. Up until then, nothing had been done to it. In the past ten years I never stopped wanting to go visit, but it just never seemed to be the right time to go.

I dream about the land often. In my most recent dream, about eight months ago, I woke up from crying. I had dreamt that it was bulldozed over and concrete was being poured.

One Saturday night, a rare thing happened. My husband and I had the opportunity to go out and we started driving. He looked at me and asked me where I wanted to go. I wasn't sure, so we just headed north and kept discussing our options. I looked at the clock and had an idea. He looked at me and said, "You want to go to Maine?" Now, remember, I live in New Hampshire. It's February. We had just had the worst snowstorm in years the day before. The farther north you go, the worse the snow gets.

The land was an hour and a half north. It was 7:30 P.M. and it was clear. I had never wanted to go so badly before and my husband had never seen the land. We went.

I was devastated. Every tree, many of them hundreds of years old, had been removed. I could see that digging had taken place and mounds of dirt were under the snow. The only thing left was the makeshift gate and fence my father had built more than forty years ago.

We stood there for a while. I cried. I was shocked. I was angry at what someone had done to the place. I knew there was a condo development going on in the area, but I had not known it was *there*! We drove around the area and found the manager's trailer. As soon as I saw it, I knew something wasn't right. I realized that there wasn't any real progress compared to what should have been done. Something had stopped the development. I decided that I was going to do a little research and find out what was going on.

On Sunday morning I started with searching real estate listings. None of the ones I had seen before were listed anymore. I figured, make the best of a situation and maybe buy one of the condos on the lake and land that I loved so much. I Googled the area name. Nothing came up from the condo developer. However, what came up was a recent newspaper article from the local paper.

It turned out an archaeologist had given a presentation to the town councilors to stop the development of the site. Artifacts were discovered that made it one of the greatest archeological finds in

North America to date. The developer did not disclose any of this information so that they could continue with their sales and building. So far, the city has denied further construction until further research on the area has been done. The developer is appealing the decision. So all of this means that construction might continue at a later date.

I have now contacted the archaeologist. I have told him about my relationship with the land. It turns out that the information I am providing him is incredibly important. I have photos and video, I remember every hill, rut, hole, and blade of grass. Well, maybe not the blade of grass, but rocks lying on the shoreline.

Apparently, the area was an Indian ceremonial and burial ground. So many things of historical importance have occurred on the land.

I now know I was there that night for a reason. I was supposed to know what was going on. My documentation and memory of the landscape will help protect the land from being destroyed. This may seem weird, but the land had "summoned" me. I have always loved it. What else would you call it when someone "visits" land? I wasn't even allowed to walk on it for fear that the owner would find out and have me charged with trespassing.

Here is another vision having to do with the person's relationship to the land. Does the land speak to us? Apparently, for these readers, it does.

THE LAND CAN HAVE A SPIRIT OF ITS OWN

When I was younger I started taking martial arts and I wanted to learn everything. Meditation was what I was in to at the time, so I would sit down with some shaman music and a couple of white candles and just think or try to understand something.

One time I could hear crying, so I looked up and in a vision was a girl in her early twenties. She was kneeling down and was crying. She looked at me, without moving her lips, and I could hear her in my mind. She looked at a field (that I believe may have been a farm at one time) and she was crying because the land was not being tilled. She kept saying, "Make me beautiful," over and over.

What she wants you to know is that you can make her beautiful in your own garden, at your home or around your town, and help to create your own "garden of Eden." Thank you.

When a spirit protects you it can send a vision to communicate with you. It may not seem like a miracle at first, but when you look at the results of that experience, you realize that it could not have happened but for the fact that it was the result of a vision.

VISION OF DISASTER

I've always had the feeling that I was somehow protected by an unseen hand. When I was sixteen I was traveling with my folks, heading out in the desert. It was a very busy night, maybe Friday, and the traffic was two long lines in both directions traveling at about fifty-five miles an hour. There was a lot of dust, and the lights from the cars were very eerie.

There was a break in the oncoming traffic, so I pulled out to pass the big rig in front of me, and as I did a huge tire came rolling out of the oncoming lane, diagonally across my path and right through where I would have been had I not been able to pull out to pass. This tire was so big I could not tell you what kind of rig it belonged on.

I was startled and pulled back into the same place behind the big rig. Mom and I looked at each other as she said, "Praise God. We would have been killed."

Here is a religious vision that seemed to pop up out of nowhere.

The Burning Bush

Riding in a car through foothills, 11:00 P.M., very dark, no structures in the area, the silence in the car was as sudden as the "burning bush" we had just passed on the side of the small country road we were traveling. The fire (flames), five to six feet high and as wide, could not have been a campfire. They appeared, maybe, two feet off the side of this small country road, very contained, too conformed for a natural fire. We (in the car) were all in agreement that what we had just passed couldn't be possible. We also agreed we wouldn't turn around for another look. The mood in the car was very subdued as we rolled on.

When visions manifest themselves as physical impressions, actual contact with the other world, then this is a powerful vision indeed. Working in the light may even make you receptive to these physical experiences as you become more sensitive.

Warning from an Older Friend

Woke up in the middle of night one night and could hardly open my eyes. When I did I felt like someone was lying on me. My whole body felt like this. When my eyes opened I saw an older lady lying on top of me with her hands folded like she was lying on them. I tried to scream and I couldn't. It was like I couldn't find the breath to scream. I was scared to death. I closed my eyes and forced myself back to sleep.

When the morning came I told my friend about it. I knew the older woman in my room was her grandma. That was how she would sleep. I was good friends with her grandma and at the time this happened my life was kind of going out of control. I was doing things I shouldn't. I think that was her warning me.

A very receptive worker describes the beings that surround her. Are these extraterrestrials, as some contactees might believe, or are these purely spiritual beings? Still others might argue that there is no differ-ence between the types and it is only our belief system that tells us how to name them.

LIGHT BEINGS

I've been receiving automatic writing for about thirty years with an ever growing circle of entities. About a year ago physical things started happening around me—lights and radios turned on and off a lot, the sofa vibrated and buzzed while I was meditating, crystals disappeared and reappeared.

I went to a psychic to see if it was my psychic energy turning on, and she confirmed it most definitely was. Shortly after that, I started receiving through my automatic writings that my guides wanted me to write a book. Consequently, I've been writing a book for the last year. That has been the unfolding of my life's purpose.

For years I've been receiving information that there is a huge cataclysm coming to earth in the next few years. Through writing this book I started channeling information from "light beings" from other galaxies. I've received many hieroglyphics. My guides or ETs often tell me what the glyphs mean. Basically, what I've been given in the writings is this: "We (the ETs) are coming to earth. You are going to introduce us to the world and tell them we're here to help rebuild earth after the cataclysmic events that are coming." I've re-ceived this same information many, many times. I find it very interesting—a little daunting—but interesting.

My life's mission according to my guides is to start a movement that's really already under way into higher consciousness. I'd like to target the beginning student, since I am a beginning student myself, in that for most of the first twenty-nine years of my metaphysical and spiritual studies I was entirely on my own, with my etheric teachers. I never felt free to discuss my interest in metaphysics and spiritual things with my husband or anyone else I knew. They were just not interested.

Since I started working on my book, I've connected with two or three "real people" that have given me guidance, but for the most part, it's been my departed loved ones, guides, highly evolved masters, and light beings that I've learned from. I've learned so much and gone through some major vibrational lifting since I started writing the book. My guides tell me I must now perfect my own light body so I can communicate freely with the ETs when the time is right—and it's growing near. . . .

The beings that come through in my autowriting seem very intent on my getting their message to the world. I'm trying to learn as much as possible about UFOs and extraterrestrials. I have quite a group of ETs that come through in my autowriting now. My favorite TV program is *UFO Hunters.*

For people who consciously decide to become workers in the light the entire world can open up to a range of mysteries and experiences. Here, a reader has decided to become a mystic and in so doing, follow a path not only of connection to the universe, but of making connections among different visions and enlightenments.

A Vision from a Meditation

I have been a mystic and seeker all my life and worked in community service all my adult life. In the fifth grade I built a Parthenon out of sugar cubes and a big papier-mâché sphinx. I started meditating at fifteen when I heard that the Beatles were hanging out with the Maharishi, followed by astrology at seventeen, Tarot at twenty-two, apprenticed in Qabalistic Ceremonial White Magic at twenty-nine, Wicca at thirty-seven.

Here is one of the visions I had while meditating:

I took a path from the astral lake I had been visiting during regular meditations. It led to a Grecian-style patio of stone where

I greeted an ancient looking, robed and bearded man. He indicated toward a large stone globe supported in a hemisphere frame of stone. As I observed the globe, it was rotating on a slightly tilted axis, as our Earth does now. Then it went through a dramatic wobble, like a spinning gyroscope that has been bumped out of balance, where the poles for a moment were almost horizontal. Then, as a gyroscope would, it returned to a stable rotation, but with the poles aligned vertically.

The man communicated to me, "In your lifetime." I was in my forties at the time.

Yet, let's conjecture. Perhaps this vision is about the future of our planet. The geophysical impact of a magnetic pole shift? The end of the Mayan calendar in 2012? Certainly fills the "stars falling from the sky" (or however that biblical thing goes). What, I wonder, would be the impact of something like this? Certainly there would be dramatic weather and water movement. But how much would we actually feel? We don't usually feel the Earth spinning around at its usual five hundred miles per hour. I wouldn't want to be in a tall building on a coast, but would a cow on the high plateau fall over? Providing we don't lose much of our atmosphere, life should go on.

Here is a vision of peace and love that came to a young boy and inspired him to be the worker he turned out to be.

A Childhood Vision

This one happened to me in the early sixties. I was about ten years old at the time. As I was playing in front of my house one afternoon, all of a sudden I started seeing a white light above my head. It began talking to me.

Naturally I thought I was having a hallucination, but it turned out I wasn't. Just as I thought I was imagining things a brownish, swirling energy came out of this white light and started moving toward a group of young boys down the street. I watched the brown energy move toward the boys, and as soon as it hit them they began to argue.

I asked the light why it did that and it replied because they were nonbelievers! Obviously I realized it was a demonstration to show me I wasn't hallucinating.

The light told me it wanted me to be a priest. I couldn't understand why it wanted me to be a priest since I didn't like, or care, about going to church. The light said if I didn't become a priest it would make my life difficult and proceeded to show me how my life would turn out if I didn't join the priesthood. I'm in my fifties now and never became a priest. Life events turned out much like I was shown as a ten-year-old boy.

I should also mention that at the time I saw the light I heard some of the lyrics to the Whitney Houston song "The Greatest Love of All." At the time I didn't understand the significance or why I was hearing those words, but I found out later in life that all art is inspired by or given from the Creator.

How many times have we heard the story about a vision that saved a person who was just about down for the count? My listeners tell me stories like this all the time. It means that there's a greater power out there ready to communicate with someone who is willing to open up to the universe, exactly as we talk about it in Worker, *and see what there is out there.*

A HOMELESS VISION

Near the end of my alcoholism it was bad. I was living under a bridge in a large city. I had become one of the invisibles—you know—one of the dirty, scraggly, unwashed, pushing a shopping cart, the ones you see but don't (because you don't want to).

One fateful day I came back from urban foraging to my steel cave—I slept inside two metal gangplanks, one turned upside down on the other—and found my world was gone, swept away in one of the city's homeless cleanups.

This was it—I had no more left. I didn't sign up for this shit. After three failed attempts to live life the way I thought it was supposed to be done, I was outta gas. I had tortured myself near to expiration on my death march of Ego. Thoroughly beaten, I sat down on a bench . . . and left this world.

I was sitting on a chair in a dimly lit room with a small table in front of me. I could not judge the size of the room, however, but I had the feeling it was immense. To my left was the glimmering outline of a door. In front of me, in a small woven basket, was a crystal ball of sorts. Not unlike the ubiquitous seeing device, but somehow different—not cold and hard but somehow robust—alive.

Father God spoke to me then:

"Choose."

And in the ball I saw a much older version of myself pushing a shopping cart. I became that older version, felt the emptiness of the shell that I had become.

"Choose death and I will bless you with no great pain or sorrow. Neither will you know joy—and you will walk to the end of it."

"Choose life."

And to my left the outline of the door grew as the door cracked open slightly, an inviting gesture.

There were no visions of me, only the slightest touch of the awesome nature of love and joy waiting on the other side.

"Choose life and thou will know life eternal."

I don't know how long I sat; time had no meaning in this place, this nexus of decision. I knew I had as long as I needed. I stood, went to the door, opened it, and stepped through. I found myself at a detox center. I had no prior knowledge of the existence of this place. I was admitted, medically detoxed, and referred to an inpatient treatment program. This was twelve years ago.

Can we see our own death? If we examine the future too closely, can we know how and when we will die? And if we see it, can we change it, and in so changing it do we change the time line itself? These are some of the questions workers in the light must think about because of the power that working in the light bestows.

A Vision of Death

Many years ago I had changed doctors, and the new doctor wanted to do a blood chemistry profile on me because my blood looked too dark. I go through this every time I change doctors because I have very dark blood. I decided to go and have the test done even though I felt fine. I was at the clinic, sitting next to some old guy who was to be next after me, waiting for the test when "something" spoke to me in my mind and said, "You will die if you take this test."

I kind of freaked out—sat there for a few minutes—and decided to get the heck out of there. I went home and told my mom. She was kind of mad at me for doing that and thought I was acting nutty.

The next day she showed me a newspaper article about the woman who took my place when I left. She had died during the routine blood chemistry test she had taken at the clinic. This was a life-changing event for me.

The following visions of warning and premonition visions of evil also serve to protect the experiencer by showing people the future that awaits them if they do not change the direction they are heading in. So many of my listeners describe this type of event that I believe it is very common.

A Warning Voice

It was on a Saturday afternoon, and I was in my house alone. I had just cleaned the house and trimmed our Christmas tree when I went to the kitchen for a break and a drink of water.

I was standing at the sink when I turned to look out the sliding glass door. I was just looking out the window, almost in a trance, when all of a sudden there was a voice shouting in my right ear.

"Doug! Doug!" it shouted. After the voice got my attention, it said, "How would you feel if you could not move your right arm?" Even though the voice was shouting at me it was the most angelic and kind voice I had ever heard.

I then looked down at my right arm that was leaning on the countertop next to the sink. I raised my arm to examine it, and said I would not like that at all. I walked away and forgot about it.

I woke up the next morning sick and by Thursday of that week I was in a hospital bed. I had been told I had suffered a stroke and was paralyzed on my right side.

It took three months to get back to normal and be able to walk and move my right arm as before.

I often wonder whose voice I had heard, and If I had paid more attention to it, what would have happened instead.

I missed my chance to listen at that time, but maybe this story will help someone else.

VISION OF HELL

I was walking through a misty, foggy field, when I started to get really light-headed and dizzy. The ground started spinning around me faster and faster and louder and louder, until I must have passed out. I quickly woke up and found myself in hell. It was like a rectangular tube where there were only human faces passing by me. They were able to see my face passing by them.

Apparently I was to spend all eternity in this place seeing other faces pass me by, all of the people who have ever lived and died and gone to hell. All the people were screaming and crying at having to spend all eternity in this place as I was also. It just seemed like eternity.

Then all of a sudden I came back to this realm and realized I had been given another chance. I was shaking and gnashing my teeth and living in paranoia for years after that vision.

I suspect that that vision might have been symbolic of people today, living their lives sitting behind a computer screen—their only interaction with others chatting online with others like them. I feel that this prophetic vision is coming true.

My next vision was equally terrifying. I was walking across the same grassy, misty field on my way home around a year later. This time I started hearing that same eerie vibration that got louder and louder and the ground started spinning around me faster and faster. Then I was lying on the grass and a chain came out of the ground and wrapped itself around my leg and pulled me off.

This was happening to all of the humans on the planet also, and the next thing I knew I was part of a human chain. We were all connected by the chains to form human chains, which were rotating within themselves in giant loops. I could see the people passing by in these rotating human chains, rotating within themselves like DNA chains. I felt as if we were being harvested and being prepared for hell.

I woke up screaming and terrified. I got on my knees and begged God forgiveness for all my misdeeds.

The fear didn't leave me for a long time. However, I have since come to realize that the doctrine of eternal damnation is just manmade nonsense. There is no sin so great that I can imagine it would justify that kind of punishment. Maybe God was trying to guide me or nudge me in another direction, because these experiences changed the course of my life. I believe that I actually suffered from post-traumatic stress disorder for a long time.

I turned more inside to myself and became more of a spiritualist. I began meditating and practicing Kriya yoga. Finally, through spiritual practices I was able to relax and make things good and positive. The more I meditate the more creative I am and also I can get a very good idea about how things will be in the future. But I don't use that ability to ego out.

I plan to write a book about my experiences of drifting through the country, living in the wilderness, and coming to where I now live in the bush. My life was and is full of all kinds of mystical and magical experiences, good and bad.

God bless you all!

Sometimes what we call a vision is really a form of premonition that materializes itself into something very specific and related to the experiencer. This is also a very common event for those who hear these stories.

A STORY OF A PREMONITION

When I was in high school many moons ago, I was on vacation with my family in North Carolina. I was the only person in the motel room, getting ready to go swimming. All of a sudden, I heard my friend Mark say my name very loudly and clearly. He was back home in Pennsylvania. I had a sudden urge right then to call him. I went and told my dad. He said to use my urges and gave me permission to call. When Mark got on the phone he told me that he was so glad I called. He had gotten bad news about his sister and was thinking about how he really wanted to talk to me.

I told him he must have been thinking very loudly and told him my story. Things like this have happened to me all my life. I never question them, just go with them.

Have a blessed day!

In Worker *we talk about the kinds of events that leave great impressions on young lives and, years later, turn out to be so important that visions are created out of them.*

THE STORY OF ARSENIO CHAVES

All day long on my sixteenth birthday I wondered why everyone I met behaved as though they forgot what day it was. However, that

night my church group proved to me that they didn't forget—
they threw a surprise birthday party for me at my home!

*At the party that evening, I met a man who was to have a great
influence on my life. He and his wife arranged the surprise party. His
name was Arsenio Chaves and he was more than twice my age, but
our common interest was music. He introduced me to his wife, and
that summer the three of us spent time working, playing, and singing
together until school started in early fall.*

Arsenio played a violin, his wife played the mandolin, and I
joined them with a guitar. We had frequent jam sessions, usually
starting or ending with his favorite old spiritual song. Arsenio's
mother said that the song was playing on the radio when he was
born.

We played in church many times and thoroughly enjoyed the
interaction. It was as though fate had drawn us together. Arsenio was
the most even-tempered and good-humored man I ever met. He was
a genuinely religious man who had a sense of purpose about everyday, small tragedies, no matter what they were, and he was thankful
for every blessing. He loved Pennsylvania Dutch birch beer, and
passed it out to coworkers after a hard day of work.

My sixteenth summer was memorable because the three of us
went together to many church functions. In the fall when school
started, Arsenio drove the school station wagon. That Christmas
we had fun caroling with the rest of the church choir.

The following year brought more good times. I passed another
birthday, although it was not celebrated with a surprise party. I
sometimes worked hard for Arsenio and he, his wife, and I learned
to work well as a team.

On a hot and humid July night, with the full moon brightly
illuminating my room, I had trouble getting to sleep because of
the typically oppressive heat. I was awake for some time, covered
only with a sheet and sweat. Both of my windows were partially
open, in hopes of finding a breath of air stirring.

My bedroom on the ground floor was arranged in such a way that my twin-sized bed was tucked tightly into a corner. It was so close in fact, that there wasn't room on the west side to slip a hand between the wooden bed frame and the wall. My head was lying toward the north wall, and at the foot of the bed there was one window. To the east, on the wall about six feet away, was another window. Between my bed and the window sat a bookshelf and a cedar chest, arranged so that they formed a miniature hallway down the side of my bed.

The hair on my entire body felt as though it was standing up and I felt as if I were waiting for something eerie to happen! Without any warning there were three raps at the east window. I tried to scream, but found that except for my eyeballs, every muscle was paralyzed. All kinds of thoughts went through my mind as I moved my eyes to look in the direction of the window.

Another three raps on the window, and I was more frightened than before. Finally, three more knocks, and in my mind I heard myself say, "Come in, whatever you are."

No sooner had my mind formed those words than I saw a bright white shape coming from the direction of the window, although the window itself was obscured from my view by the bookcase. The thing moved to the end of the cedar chest and then glided toward the bed until it stood on my left side. The form looked down into my face, and it was Arsenio—smiling. He spoke a word out loud, "Good-bye."

Arsenio's specter then moved across the foot of the bed and came alongside me on my right side. Again, he spoke a word, "Good-bye." With that done, he returned to the window through which he had entered and disappeared from my view.

As soon as I was able to gain control of myself, I got out of bed and made a large X on the wall calendar above my desk and noted the time. It was not a dream. I had not been asleep.

I never mentioned the experience to Arsenio because I did not believe in ghosts of living men, but I couldn't resist telling his wife. It bothered me too much to keep to myself. She laughed and said that it was all just a dream. I insisted that it was no dream; I was fully awake when it occurred.

The rest of the summer was largely uneventful, and I tried desperately to put the memory out of my mind. When September rolled around, Arsenio again drove the station wagon that picked up rural school students and transported them to a central point. I was the first student to board every morning and sat in the front seat talking to him until the bus reached the transfer place. Those who were going to high school changed to a bus and were taken there.

One morning in October, three months from the dreaded encounter, Arsenio's sister was driving the station wagon. I was greatly surprised that she was taking the bus run and I asked her what was wrong with Arsenio. She assured me that he just had a "little stomach upset," but would be back the next morning.

The next day he was still sick. She said that it was just a "touch of the flu" and my friend would be recovered enough to take the wheel by the next day.

Arsenio was removed from his home and taken to a hospital the next morning, and soon thereafter was transferred to a special clinic. An exploratory surgery was performed, but they didn't find the reason for his sickness and pain.

His condition continued to worsen. His wife stood vigil, never leaving his side until the last day when the desperate surgeons performed another exploratory operation. As she sat in the waiting room, she heard the familiar strains of "It Is No Secret" over the hospital speaker system and knew in her heart that he had died. At that moment, one of the surgeons came through the door from the surgery theater and made the announcement.

Arsenio was dead three months from the time he appeared to me, had been sick nine days, and "It Is No Secret" was playing at the moment of his death, just as it had been playing at the moment of his birth at home thirty-four years before. It was his favorite all during his life.

After the funeral I saw his wife in the back room of the church. She wanted me to tell her again about the "dream" I had related to her twelve weeks before. Again, I described the experience to her in detail. She screamed and ran out of the room.

The minister of the church came to me and said that it was the devil I had seen and I was no longer welcome in his church. I was "contaminated."

The story rightfully should end there, but it had such a traumatic impact in my life that it was impossible to forget, and it is as much alive in my memory today as it was when it occurred. In the years since Arsenio's death, I have resolved some of my questions about the experience.

It was not until the late 1980s that I discovered the name for what I had seen. When a customer brought a Rolls-Royce Silver Wraith automobile to me for service, I looked up the definition of "wraith." *Webster* defines it as "an apparition of a living person, supposedly portending their death." So that's what it had been. The memories of that experience still make the hair stand up on my arms and neck. In doing research in the late 1990s, I also found that what I had probably seen was his astral body, and that he most likely was having an out-of-body experience (OBE).

I had a hard time understanding why his wife screamed, but through the counsel of others, I have come to realize that she probably screamed because he appeared to me instead of her. Considering that, her action was understandable.

The reverend made the remarks he did out of pure ignorance. Anything he had not witnessed must have been evil and therefore from the devil. His philosophy: If you can't explain it, condemn it.

While the meaning of the experience is totally open to individual interpretation, this is my own belief: Arsenio appeared to me and smiled because he wanted to show me that he was not sad about leaving this life. If the three series of knocks meant three months, and the three raps three times meant nine days, he was trying to tell me what to expect. That meaning was not apparent to me when I was only seventeen, and was not experienced in spiritual matters. Although the man has served as a guiding beacon throughout my adult life, the experience as a whole has haunted me and sent me on a never-ending quest for answers. I believe that in the later years of my life I have discovered at least some of them.

Listeners sometimes relate stories of visions that stretch across the years and are prophetic in nature. These visions reveal the plans people make for us—people who have great impact in our lives.

THE WOMAN IN THE FLOWING DRESS

My father passed away when I was nine, and my then ten-year-old sister Melissa and I went to live with my oldest sister Brenda, twenty-five years my senior, and her husband. Melissa and I were the two youngest of twelve siblings, and Brenda was unable to have kids of her own. I found out in later years that my dad had asked her to take us in, should anything ever happen to him.

The summer that he passed away, Brenda had arranged for Melissa and me to fly to her place for a two-week visit. I was packing my suitcase and chatting with Dad, and somehow we got onto the subject of "someday, when I grow up and get married . . ." I don't remember exactly how the conversation went, only that I made a statement to him that clearly indicated I did not expect him to be around for my wedding. I remember precisely knowing that he would be dead by then, and whatever I said prompted him to question, "How do you know I won't be there?"

I remember feeling guilty about the fact that I just assumed he would die before I grew up and got married, and that I told him I didn't really know why, I just thought so. While we were visiting

Brenda, my dad died quite unexpectedly. My mother was far older than Dad, and the family agreed it would be best for my sister Brenda to take in Melissa and me. My mom passed away two years later from a stroke.

Within about six months after moving in with Brenda and her husband, I had an interesting "sighting." Melissa and I shared a bedroom, and we could see through our doorway into the living room. There was a bookcase in the living room with a Buddha statue. Brenda wasn't a Buddhist, but she liked the statue for the decor. It was 1973, and I think that was a popular thing at the time.

I woke up one night and looked out the doorway into the living room. I saw a figure floating slightly above the floor at an angle facing the Buddha. I couldn't see the statue itself, but the figure was floating toward it, and it had long, flowing, ornate robes with those long, bell-type sleeves, a pointy hat with long scarves on it, flowing down the back, along with the rest of the robes.

The figure had almond-shaped eyes, which were closed, but I could see enough facial features to know he was Asian, and he had his hands together in prayer. He just floated by and I dove under my covers, scared to pieces. I just prayed that God would keep me safe and make it go away, and I cuddled up close to my sister. I went back to sleep too scared to look again.

I didn't tell Brenda about what I had seen until about three years later. After I recounted the story, she told me another story that she had never told Melissa or me, for fear it might scare us. We had a neighbor in the apartment complex who was nice, but kind of odd. There was something Melissa and I sensed about him that made us think of him as a little weird. Maybe it was his tone, his little dog, or just his general manner. He had to walk past our downstairs apartment doorway to the stairs leading to his upstairs unit. He told Brenda that when he passed our door, he sensed "a protective spirit in long, flowing robes." As you can imagine, when I told her about what I had seen in the apartment, she was pretty dumbfounded, and so was I when she told me what the neighbor had told her.

Another experience I had occurred in a different home we lived in about a year after my dad died. I woke up one night and saw a glowing white-light figure of a woman wearing a hooded robe and standing on the right-side of my bed. I couldn't make out any facial features, only the general shape, and that her arms appeared to be held in front of her, across her stomach. Again, I was scared witless and dove under the covers. By then, my sister and I still shared a room but had twin beds. I remember staying under my covers and praying for God's protection, too afraid to look and see if it was gone.

Eventually I went back to sleep. I should add that I have had "waking dreams" where you wake up after a vivid dream and realize that it was only a dream. On all of the occasions I'm recounting here, I was wide awake, and have no doubt that I was not dreaming.

UFOs and ETs

I n *Worker in the Light*, we never included the hunt for UFOs or contact with extraterrestrials as part of our discussion because the book wasn't about UFOs. However, the response from listeners and callers about UFOs was overwhelming. Whether the phenomena people saw around them were UFOs, spiritual manifestations in the form of orbs, ETs, light beings, entities from another dimension, or angelic spirits, we can't tell you. Only our contributors can speak for themselves about the astounding visions they had about what they saw when they connected to the universe.

What we can say, however, is that UFO contact experiences, visions, encounters with life forms in UFOs—regardless of whether they're ETs or beings from another dimension or time—are part of the experiences people do have when they reach out to the universe, even if they are doing it unconsciously. Take the case of one contactee in Virginia, who had seen UFOs when he was in the military. He had the very strange feeling, a feeling he shared with only one or two others in his barracks, that the UFOs knew he was there and were showing up for him. No creature came out of a craft, announced it was from Venus, and promised to take him aboard, but, nevertheless, this soldier knew that there was a communication between himself and whatever was inside that craft.

After he left the military—they say because he had medical problems, but it might be because of his UFO experience—his sightings continued, only this time they were even more intensive. It seemed that he would know in advance when the craft, luminous, colorful orbs that were affixed to triangular-shaped craft, would show up. He would awaken in the middle of the night as if summoned and go to his window where he would see them. Sometimes he would follow them and see huge triangles floating over sections of the town.

When he began to post some of the videos he had taken of the craft on the Internet, a strange person contacted him, claiming to be a government contractor, who wanted to know about his sightings. But when he agreed to talk to her, she only asked him questions about himself and not about what he was seeing. Soon, she revealed to him that he was, in fact, summoning the craft and demonstrated how they would come in response to his mental requests to see them. He admitted that he sometimes felt lonely just before the craft showed up, and then much better after they left.

Soon he began experiencing missing time, periods when he lost all awareness of what he had done or what had happened to him. And then he began exercising forms of telepathic powers, vastly enhanced abilities that he had exhibited as a child but turned away from because they had scared his parents. This young man was making contact, reaching out to the universe almost reflexively instead of consciously, but, nevertheless, reaching out.

In another instance, the contact with a craft and its occupants was truly violent. A private pilot, flying with his cousin off Catalina Island off the coast of Southern California, spotted a bright light just beneath the surface of the water. When he descended to a thousand feet to take a look, the craft hit him with two bursts of a powerful bright light—a light so thick that it seemed almost gelatinous. As the pilot fought his way through what seemed like a colloidal suspension of light, the plane hit the water and was completely destroyed. Miraculously, the pilot was thrown from the cockpit—how he does not know—and was rescued by Baywatch divers. It was also a miracle that he was still alive after being underwater for almost twenty minutes. His cousin, unfortunately, who was already dying from cancer, perished in the crash.

From the moment of his rescue, the pilot began experiencing contact with strange entities—balls of light that made their way into his bedroom at night, voices that seemed to play out in his head. He heard, not words, but a presence announcing itself. You might think these were straight-out psychological reactions to the crash, but they weren't. The voices have been with him, off and on, since that crash, beckoning him, he says, to explore what they are and what they want of him. They are benevolent, he says, taking responsibility for him now that he is alive, taking credit for having saved him. He is on a quest to find out what he has to do to facilitate even more communication with them.

If I told you how many people told us about their alien communication, it would astound you. We've heard from people who talk about events in their lives so bizarre that it would make no sense, except for the large numbers of similar stories. We've spoken to self-described extraterrestrial hybrids, people with blood types so rare that even their doctors scratch their heads in disbelief. We've spoken with people from vastly different backgrounds and family histories, who describe the same types of events in their lives and, then, after some rudimentary blood tests, find out that they have some of the same blood chemistry.

We've spoken with people, whose conscious memories of alien contact, and their own belief that they've descended from marriages between extraterrestrials and humans, have left them completely confused about who they are and why they're here. They speak of their alien fathers and earth fathers, their mothers who had been taken by spacecraft when they were little children, and their children, who report strange, buglike, shiny entities in their rooms at night.

We've seen video of strange beams of light coming down from the sky and creatures suddenly disappearing who have walked through the spots where the beams hovered above, but did not touch the ground. And we've spoken to callers who have witnessed craft over their heads in Phoenix, who then report an unmistakable sense of peace and calm as they watch the craft float on by.

I can tell you definitively that you cannot speak to so many people, hear their voices on the air at night, read their stories as they come to you in letters and e-mail, or face them in interviews on camera, and not believe that something is out there that we can communicate with and that wants to communicate with us. The stories of our contributors, who have taken the steps to reach out to the universe and exercise their communication with these entities, are fascinating stories—stories of courage, and stories of wonder. The stories are so numerous that they would fill many, many books, and still people would be astonished by them. We can categorize them, of course, but even that would do them a disservice because each one is a unique story of contact, of witnessing, and of reaching out to communicate with a species that is right here, right beside us, just a dimension away, separated by a thin tissue of invisibility. Even these entities, we have come to believe, could be workers in the light. But what light and where is it from?

There are people who have extended experiences with UFOs as if the entities in the craft know whom they are contacting. It tells me that UFO contacts aren't random, and that people are either tagged from an early age or have the ability to summon them. Many of the contributors to this chapter have written of this very phenomenon.

ALIEN CONTACT

It was the summer of '79. I would like to say I was camping, but the truth is that where I lived there was a gang fight between us surfer boys against the Mexican low-riders. People got hurt and the cops were looking for me and some of my friends. So, truth is, I was hiding out in the mountains by the high desert.

I was alone on the desert side. I was hunting on the low side as the desert seems to start there. Rabbits go there as there is more grass to eat going up the mountainside and are easy to pick off with my bow.

The sun was almost gone so I started to hike back to my camp before it was too dark to see well. Then light seemed to be all around me and the area I was at. I looked up and saw this very large ball about thirty yards away and about a telephone pole height in the air. It was about fifty feet round or bigger, and light was all around it.

I looked at it for some time and did not know what it was or what the hell was going on. I thought it was some balloon, but then it moved very slowly and beams of light where moving around on the ground like a scan.

I took off up the hill toward where the trees started, looking for cover and moving fast. The light beams came on me and the ball moved toward me. I got to the trees and got behind one, and then the lights stopped. The ball moved back to where I first saw it. I had a very clear view of the ball. It was hovering, and I was higher up the hill. It was lower than I, so I got a good look at it. Then, like a lid on a jar, the top came off, but it was the disk-shaped UFO.

It came right at me. While I watched I had put my string back on my bow and screwed a four-edge razor-tip point on an arrow and had it at the ready. When it came I drew my bow and took a shot. I hit it but it did nothing, of course, and I took off like a bat out of hell. I got to my camp and was a bit scared, so I set up for bed, got in my bag, and went to sleep.

When morning came I woke up in my bag, but I was almost half a mile away from my camp. I was very confused. I rolled up my bag to head back, and in the bag was the arrow I had shot but the tip I had put on it was gone.

I hunted in other areas and did not go back to where I saw the ball for almost a week. But I needed food so I went back to the spot so I could pick off some bunnies. I got behind a bush, got my bow ready, and sat still waiting for "Bugs" to show up. It was just before afternoon when I felt very light-headed and had a humming noise in my ears and head. A few minutes later the ball showed up and again I sat still. It was about thirty feet away.

The buzz in my head got louder, then the ball started to descend and stopped about a foot off the ground. I saw three people (ETs?). Two were little and one was taller but still short. The tall one looked like he had a spandex suit on. The two little ones looked naked and their arms were longer then the tall one. I could not see the side where they came out of the ball.

I had a million thoughts run through my head. I had figured I was screwed so I stood up and took aim at the big one. He held up his very skinny arms in a "No, don't, stop" motion. I got a good look at his face. He sort of looked like the pictures on TV, with big eyes but not as big as the ones on TV. He bent over and put something down on the ground, turned around, and then he and the two little ones went back in the ball. I just stood there. It was about ten minutes before the ball went up and took off.

I could hear noise behind me. I turned and saw a military chopper heading for it. I watched it, and the chopper. It would move ahead, the chopper would get close, and it would move ahead again. It looked like the ball was playing with the chopper—cat and mouse—then it took off toward the desert and the chopper went after it. I went to see what the ET had put on the ground. It was my four-razor-edge arrow tip.

I went home two days later and tried to tell a few people, but all I got was, "You were on drugs" or, "You're nuts," so I never spoke of it again.

In July 1994, I was riding my horse in Houston, Texas, and stopped at a favorite spot near the cliff edge where there were nice trees and a great view. I would stop, rest, let my horse graze, then head back to the stables. This time I was just sitting there thinking. I had just broke up with my girl.

I got light-headed and a bit dizzy and then that buzzing noise in my head started again. I don't know where it came from, but a classic UFO disk was there, which looked just like the one from the ball but much, much bigger. I just sat there as the buzzing got louder then it stopped. The disk took off. I watched it as best I could.

I can't be sure, but it looked like it went right into the water. I did not know what to think. What could I do or who could I tell? Everyone would think I needed to be in a padded cell if I told what happened to me, so I tried to forget it and get on with life.

In the summer of 1996 I worked with people's horses at their homes. One customer's nice home had its backyard facing a lake and had lots of pets, so I took my girlfriend at the time to help me.

One day I was outside feeding large macaw parrots in a big breeding cage. My girl was in the house feeding the dogs and fish. I was bent over filling the water dish when I stood up and got light-headed again, but I thought it was from standing up too fast. I got out of the cage and then the buzzing in my head started again. Then from lake view side a disk was there, looking like the same one I had seen before in '94, and was only about one to two miles from the '94 spot. It was close, about seven feet from me. My girl came out the back door. She freaked out, screamed, went back in the house, and slammed the door. I stood there. I was not scared this time at all. The buzzing would stop and start again, stop and start. This went on for about three minutes. I started shouting at it but can't remember what. I yelled, but as before the buzzing stopped. It took off, but this time it went too fast for me to see anything or where it went. My girl was freaked out for a long time and she did not want to talk about it with anyone, even me, and I was there! She started studying the UFO thing and became a little spooky. As for me, I went on with life.

In October 1999, I was moving out of state. It was evening. I got the light-headed thing again so I pulled over and got out of the car. This time I expected to see something. The buzzing started a few minutes later. I looked up, watching for it and then it showed.

It was a disk that looked bigger then the last one I had seen, very high up, with lights all around it. The buzzing got louder on and off, then just stopped, and again it took off.

I got in my car and started driving when about a half hour later the light-headed thing started again, then the buzzing. I did not stop this time but then I saw it. It was not high in the air this time, but it was following me for a few miles. The buzzing stopped. It took off. I kept driving.

It often takes only one sighting to turn anyone into a UFO enthusiast or at least a researcher. This is how many people begin to study the field.

MY UFO SIGHTING

I've been interested in UFOs since I was a late teen—I'm fifty-five now—because of a sighting in the late '60s, which to this day I think about now and then. Yes, I saw three occupants in the craft's bay window. It wasn't a landing or anything. It was just hanging in the sky. I was just amazed at seeing something that wasn't normal, at least by our standards, and shouldn't exist. And I remember the feeling of stillness, like a vacuum, as this thing was in view. I then broke my gaze from it to try and get somebody's attention to see what I was seeing and to validate I wasn't imagining it. I looked back at the spot where I had just glanced at it and it was gone. I never, ever saw anything like that again. In the weeks and months that followed it affected me by way of dreams I would have of saucers. They were more like nightmares.

When groups see a UFO together, it is an entirely different experience. It's shared, and the moment becomes imprinted in their minds.

A MASS SIGHTING IMPRINTED IN OUR LIVES

My current wife and I were at a friend's house at a bonfire. Ten of us were sitting around the fire. I was getting bored, so I relaxed more into my chair and looked up. It was dark, around 9:30, and I observed this craft. It was black and gray. I don't know how I saw it against the dark sky being the color it was, but I knew it was huge, arrow shaped, and moving very slowly across the sky. I looked at my wife, who also saw it, and I then said, "What was that?" My friend Henry said, "It was probably a shooting star." My wife nudged me in the knee and just motioned for me to be quiet. It was no shooting star. No lights were on the craft, yet it was moving very slowly, and it was no stealth bomber, either. The arrow-shaped front part was gray and the back section was black.

I had watched it moving across the dark sky for about one minute before I said anything. I have never seen it since or anything like it.

Quite recently my wife has seen different crafts where we live. She was coming back from the grocery store about 8:30 at night, and noticed a real bright light, like a helicopter light, but it was no helicopter. She knows the difference between helicopters and bright lights since she grew up in a military family. She was close to home and watched it dart around the sky. She had no camera to capture anything. As she drove into our driveway (we live next to a very wooded area), she noticed it hovering about a mile into the woods, it veered off to the right and immediately was gone. She ran into the house and told me about it, but by the time I went outside it was gone.

Another incident occurred back at our friend's place—the one with the bonfire, when my wife was taking a friend for surgery and then staying overnight there. Her husband had gone out of town. They had a picture window in the living room, where my wife was sleeping on the couch. She was awakened by this bright light moving around the farm area. They have one hundred acres of farmland, but no cattle. She watched it for about ten minutes as it slowly moved its light around the area. It came very close to the window and she tried to look up but could not see where the light was coming from. In just that instance, it was gone.

Many people have told me that their first experiences with UFO contact was much more than a sighting. It was a spiritual experience as well. I have come to accept that as a valid reaction that changes your paradigm and opens you up to the universe.

MY UFO SPIRITUAL EXPERIENCE

The first time I saw a UFO was with a friend of mine, Gus. He had just come back from vacation and one day, without giving me a valid reason, he asked me to accompany him to the beach in the evening. At the time we had just moved to California from Minnesota so I thought, what a nice thing, informed my husband at the time, and with his approval, off we went.

As we were sitting on the sand he said, "Look up, what do you see?" I was somewhat amazed, because the stars looked like they were dancing. He said to me, "Those are not stars, stars do not dance. Those are flying saucers. Just wait and see what happens when they're finished dancing."

To my surprise, within less than five minutes, the dancing stars sped off at extreme velocities and were seen no more. Gus informed me that he first spotted them while on a trip to Mount Shasta. I was too busy with my new life to pay too much attention to what I witnessed.

I didn't pay too much attention to any such phenomenon until I had a spiritual encounter of sorts in 2005. It was autumn and the evening was especially humid and the air was so dense. I remember sitting on the front porch of my house when a light blue aura in which something appeared to me that looked like the Lord Jesus Christ. He said to me, "I want you to save them." I didn't know what to do, so I voiced my complaint, not verbally but telepathically, "Save them? Who are you referring to?" He stated, "You know who they are." I said again through thought, "They don't want to be saved." "Follow them," he stated, "wherever you have to go." The next day, without any reason, I got in my vehicle loaded with all my stuff and money and drove for no less than twelve hours, stopping only to purchase food and fuel. I found myself driving through mountains, my eyes wide open, seeing more "dancing stars." I felt as if they had followed me and were trying to guide me to their plight (if in turn they have a plight). These are just a few of the instances when I have had strange encounters not easily explainable to a nonbeliever.

Since that time I have traveled the eastern and midwestern regions of the United States and most times have encountered the dancing stars (as I call them now). I have also seen a very bright light that went from west to east and hovered over the eastern part of Santa Monica for about two minutes. At the time we lived about two and a half miles from the ocean. My ex-husband's wife also viewed it with me, and we watched it disappear flying off toward the east at a very high rate of speed.

During my travels I was led to areas where UFOs have made their mark. In the process, I was instructed to dot the intersecting lines of my graph notebooks, and I believe the spirits of these dead aliens guided my eyes to draw connecting lines, in the process creating a visual rendition of their crafts. Sometimes I would be told about systems of their UFOs and how they fly. I have been guided to draw no less than one hundred pictographs of this sort as well as having been given logical understanding of alien mathematical notations, which I also took notes on.

I thank you for your interest.

Sometimes, as in the previous reader's contribution, a single UFO sighting can be the beginning of an entire spiritual consciousness-raising.

A Spiritual Awakening

I have experienced a spiritual awakening that lasted about ten years, and I'm still working things out. I look back and still can hardly believe it myself. I am going to try to touch on everything the way it happened in a chronological order. Okay, here it goes:

It started: One morning I left for work early so it was still dark, and I saw a light in the northern sky, low on the horizon. It was circular and still and flashed green, red, and white. At first I thought it was a plane but planes do not stay still. I didn't think much about it until March of that year when I was coming back from shopping. I live on a farm, so there is a large area of the sky that is cleared. It was in the middle of the afternoon and it was a strange day. The airport had computer difficulties so they had halted plane travel. The air space over our farm is one of the routes incoming planes use, so the sky was quiet.

I was driving down the driveway and noticed a metal disc that I thought was a plane. I parked and got out of the car, looked up again, and noticed it had no wings or tail. It was a silver disc. I turned around to get my groceries out of the trunk, then turned around to look again as I was curious, but the disc was gone. If it was a plane there is no way it would have disappeared; planes do not fly that fast. I was curious. I thought to myself, *Did I just see a UFO?* but once again dismissed it.

I cannot remember exactly how long it was after this sighting when I had a dream. No, I had a vision. It felt more powerful than a dream. I was standing at the water's edge, it was dark, and above me coming from the north. (I don't know why I feel so strong that it was from the north but it just feels right.) There was a V formation of exactly the same craft that I saw earlier that flew over my head and once again flashed the colors of green, red, and white. Then a second formation flew over my head, flashing the same colors, but this time dropped a baby bottle full of milk.

Time went on and I was feeling very anxious, working with all kinds of emotions. By the summer of 1997, when I decided that I wanted to leave work, dreams and visions were happening. I obtained some counseling but mainstream psychology does not accept this kind of experience or reality. Luckily, my wife was fine with this and was willing to support me.

I connected with a local woman who was very interested in UFOs and spirituality, and she gave me a book called the *Keys of Enoch*, where I saw a diagram of the spaceships I saw that afternoon and in my visions. They called it a Merkaba Vehicle. I felt validated. I was not going crazy. Also, martyr was defined in the book as someone who puts humanity's needs before their own. Then things began to make sense. I opened a door that, believe me, I was not ready for.

As time went on I explored and researched many beliefs, and my kundalini was activated. Now, I was raised Christian so a lot of our belief structures were in place. So this was my reality.

Shortly after this I experienced a soul transfer. The feeling was weird. A tingling started in my toes, went up my body, and then—whoosh—it felt like my soul left through my third eye. Around two nights later I was semi-awake and lying on my side when I felt a soul literally walk in. Shortly after this I had an out-of-body experience. I felt myself leaving my body and the next thing I knew I was walking behind a being in the Milky Way. It was like a spirit; we were not in the physical. It was a small being with the large almond eyes. The being turned around and spoke to me and spoke to me telepathically and said, "We do not need spaceships."

I have been back to work for around two years now and I'm a totally different person. There are a lot of personal issues I worked out and I find that my belief structure has changed. I accept what feels right to me—a little of this a little of that. I'm working in a different job with similar equipment and have no more infections.

I approach life with new eyes, I can truly say that I have been reborn. Extraterrestrial and religious experiences have calmed down.

Many encounters with UFOs and their inhabitants start in a person's childhood and are also often the result in a family history of UFO contact. Contactees wonder whether they are part of a long evolutionary process in which humans eventually will join with their star seeds in what Arthur C. Clarke called Childhood's End.

Childhood Visitations

I have been subject to powerful, vivid dreams of "visitors" since I was old enough to store memories. When I became a bit older, say in my late teens, I began to have paralysis dreams several times a week. I have never thought much of them. In fact, I always dismissed them as dreams and shrugged them away. For some odd reason, dating back to my early childhood I had always contained this feeling that I was being chased by aliens or UFOs.

Too young to really put much thought into the nature of this phenomenon, I had always dismissed this feeling as childhood fantasies—the monster under the bed, if you will. I even wrote about seeing these aliens for a free journal topic as early as the first or second grade. I could never really figure out where, why, or when the source of this "childhood delusion" stems from, but dismissed all this as nothing important during my whole childhood and teenage life.

Who would take much stock into such dreams? My parents never told me about any such things. I didn't have bad nightmares from horror movies and candy. I can't explain why this thought of being somehow involved with a nonterrestrial force entered my head. "Just dreams" became my excuse for having these vivid dreams or paralysis dreams, especially after I had educated myself on the subject of paralysis dreams, and it all seemed more likely that it was all imaginative.

There was, however, a single experience that I can recall as being more than a vivid dream of this experience. In the summers, I slept a lot till noon, being a lazy teenager. Bear in mind that I was having several paralysis dreams a week in which I would see these visitors, but one afternoon while snoozing, I was startled out of sleep by a noise. I thought for a moment that it was my mom opening or closing some door in the house and even checked the clock. There was no possible way that anybody was in the house at this time, being around midday.

Now to the actual experience: After checking the clock, I closed my eyes and attempted to fall back asleep when my bedroom door clicked open. Also bear in mind that this was distinctly *not* a paralysis dream or a vivid REM dream. I was clearly conscious, awake, and alert when I opened my eyes again upon hearing my door open.

I saw a strange, short, dark figure standing in the opening of the doorway. It was nearly enveloped, or cloaked by a dark fabric wrapped around its entire shortened stature. It had a dark, small face with dark eyes. I cannot recall many details of what this creature looked like as my eyes were slightly blurred from just coming out of sleep. As soon as we locked eyes, I passed into blackness only mere seconds after witnessing my door close slowly. I slept for hours and hours after this.

This was very real and distinctly *not* a dream or fabrication in any way. After years and years of dreams, I have had one *real* experience of some sort of possible alien visitors. The only other details worth adding to this story are almost negligible, but I will let whoever reads this make their own conclusions.

In addition to my lifetime of strange dreams and notions of being somehow involved in something that I was not aware of, I have had many occasions in which my memories seem falsified. I will strongly recall a memory, but upon further mental examination, find such memories to have never existed. I have never experienced lost time, but I often experience lost, inaccurate, or falsified memory.

It's as if the memories of my lifetime experience do not add up somehow. When I was younger, I often had these mystery noises or happenings which I always dismissed as the "monster under the bed" cliché. I have always had several of these experiences, but do not feel that it's necessary to share them as they could very well have been nothing more than my imaginative fears taking hold of me.

I have no reason to believe otherwise. However, one time in particular during childhood, one experience was real, although still unexplained. I cannot recall the exact age and will guess between seven and ten years of age. My older brother and I stayed up late one summer night (about 3:00 A.M.) and heard some strange and unearthly noise. We were both scared as it sounded so unfamiliar and quickly decided to hit the lights and go to sleep.

The next morning, both he and I had pains behind our ears and very small, needlelike scabs posterior to our ears. Aside from this experience and the above-mentioned experience, I have never had any sort of physical encounter. Everything else has been . . . just dreams.

As far as family members sharing any of these experiences, none have ever had any unusual happenings and do not believe in "visitors." The exception to the previous statement is the single experience of my mother and her three siblings during their childhood: All four claim to have seen a UFO touch down in the very small town in which they grew up. I have no reason to doubt the sincerity of their claim.

I am medically sane; however physiologically, I was ill during my teenage years with cancer.

Sometimes the memories of the actual craft itself, especially when experiencers have been aboard it, can be quite vivid and compelling.

I Dreamed Myself Awake

I haven't seen the maintanence guy in a long, long time. So long, in fact, that I can just barely remember him or the last time we met.

It was about twenty-five or so years ago. It was a sunny day and we met outside the ship. I don't remember much of the conversation—we exchanged pleasantries—and he pulled out a bag of herb. It had an odd sort of color, purplish, and I asked him where he got it. I don't remember exactly where he said, but I *do* remember declining, worrying just a little as to the compatibility with my system. He told me a little about his travels on the ship, grumbled a little about his job—dirty and such.

I listened and nodded as I could relate to dirty jobs. I suspect this was the thread that connected us—made us friends. I did consider him a friend at the time. Thinking back, he was one of those friends that one could go years without hearing from and when we got together it seemed as if it had only been last week since we had seen each other. After a while he said he had to get back to work. He told me it was nice to see me and he meant it. He turned and left, walking up the ramp of the ship.

I don't remember if he said he would see me again. I haven't. Nor have I seen the ship.

I used to visit the ship from time to time when I was younger. It would land in a big green field near a hill and open up for those who were "drawn" to it. This drawing seemed perfectly normal and as often as not either Barbara or Tom (Ted?) or both would greet me (us). If not, I (we) were welcome to come aboard and make ourselves at home. I distinctly remember others about me, but I don't remember a single one of them personally.

The ship was very large, with more than several floors of space inside. I remember there was an administration floor, as well as a floor with rooms for teaching/meditation. These rooms were arranged in a circular fashion around a central room, which served as a gathering room. I never got to navigation or any other levels on the ship. This wasn't because they were off limits or anything like that. I just had no reason to see them at the time and I always felt there would be another time for that.

Barbara and Ted (Tom?) were tall and fair-skinned, blond humanoids. Other than their height, the only features that stood out and let one know they were not of this planet were the nose and ears, which were just slightly different than ours but not grotesquely so. They were very . . . benevolent is the only word that comes to mind. Patient, kind—these were traits that were a part of this aura about them. They knew me, but it seemed as if they knew me as part of a larger group or something, like teachers who know each and every one of their students—and had a great many students—but this did not diminish the knowledge of who I was, individually.

I do not remember the first time I met them. I do feel as though I was young, possibly very young, when they first made their presence known to me. I do not remember individual lessons or instruction, although I believe I received some because I do remember the primary purpose of the visits was instruction/selection.

The last time I saw them I was led into the gathering room aboard the ship. In the middle of the room was a ball of the purest, brightest light one could possibly look at without burning out one's retinas. It was painful for me to look at it. I looked around the room. There were others touching the light, staring into it. There was the feeling of the presence of love—of God the Father/Creator in the light. I could not stand to be in the presence of this light and left the room—and the ship. I knew I had failed a test of some sort and the lessons were over, for a time.

I was left, however, with the knowledge that there is more—so much more—than the reality of this human existence. The essence of this knowledge is hope.

The ship hasn't returned as of this writing, although I feel as though it will again someday, possibly sooner than later as I have felt my inner consciousness pressing forward—hard—lately. I am hoping this is a signal or something to begin the process of letting go of this world (be in it but not of it) and someday regaining my opportunity to gaze into the light again and see my friend, the maintenance guy.

Still other contactees report the classic abduction scenario, which is so challenging to reality that even they deny that it could have happened to them. Sometimes it takes years for a person just to accept his own abduction reality to the point where he or she can try to put it into some sort of healthy perspective.

ABDUCTION

I have to get this off my chest.

In 1992 I was working construction, building the town hall. After a long day I drove home and couldn't wait to just lie down and relax. I had a lot of things on my mind and couldn't sleep if I wanted to, I was completely awake. I saw a light coming down my driveway. It had to be a car but it was a little late for company. I sat up in my bed and tried to wake my wife because the window was on her side of the bed.

As fast as I tried to shake her I became somewhat paralyzed. I could barely move. I saw a cobalt blue, swirling ball of light enter the wall of my house and stand by the foot of my bed. Next thing I knew I was lying on my back and something was standing next to me. As I looked I saw two weird-looking gray things that seemed surprised that I was somewhat alert. All of a sudden my opposite hand was forced down and I felt a sharp pain in my thumb. I fought to turn my head and look over and see what was causing this and I began to panic. There were two tall, dark (scary looking) beings reaching over my wife. One was forcing down my arm and the other was doing something to my hand, like sticking a pin in it or something. I began to panic and fight what I could only describe as paralysis.

The dark things, which were very terrifying, seemed to be pissed off at the gray things, and in a split second the ball of light was leaving the room and I was able to move again. I jumped up and ran into the bathroom. As I turned on the light, I looked in the mirror and began splashing water on my face, wondering if what I thought was real was really a dream, and noticed pink streaks running down the right side of my face. I looked at my thumb and it was bleeding. I spent the rest of that night in the bathroom and didn't come out till morning. They could have taken my wife for all I knew, but there was no way I was going out to check. I was terrified.

I told my wife of the account the next day and she told me I was nuts. I told a couple of other people who laughed at me like I was telling a joke. From that point on I rarely spoke about it at all until now.

Several months after the incident, while watching a show on alien abductions, something I was never interested in, a woman described how a glowing ball of blue light entered her house and she was abducted. The hairs stood up on the back of my head. Recently I had moved, having bought thirty-five acres and built a new house. I have this urge to be far from cities and close to nature.

I don't know how to say this, but something major is going on. Something is going to happen to this world as we know it but I can't quite describe it. I think we are all in big trouble. I fear dreaming in that state but feel it's now my duty to tell what I see.

In other abduction experiences, the contactees can be more awed by the nature of the ship itself and less fearful of the process of the abduction.

INSIDE A STARSHIP

One night, after a good day surfing in the clear blue waters of Maui, I lay down on my bed to go to sleep. Before falling unconscious, I began to feel a very unusual spinning sensation. It felt as if my entire body was gyrating in countless cyclic patterns. As my mind began to clear after this experience, I suddenly became aware of myself standing inside what I assumed was some type of spacecraft. Incredulous with my present situation, I received a mental greeting. "Yes friend you are truly with us. Now allow your mind to relax, and we will be most happy to shed some light on your present predicament . . ." My mind was reeling in the most tremendous state of mental excitement and anticipation I had ever experienced!

The surroundings in which I found myself were pulsating with a brilliant luminosity that was literally emanating from everywhere about me. And here, directly in front of me, was a group of seven beings, both male and female, standing around and manipulating what appeared to be some sort of control panel. One particular soul, human in appearance and dressed in a pure white space suit, was looking at me with the most intense, penetrating eyes I had ever seen. He seemed to be able to pierce directly into my mind— and I knew this was no human being, in my normal frame of conception.

There was a beautiful glow surrounding all of these beings and I noticed such a warmth and tremendous sense of peace that was in stark contrast to the absolute excitement I felt as I began to truly realize: I was standing inside a starship from some distant planet!

As I now reflect back on this experience some nineteen years later, I feel very fortunate to have been contacted in this way. It was not long after this encounter that I began having many psychic experiences that shook me loose from many of the limited and rigid thought patterns that for the most part are all based on the fear of the unknown.

I began allowing myself to be guided more and more by my own intuition. At age thirty, having never painted or been involved in creative expression of any kind, I awoke one morning with the desire to draw a starship. I began to feel a beautiful, uplifting transcendence every time I sat down to paint and now consider artistic expression to be a large part of my life's work.

I have related my UFO experience to thousands of people in the past nineteen years on television and radio shows and have encountered many skeptics, some very hostile. But every time I have an opportunity to relate my experience, I again feel the beautiful, transcending state of mind that has become so familiar to me in the many years since my original encounter, and I know the truth will someday be made known . . .

Often, the color blue seems to be most associated with UFO contact or just plain sightings. But even ordinary sightings—if they can be called ordinary—have such a transformative effect on a person that it can change his or her life permanently.

A SIGHTING

Around midnight I was observing the annual Perseid meteor shower. I am an amateur astronomer, and have studied this all my life. I love the night sky. It has always entranced me.

While in the front yard looking for meteors, my dad spotted it first. It was a glowing blue disk about twice the size of the full moon, with a bubble of some sort on top. It was impossible to say how big or how far away it was, since there were no points of reference to go by. It was practically edge on and about sixty degrees altitude above the horizon in the southeastern sky. It was clearly three-dimensional and seemed to be stationary or to hover for a minute. Then it moved in a slow circular pattern before streaking off toward the northeast at an unbelievable speed. That was the last we saw of it. My original drawings have since disappeared. My memories haven't. I never forgot that night.

Since then, many things have revealed themselves to me, which make me believe that my life is somehow tied into that event. It was clearly meant for me to see the UFO. I have only recently been compelled to get my story out. My mom reported this to the nearby Army base after it happened, but no one ever followed up, to my knowledge.

I believe I may be responsible for the UFO appearing that night in that place. The hoof beats of the event that spawned my synchronicities are getting louder every day.

One of our readers also talked about her UFO sighting, remembering the impression that it made on her that lasts to this very day. People fortunate enough to see UFOs have no doubt about what they saw.

MY STORY

My story goes like this and I can't believe I'm finally getting the chance to talk about this because this sighting has been on my mind for sixteen years. I work at night and was driving home when I saw in the distance what looked like two large car headlights, but were in the air hovering above a small building about a mile away. I thought to myself, *Boy, that plane is flying very low.* So I kept my eye on it and seconds later realized it was a black UFO just sitting there.

This craft was very sinister looking, like the Stealth—not a sound—so I pulled over on the right side of the highway to watch it, wondering, why would aliens come to some inconsequential town?

I got the feeling it was watching and listening to something from the direction I just came from. I looked up the road and two blocks up there was a police officer who was out of his patrol car talking to a man sitting in a black unmarked car. I turned back to watch the UFO and realized it was listening to them talk from a quarter-mile away, probably about the UFO. This lasted two minutes. As soon as they were done talking it silently turned and flew away and was gone in seconds.

Sometimes, when a contact event is so powerful, the contactee is literally yanked out of one type of existence and planted into another.

MY CONTACT

I never imagined being the author of what is to follow. I am not a psychic; I grew up in Boston watching Celtics and Patriots games. I do have fond memories as a little boy of sitting on the sofa with my father and studying clippings of UFO sightings. I remember enthusiastically giving a report on UFOs in the second grade. Forty years later I have unexpectedly returned to the subject.

It started when two friends on separate occasions said that I would be doing a book on ETs. This was one of the weirdest things I had ever heard, and from two people no less. It turned out being the strangest assignment I have ever had.

One friend elaborated and said that an invisible ET communication device was being built in my backyard. The project would take nine months, and once the device was complete, I would be able to start the book. Where else can you get information like this but Sedona? So, after nine months, I gave it a shot and commenced the communication process.

At first, I just asked the ETs questions and listened to their responses. I would ask them about their life, their thoughts, their science. Many of the questions were mental in nature. After a month of this, I started to feel that this was off track, that I was fumbling around. There wasn't a depth to their responses. Furthermore, my mind was subtly interfering. After seeing countless versions of ETs on television and in the movies, I had brought with me a package of expectations. So I took a hiatus to regroup and figure out how I would proceed.

During this break, I determined that they not only wanted to answer the questions, they wanted to pose the questions as well. They had specific things they wanted to address and that was it. They weren't interested in expounding on matters or having a general discussion. They weren't interested in witty rapport or clever banter.

So I started once again, listening both to their questions and answers. I also made one additional change, which supported the process. I said a prayer before each interview, which seemed to open things up and allow for greater clarity.

As I proceeded, I found that I could barely last fifteen minutes, it was so exhausting. There was a very finite time limit to these interviews and once the time elapsed, I could go no longer.

Compounding that, it took me, in general, several minutes to receive the appropriate question from them and then several minutes again to get their answer. I was not getting very far and started to think that I might be inadequate for the task at hand. Another friend—my friends are on the intuitive side—then explained the process to me, which made sense. A new part of my brain was being utilized to connect with the ETs. It was like using a muscle for the first time, so I must be patient. This took a lot of pressure off. As the conversations progressed, I was eventually able to hold longer interviews.

As I listened, I would verify the information by muscle-testing or using CKT, a technique many chiropractors use to verify information. I would press my left hand against my right wrist. If the wrist went down, the answer was yes; if it stayed strong, the answer was no. After I wrote down the information, I would double-check the accuracy with the help of another person adept at muscle-testing. The more outrageous passages, particularly at the end of the book, were triple-checked.

This diary consists of thirty-four days that occurred over the course of approximately six months. It was often appropriate to take breaks of one, two, or three weeks to change my train of thought and to open myself to new material that would be presented. The pauses were needed in order to more fully capture their three dimensional nature. Moreover, I needed the break because I had to shift, grow, or change in some way to allow the next piece to come forward. For example, I found that the interviews were more effective if I came to them in a more lighthearted way. Seldom was I in a mental comfort zone. I was not in charge here.

I am a clergyman, so I was not surprised by the spiritual content of some of the entries. It did surprise me that these warm, sweet, and calm moments would come forward as I was conversing with them. These conversations often felt like a holy gathering.

I had a completely different expectation regarding the content of this book. I expected the book to be totally about them, what they do, their spacecraft, and other aspects of their existence. I saw myself as simply a recorder of information, an observer. I was very surprised that I would come to play a part in the story. I did not anticipate having extraordinary experiences outside of the interviews. I was astonished with the dreams I had that related to the ETs.

As I was feeling things kinetically and emotionally, having unusual occurrences outside of the interviews, finding that my perspective was shifting and my intuition growing, these conversations became very real for me. It was a multi-dimensional experience.

Within all this chaos there remained the peacefulness of their presence. Connecting with them became a joy. Somehow, these beings from far, far away had come into my life and touched my heart.

Here is the actual diary this contributor wrote about his contact with ETs.

MY DIARY OF ET CONTACT

This is the diary of my contact with them:

1

Day 1—Friendship
Who are you?
We are eight ETs. We are hovering over Earth. We
    have been here seven years. Right now, we are
    above Utah.
What do you want?
Friendship.

Day 2—Love
What are you doing up there in the sky?
We compile a huge array of scientific data about Earth
    and its inhabitants, for one.
Do you love humans?
Yes.
Why?
We see through their vulnerabilities to their hearts,
    their kindness, their strength.
Would you say it is easier being an ET or a human?
It's easier being one of us.
Why?
Humans are very complicated. It is much easier for us
    to live in peace and harmony.
Are you superior to us?
No, not at all. Even though our science, our minds,
    our culture are much more developed, humans
    have the capacity to be closer to God.
Why is that?
God loves humans most of all.

How do you know this?

We are aware of what goes on not just in this universe,
but in many universes. We see and hear incredible
things. We know this.

Day 3—"We Would Put a Halt to it."
Did you follow the gigantic tsunami that hit Asia?
Yes.
Did you know this was going to happen beforehand?
Yes, we are very aware of what is going on with your
planet.
*Would you ever intercede if you saw that a horrific
disaster was about to transpire on Earth?*
Yes, most particularly in the case of nuclear disasters.
If we saw that a nuclear disaster was about to
transpire and we knew that this was wrong for the
planet, we would put a halt to it.
*How do you know if a nuclear disaster is right or wrong
for the planet?*
We would have a telepathic conference with the
chieftains of our planet and they would direct us
accordingly.
How would the chieftains know?
They would have received the information from high
spiritual beings.
Like angels?
No, various spiritual heads of your planet and solar
system.

Day 4—Service
Who do you serve?
We serve your planet. We serve our planet. We hope
to serve in every way that which is good.
Does everyone on your planet serve?

No, approximately 68 percent serve like we do.
*What are the other 32 percent like? Are some of them
    criminals?*
No, they just aren't as clear in their consciousness.
What percentage of people here on Earth serve?
Twenty percent.
*What percentage would we need to have a peaceful
    planet?*
Fifty percent.
*Your planet must be very peaceful to have so many who
    serve.*
Yes.

Day 5—"Not from a superior place"
Tell me something about yourselves.
We love to laugh. We have plenty of laughs up here in
    our spaceship.
Are you laughing at what you see down here?
Yes.
Can you give me an example of what's so funny?
Yes. From where we come from, we don't have
    bathrooms. We find the act of going to the
    bathroom funny.
You laugh at us pooping?
Yes, but not from a superior place.

Day 6—Arizona
How far is your spacecraft from me right now?
Six miles away.
So you are over Arizona?
Yes.
What are you doing in Arizona?
We are talking to you. We can, however, talk to you
    from Mars, Saturn, or even much farther away.

We like Arizona. There are certain places we can go
where we receive and Arizona is one of those
places.

What do you receive here?

There are a number of good people in Arizona.
Through their works, their goodness, their
spiritual practices, they have created patterns of
positive energy that we receive from.

Do you work outside of the United States?

No, all of our work is done over the United States.

What are you doing that is so specific to the United States?

Monitoring nuclear energy.

Day 7—Experiences

How are we doing as a planet?

Very well.

Based on what criteria?

If you are alive, you are doing well.

Why is that?

There is so much to be gained by living on Earth.

What is gained?

Experiences.

Why experiences?

All experiences ultimately lead to God.

Day 8—ETs

*Do you see other ET spacecraft that are not visible to the
human eye?*

Yes.

How many different kinds of ETs hover over Earth?

Hundreds.

What sets you apart physically from the other ETs?

We smile more. We are about a foot taller.

What sets you apart mentally and emotionally?

We are at the high end mentally. Emotionally, we are
predominantly neutral.
What distinguishes you spiritually?
We are of service. About 60 percent of the ETs here
are of service.
What are the other 40 percent doing here?
The universe is attracted to Earth. Humans are God's
grandest creation. Most of the remaining 40
percent are simply observing. A very small
percentage are up to mischief. Due to the laws of
the universe, they cannot, however, do very
much.
Mischief, as in abductions?
Yes, there have been abductions. We do not condone
them.

Day 9—Dreams
What are your dreams, your aspirations?
We aspire toward peace and harmony. We aspire
toward oneness.
Our existence, our lives now are very peaceful. We
have love, we have community, we have mental
stimulation, we have the joy of service.
Our dream is not of this place, but of another world,
another life. In our dream, the love we experience
now is magnified many times over. In our dream,
we walk with God.
The dream is of going back to God?
Yes.

Day 10—Helping Each Other
*I have a sense that you are helping me in my life. Is that
true?*
Yes.

How are you helping me?

By communicating with you, pathways in your
consciousness are opening up. If you can hear us,
you can hear many things. If you can give us a
voice, you can give a voice to many things.

Am I helping you in any way?

Mankind has a very special radiance. Through you, we
now have direct and personal contact with this
radiance, the divine spark of man.

Day 11—Communication

*If you could be human for a day, what would you like to
do?*

Talk to many people and connect with them.

*You wouldn't want to partake in the physical pleasures
here?*

No, that would be of no interest to us.

*If I could be an ET for a day, what would you advise me
to do and experience?*

To plug into the universe and connect to the universal
consciousness. To share with others telepathically.

Why do you recommend that?

It provides a tremendous sense of connection. It
makes one strong and wise. It opens the heart and
is fascinating.

Day 12—Vision Stories

As friends, what can we do today?

Tell us something close to your heart.

*I play sports with kids. I greatly enjoy this. I love to see their
spirits shine. They are so beautiful, free and innocent.
It's touching and incredibly sweet to be with them.*

We also have an activity where our spirits soar. Back on

our planet, thousands of us will gather in a large hall. One of us goes to the front and ascends a stage. Silently, telepathically they share a deep, beautiful experience. It may be a wonderful moment of love, a special time with a child or spouse, a vision of another world or a vision of God. Or, they might communicate a joke or something that is humorous in nature. When that one is done, another ascends the stage and communicates their vision story to the group.

Day 13—Laughter

Do you play games up on the spacecraft?

Yes we played one just recently. When a crew member goes to sleep, the ones who are still awake visit him in his dreams.

What is the point of the game?

To make the dreamer smile. In so doing, we try to be imaginative and creative in how we position ourselves in the dream.

I keep seeing these images of you giggling. Are you the ETs of laughter?

Yes.

How can you be so smart and yet laugh so much?

This does tend to set us apart from much of the universe.

I would like some of that to rub off on me. What do you suggest?

Try laughing, even if nothing is particularly funny. Invest yourself in that laughter, let it out. As you laugh, the laughter will respond to you. Listen for there is wisdom in that laughter.

Day 14—We are all One
These interviews give me a sense, in no uncertain terms,
    that we are all connected in the universe.
If you could only see, as we do, how we are all one.
Please explain, what do you see?
We are a culture, a planet that has lived a long time.
    We have seen worlds created and worlds
    destroyed. We have seen the beauty of birth on
    many galaxies. We have seen souls incarnate from
    one world into a completely different world. We
    have seen holy angels at work. Amid all the
    change, all the birth, the death, the destruction,
    the transformation, the growth, we have known
    the smile of God. God smiles upon all of us and
    loves all his creation.

Day 15—332 Spaceships
Are there many of ET spaceships over the U.S.A.?
Yes.
How many are over the United States right now
    [February 23, 2005]?
Three hundred Thirty-two.
Which state has the most spaceships over it?
Arizona with 60.
Which state has the next most?
Nevada with 42.
Of the 332 spaceships, how many are visible to the
    human eye?
Twenty are visible and only at certain times.
At what times?
A combination of factors are involved: Who's looking;
    not everyone can see a UFO as clearly. The speed
    of the ship. At certain high speeds they can't be

seen by the human eye. Atmospheric conditions such as cloud cover, amount of sun, air pollution and a variety of other factors.

Has anyone ever seen your ship?

No.

Why is that?

Our ship exists on the sixth dimension.

Has anyone ever seen you?

No.

I would like to see you sometime. Is there any chance of that happening?

Our first impulse is to say no, for it is not allowed. In your case, we will just have to wait and see.

Day 16—Aron

ETs are generally thought of as cold creatures. Are you affectionate? Do you touch those you love? Do you lead lives of warmth?

Humans lead a life that is much more physically based than ours. Your lives are ten times more physically oriented than our lives. On the other hand, our lives are much more mentally based. Our mental orientation is one hundred times greater than yours. By physical standards, you might not consider our expression to be warm. This does not mean we love our children or our spouses any less. We just have different tools to work with and different ways of expressing love.

How do you express love?

We can send the feeling of love to another. We are still very much in touch with our families back home. The love they send us and the love we send them is palpable.

(*A specific ET comes forward to speak:*)

I have a wife, a son, a daughter. I am in touch with
them every day. I can see what they are doing. I
can talk to them inside myself. Although
physically we are apart, the expression of our love
is not diminished.

Who are you?

I am Aron. I am one of the three captains of the ship.

Day 17—Ability to Transform

Why do you want to make contact with me?

We spend so much time observing Earth, serving it, it
is natural for us to want to make contact, to
connect, to share, to get personal with someone.

What do you experience when we converse?

Peace.

*You are much more intelligent and psychic than I am. Is
there some ability or quality within me that you
admire?*

You, and this goes for humans in general, have this
marvelous ability to transform and improve
yourselves. And as we have mentioned before, you
are very close to God.

What does that mean, "close to God"?

You can be so utterly beautiful in your expression.
When a human shines with the *light,* he shines
with it so magnificently.

Day 18—A Gift

*I am open to taking our relationship to a higher level.
What can I do to expand our friendship?*

There is something we do to celebrate a friendship. It
is like a handshake, but in this case one's hand

extends to the other's elbow and vice versa. You can do this in your imagination now.

With each of you?

No, do it with Aron.

(We do the special handshake.)

I feel somehow different now, I feel very relaxed and peaceful.

We are peaceful and relaxed. This is a gift from us to you.

Day 19—Hollywood

If Hollywood wanted to make a realistic movie about ETs, how would you advise them?

Most of the ETs hovering around Earth are good in nature. Most ETs are supporting your planet. They admire and honor humans. By and large, we cannot be seen by the naked eye. A very small percentage of the ETs create crop circles. (We don't.) Crop circles are good for the planet. ETs do not need your natural resources. There are hundreds of varieties of ETs. ET spacecraft do get spotted from time to time. Although flying saucers do exist, we don't fly in one. Our ship is huge and has several layers to it.

We have a sense of humor, but most ETs don't.

Day 20—Joyful

I am going to list a number of descriptions that I believe characterize you. Tell me which adjective is most prominently missing from this list.

Loving

Of service

Intuitive
Psychic
Brilliant
Good
Calm
Mental
Peaceful
Community-oriented
Spiritual
Lovers of laughter
Scientific
Gentle
Non-materialistic
Neutral
The adjective that is most prominently missing in
    describing us is joyful.
Your lives on the spaceship are joyful?
Yes, very much so.

Days 21 and 22—Angels
*You remind me to a certain extent of the ETs who show
    up toward the end of A.I. Artificial intelligence to
    help the robot boy. They are standing on a balcony
    overseeing the boy and assisting him in conjunction
    with an angel. How close of an approximation are
    those beings to who you are?*
Eighty-two percent
How is that depiction off?
We do not as a rule come down physically to Earth.
*In that scene, the aliens are shown working together with
    an angel. The angel appears to be in charge of the
    proceedings and the aliens are backing her up. In*

reality, Angels don't ask us for support. If they
need support, they ask God. You wouldn't find us
in a position where we are backing up an angel.
However, on occasion, we do ask angels for their
support.

Under what circumstances?

When we are assisting humans, sometimes we will call
on the angels to help the humans as well. For
example, if we are trying to protect a person or a
group of people, it may be wise for us to call on
the angels.

Why?

Because they have a direct connection to God. They
can do some things that we just can't do.

How is your power different from the power of angels?

Let's say a pedestrian is in harm's way. We would use
our technological expertise to save him. We could,
for instance, slow the advancing vehicle or stop it.
If need be, we have other technological options
available to us as well. We could also use the
power of our minds to alert the driver or alert the
pedestrian. Angels, on the other hand, might just
pick the pedestrian up and remove them from
harm's way. The angels could create an unusual
weather condition, like a strong gust of wind, to
alter the chain of events. Our efforts would be
primarily technologically based; their efforts often
transcend the laws of the physical universe. Their
work has the signature of being effortless, poetic,
and compassionate.

*Let's look at a different scenario. Say you are helping an
individual achieve some kind of goal like buying a*

house or getting a book published. How would your methodology differ from an angel's?

An angel might whisper affirmations and do this ceaselessly until they made a great impression on the person's consciousness. Angels have a great ability to connect people. They could connect a buyer to a seller, a writer to a publisher, and so forth. Angels can alter energy. A person might all of a sudden find this very sweet energy around them and with this energy create the success they desire. How would we help someone create a success? There is a universal consciousness that we are all connected to. We would place as an intention, say the publication of this book, into the universal consciousness.

Have you done that for this book?

Yes.

Day 23—Chosen

When did you choose me as one who you would talk to?

Not until recently, last year.

How did you find me?

Through an angel.

What did you tell the angel you were looking for?

There were four criteria:

1. An open person.
2. A person we could consider a friend.
3. Someone extraordinarily linked to us.
4. A lover of all life.

How am I extraordinarily linked to you?

That will be revealed.

2

Day 24—Crusaders

*I have been watching the television show 24 (season 4)
this year, and it has been a very intense experience for
me. In the program, several nuclear power plants in
the United States are on the verge of melting down.
My legs actually shake throughout the show. You have
stated that your main job here is to monitor the use of
nuclear materials. What kind of nuclear power are
you monitoring?*

We are monitoring nuclear power plants in the United
States.

*I also had a memorable and unusual dream recently
where I was speaking out against the misuse of
nuclear energy. I need to ask this, am I involved in
your mission?*

You became involved with this mission when you
became involved with us.

How did that happen?

You are a good soul. Your soul agreed to help us out.

How am I helping?

You as a physical person are not involved. Your soul,
however, is involved. On the other side, where
there are dark forces and the forces of *light*, you
represent the *light*.

*Are you saying that there is a spiritual battle going on here
on Earth revolving around the use of nuclear energy?*

Yes. The forces of darkness are very much attracted to
nuclear energy.

So, we are a group of crusaders, alien and human,
fighting against the misuse of nuclear energy?
Yes.

Day 25—Greed
You've mentioned dark forces. Is the negative power
working here in the United States and if so, how?
The negative power has a greater foothold in the
United States now than it has ever had before.
This negativity is manifested in the worship of a
false idol. That false idol is money. The negative
power is expressing itself in the United States
through greed.
Are you down on the United States?
No. There are over one million highly positive,
evolved people in the United States. They more
than balance the negative foothold.

Day 26—Time Travel
Do you time travel here?
Yes, we time travel for scientific study.
How far back are you traveling to?
1942.
Why do you need to study that time period?
It marks the beginning era of the atomic bomb.
What are you studying?
We are studying one particular element, element O.
Why?
The negative power is using that element to do
damage. We are trying to balance what the
negative power is doing with that element.

Day 27—Proof
Why is there no conclusive proof of ETs here on Earth?

The human consciousness is not ready to receive this
information. However, in one hundred to two
hundred years' time conclusive proof will come
forward.
*Will this conclusive proof coincide with anything
happening here on Earth?*
Yes, there will be a series of dramatic Earth changes.
The landscape in many areas will be altered.
Why would the proof come then?
At that point the human consciousness will be more
open and flexible.

Day 28—Physical Appearance
*The generic physical image we have of ETs is that they
are four feet tall, gray or white in color, with big
heads and big eyes (that often extend to the side of
the face) and webbed fingers and feet. They have no
hair and no clothes. How accurately does that
describe you?*
That is 78 percent correct. We are closer to four feet
ten inches tall. We are bluish white. Our eyes are
big, but they do not extend to the side of our face.
You have webbed feet and webbed fingers?
Yes.
*Are some ETs here because their race is dying out and they
want to get something from planet earth?*
No, no, no. Most ETs exist on a different dimension.
What is here on earth could not be transferred to
their home planet.
*Is that one of the reasons why there is no physical evidence
of UFOs or ETs, because ETs exist on a different
dimension?*
Yes.

Day 29—Healers

*I heard a woman state that ETs had healed a grave illness
that she had as a little girl. Do ETs get involved with
healing human sickness and disease?*

On an individual basis, yes.

Is that one of your jobs?

No, it is not our responsibility. We do it as a service.

*How many people has your crew provided a healing ser-
vice for within the last year?*

Three hundred eighty-eight.

Day 30—Flying

*What is something that I do not know about you that you
would like to share?*

We are a much older culture than yours. We have
720,000 years of recorded history.

What else?

We can fly.

That must be fun. Where do you fly to?

Wherever we have to go—a friend's home, to work.

Do you ever fly just for the fun of it?

Yes, all the time. We like to fly in formations and do
artistic movements together in unison.

Day 31—The Fan Club

*I have been having a series of similar dreams lately that
have coincided with these interviews. In these dreams
a very cute young woman will appear (someone I am
not familiar with) and she will behave in a physically
affectionate way toward me. They are not sexual
dreams. I get kissed and hugged like I am one of the
Beatles. It feels like I am on the receiving end of
innocent teenage love. Can you tell me something
about these dreams?*

The women in these dreams are ETs. They are
attracted to you. They know you through us and
the communications we have been having with
you.

Are they from your planet?

No, they are from sister planets that we are in touch
with telepathically. These are good planets with
good beings living on them.

How many different planets are these ETs from?

Four.

Why are they attracted to me?

They see your goodness and your sweetness.

*Why do they choose to communicate with me in the form
of charming young females?*

So that you can connect with them.

Are they actual ET females?

Yes.

Who are actually this attractive in ET terms?

Yes.

What do they want?

They just like you. You are cute to them. They want to
connect.

*Why is it that female ETs are coming in my dreams and
not male ETs?*

Certain ET females have crushes on you. The men
don't.

*Last night, I told a cute blond ET not to kiss me on
the lips. In the dream, my wife was standing
right next to me. The ET kissed me anyway. How
come?*

She was caught in the moment and meant no harm.

Do these ETs want to date me?

No, they want to adore you.

I have an ET fan club?
Yes, many care for you.

Day 32—God Smiles Back
*I have become aware of how deeply I am connecting with
  people, animals, and life since we started our talks
  together. I think you have had something to do with
  this.*
Yes, the part of your brain that you have used in order
  to communicate with us has greatly expanded
  since these conversations began. This aspect of
  your brain (on the right rear side) gives you the
  ability to connect deeper with life. It is a sacred
  portal into the infinite.
*You have become real in my life. I talk to my friends
  about you. I pray for you.*
We pray for you as well.
How do you pray?
We do not ask for things for ourselves. In our prayer,
  we connect to Spirit with our love, with our
  depth, our inner knowing. We already know that
  it is all perfect. We smile to God and we allow
  God to smile back.
How have you prayed for me?
As we smile, we carry you in our hearts.
*You are good and pure. Since talking to you, I feel like I
  want to connect more with those who exude goodness.*
Goodness is a universal language.
There is a stillness in the room. I feel like I am in church.
This is how we pray. God is smiling back.

Day 33—The Brown Horseman
What is it that you wish to speak about?

The Book of Revelation.
You are aware of that book in the Bible?
Yes.
What do you want to say about it?
The Brown Horseman has descended on Earth.
(After doing some research on the Internet.)
There is no Brown Horseman specifically mentioned in
the Bible.
The Brown Horseman comes between the White
Horseman (of Conquest) and the Red Horseman
(of War). It is the Horseman of Greed.
Why are you telling me this?
After you die, you will be involved in the unfolding of
the Book of Revelation. We both will be together.
I will be involved with the apocalypse?
Yes.
That's a strange coincidence; just the other night I heard
someone comment that after the apocalypse, the only
ones to survive will be "cockroaches, Tammy Faye,
and Cher."
It won't be that brutal.
Are you making a joke?
In part.

Day 34—Someone to Watch over Me
Sometimes in these conversations, you will bring up a
highly interesting subject, like element O or the
Brown Horseman, and you won't expand on it very
much. Why is that?
There is only so much that we are allowed to say.
Is this our last day together doing this?
Yes, we are tremendously pleased to have had this
experience with you and now it is done.

The communication does feel absolutely complete. I am
   starting to observe a peace and quiet inside of myself.
   I feel the oneness with you. The oneness runs deep.
   What's our next mission together, the apocalypse?
Yes, in the meantime, we'll be watching over you.

AND FINALLY:
THE GEORGE NOORY
CONSPIRACY THEORY

Y ou knew this was coming.
You knew that this had to be said.
"There are no coincidences."

Saying this many times on *Coast to Coast AM,* I sometimes forget the real implications of this statement. It means that in the great universe, even given the wobble of chance and possibilities, things tend to connect with one another, quanta of matter flip in reciprocity with each other, and what we expect to see is, indeed, what we see. Therefore, when folks tell me about synchronicity, a nonfortuitous correspondence of things, I always respond with my theory that chance is something we blame for things over which we've relinquished control. In other words, casting your fate to the winds, especially when you're sailing, is tantamount to courting disaster. It's similar to the statement that to seek permission to do something, especially inside a bureaucracy, is to seek denial.

I believe, and in light of what our contributors have written, that for those who open themselves up to the possibilities of messages from the great universe, all things are achievable. You can see the future, use your intuition as a homing beacon as well as a radar signal, tap into the minds and emotions of others, and communicate with just about anyone. So, if you can do all this, if human beings have this wonderful power, what's stopping them from using this law of attraction to become workers in the light?

I believe that what's stopping them is a concerted effort by those who want to keep human beings spiritually enslaved, spiritually blind to the possibilities that exist for us. Is this a conspiracy? Yes, and I call it my own George Noory conspiracy theory, and it goes like this: the more you can get people to worry, the more you can instill seeds of fear in a mass population, the more you can get people flustered with the business of day-to-day living, then the more you can keep them from figuring out what to do to empower themselves.

This conspiracy has been around for a while, at least since the end of World War II, but probably even before it. This conspiracy probably began to emerge as our population, at least in this country—but we saw it actively at work in Germany, Italy, and Spain in the 1930s and in Russia during World War I—as it gradually shifted from an agrarian economy of small farms to an industrial economy based in cities. The conspiracy also probably grew out of the influx of immigrants to America from the early 1900s right through the end of World War II because people from different ethnic backgrounds and value systems needed to be manipulated into a homogenous mass of consumers not only of product, but of government services.

I don't see this as a kind of deliberate Orwellian conspiracy, or the kind of conspiracy to deaden the minds of the masses that George Lucas portrayed in his 1971 *THX 1138*. I see it as something that almost came together by itself as a result of the self-interest of a number of groups. For example, down on the farm circa 1920, people were self-sustaining for the most part, except for the need of banks for credit to buy seed and equipment. In a stable economy, the cycle of borrowing, growing, selling, and paying back was timed to the cycle of the seasons. But let one or two major events trip up this cycle and the economic dominoes start falling. Banks collapse and have to call in loans to other banks, who, in turn, call in loans to direct borrowers. Suddenly everyone looks around to discover that they've lent so much money out on insane loan-to-value ratios that there's not enough money in the properties to pay back the loans. As lenders collapse, so do the banks that lent them the money to lend. Sound familiar? It's happening now.

Then there's the weather. If you know the story of the Joad family in *The Grapes of Wrath*, then you know that in the 1930s, much of Oklahoma suffered extreme drought and became a dust bowl. If people can't grow crops, they can't sell crops. And if they have no crops to sell to bring in a revenue to pay back their loans, they default. Too many defaults and the banks that were relying on the repayments default on their loans. They collapse and the collapse goes right up the line until all of the banks that have lent money go down. Again, looking at the subprime mortgage collapse and the collapse of the derivative financial instruments based on those mortgages, we are in a very similar situation.

The famine caused by the dust bowl and the collapse of the financial markets became a perfect storm in the 1930s, further pushing people off the land and into cities, where the masses had to be fed, order had to be maintained, and, above all, people had to be controlled. Suddenly, people were looking at ways that mass populations could be manipulated, moved, kept from thinking dangerous thoughts, and, above all, milked for their votes and what money they had.

A key experiment in the mass control of populations, a way to keep people from thinking for themselves and thinking the way those in power wanted them to think, was the 1938 Mercury Theatre on the Air broadcast of H. G. Wells's "War of the Worlds." Most people still think that this wild and wacky broadcast was the sole brainchild of producer Orson Welles. Only three years away from his masterpiece, *Citizen Kane*, a young and fiery Orson Welles was actually financed by a Rockefeller-associated group at Princeton University through Frank Stanton, who later became the president of CBS. Frank Stanton was the marketing genius who invented modern, demographics-oriented radio and television programming. He looked for and found ways to test audience response and broadcast news and entertainment directly to that response. And "War of the Worlds" was one of his early test cases.

As a radio broadcaster and former television news producer, I am still fascinated with the "War of the Worlds" story and the story's aftermath—also a Frank Stanton creation. The broadcast, strangely associated with the Rockefellers, posed the question, a question still posed today: could a radio broadcast so create panic among listeners that they would abandon all logic and believe what was on the radio rather than simply calling up their local police or even looking out a window? Apparently Stanton found out that it could.

At the same time, too, the people at the Rockefeller-associated group gained some valuable information about how people might react to an extraterrestrial invasion, information that might have prompted Laurence Rockefeller almost fifty years later to fund the Pocantico Hills conference on UFO phenomena and for Rockefeller to urge President-elect Bill Clinton in 1992 to push hard for getting into the UFO records kept by the U.S. military and intelligence.

You don't have to be a broadcaster to appreciate the power of the media back in 1938 to mold mass opinion as the world girded for war. But to a broadcaster, that immense power to get people to believe in something that was not happening was very instructive. All you have to do is gain the trust of your listening or viewing audience and you can use that trust as a highway to deliver any kind of message you want, true or false, healthy or harmful, but always inuring to your benefit. For example, go back to those innocent days of the 1950s when advertising companies on Madison Avenue were able to convince medical doctors to go on television to extol the pleasures of cigarette smoking, even as data had begun to trickle out linking cigarette smoking to lung cancer. Seem far-fetched in the savvy world of the twenty-first century? Not so much.

Consider an evening romp through the television evening news cycle. It might begin with ads for all those quickie fast foods you can slam together for your family because you and your spouse are both working your heads off just to support the family and fill a gas tank. You've eaten the food you've seen advertised, eaten it, probably, while watching television. As you're eating and fretting about settling the kids down from all the sugar they've consumed at dinner, you begin to watch all the commercials for pharmaceuticals for indigestion, acid reflux, headache, anxiety that deprives you of a good night's sleep, assorted analgesics, and finally a good sleeping aid. You're programmed with the old one-two punch. How can you assert any control over yourselves and your lives when you have these messages crashing into your brain? And that's not all.

You take to bed with you each night the demands of your job, the demands of your family, the demands of your kids' schoolteachers, who, themselves, might be recommending medications for a child who causes too much trouble in class. With all this weighing on your mind, how can you even begin to reach out to a universe of love, hope, potential, and self-empowerment? And that's my point. You don't have to have an organized conspiracy to define how you think and react. The very pressures of the need to control mass populations, usually through mass media—as Frank Stanton invented it—is effective enough.

And all of this is what I call my own conspiracy theory. You can see examples of how this works all over the place. It is like the opposite of the Jungian shared collective unconscious. In this conspiracy, conspirators seeking your money, your vote, or your allegiance to something need only to tap into an ongoing conspiracy machine for a timeshare. I see this happen every day all over the place, but because this is also part of the American marketplace, it supports the very work I do.

Seeing the full picture, the vast magnitude of how people can be programmed into denying the very essences of themselves, I want to do something about it. I want to find a way to reverse the programming. I want to find a way to start a quiet wave of independence that results in a spiritual awakening, a kind of self-empowerment revolution among my listeners wherein folks can tap into a universe that's all around them, use the inherent power of their senses, and become what human beings are, but don't know they are: free.

Once you realize that there is a conspiracy-by-default, even if not by design, to keep you from reaching your potential, you have a choice to make. Settle back into the warm comfort of being handled, convincing yourself that those handling you will take care of you, yet still hoping for the best, or take upon yourself the responsibility of empowering yourself. Don't think this is that easy a choice. Knowing the truth may set you free, you think, but knowing the truth also presents you with the awesome knowledge that you have to do something about what you know is true. Not so easy!

My suggestion is to do it in baby steps. Let revelation come in small doses so that when the truth about the nature of the power you wield stares you in the face, you will be ready for it.

Look at how the truth impacted upon the lives of our contributors. All of them, in their own ways, found themselves face-to-face with the awesome power of the universe. Some of them willingly chose it. Others were chosen to see it. But all of them stepped right to the edge of the world we take for granted and then, in a moment, looked over that edge to discover such things as: we don't die, the spirit lives on, angels speak to you, you've lived before, your body is just a shell and you can leave it and come back to it at will, time is an illusion because the future creates its own past, and our Creator embraces each of us with love. These are stories of people who learned these things as facts. They experienced things that they always had the power to experience, but never knew it.

How long will you wait? And why wait at all? The universe is waiting for you, and you, without knowing it, are probably waiting to embrace the universe. Take the step forward, find your mantra, practice your breathing, focus on your breathing, send unpleasant thoughts and fears floating downstream, and open yourself up to the limitless possibilities that await you when you exercise the power of your own consciousness.

INDEX